WEBSTER'S
NEW WORLD™

VOCABULARY
of
SUCCESS

by Mike Miller with
William R. Todd-Mancillas

MACMILLAN • USA

To John Schwegman, who taught a class on Greek and Latin derivatives when I was a student at Ben Davis High School in Indianapolis in the mid-1970s. Mr. Schwegman, your enthusiasm for words and their history and usage was contagious, and I hope some of that love for language made its way into this book.

Acknowledgments

My thanks to William R. Todd-Mancillas for getting this project off to a good start.

Contents

Part 1 Words Day by Day

Part 2 Top 20 Words To...

Introduction

This is a book for people who love words—and it's a book for people who don't.

Let me explain.

I love words. I get excited when I trip over new words in a book or magazine or overhear new words in a conversation. If you're like me, you'll like this book because it has a lot of words that will probably be new to you—words that are common but are used generally or imprecisely, words that are underused (but undeservedly so), words that come from the lexicon of specific professions, or words that have for other reasons only recently come into common usage. So, if you love words and love using words, you'll have fun with this book—and learn new words along the way.

But, even if you don't love words—or perhaps especially if you don't love words—this is also a book for you. If you just want to learn the right words to use in a given circumstance, if you want to be able to understand what successful people are really talking about, if you are entering a new profession and need to quickly learn the lexicon—in short, if you want to sound successful in a variety of situations—reading this book will benefit you.

Reading *Webster's New World Vocabulary of Success* is a great way to learn words that you will use in the real world. You don't have to be a linguist to enlarge your vocabulary; having a broad and impressive yet still practical vocabulary can truly help you progress in life and in your career. This book shows you some of the words you need to know to effectively communicate with people who are successful and can help you in your own quest for success.

Would Have, Could Have, and Possibly Even Should Have—But Didn't!

Let me get something out of the way before you start sending me letters. If you're a language purist, you might not particularly like parts of this book. That's because I didn't limit myself solely to those words that appear in dictionaries. Many words and phrases that you hear in the business environment, in specific professions, at cocktail parties, and on the streets are words that have informally developed and have not yet been accepted by the professional lexicographers who compile dictionaries.

I believe that language isn't set in stone but is flexible and exists for our use, to work for us, not to dictate to us. We should not be slaves to a strict and unbendable set of rules, but rather should use this wonderful tool we call language to our best advantage. Sometimes that means taking words from other languages and adapting them for our use. Sometimes it means taking a word and using it in a slightly different way to better express a certain thought. Sometimes it means embracing jargon and migrating it into common parlance. Sometimes it even means taking a noun and turning it into a verb—"verbizing" it—because it's a better way to quickly get our thoughts across.

Not that I excuse sloppy use of language—I've threatened to do bodily harm to people who say "I've got" instead of "I have." Yet I'm not above bending the language to my needs, such as verbizing the noun "attrition" into the verb "attrit" or speaking in acronyms or verbal shorthand to get my point across quickly. (Yes, the verb "verbizing" is itself verbized from the noun "verb" and isn't formally recognized by the Webster's lexicographers—but isn't it a wonderful way to express this specific action?)

This book includes more than 1,800 words. These are not the only words that could have appeared in this book. I'm sure you can find a hundred words that you would have chosen that aren't included and a hundred that are included that you wouldn't have chosen. Frankly, so can I. Choices had to be made, however, and I made them based on two overall criteria for the vocabulary of successful people: actual use and impressiveness. However, if enough people buy and enjoy this book, then I could write a second volume and include another 1,800 words!

How to Use This Book

The format of this book is unlike most other vocabulary books available today. There are no lessons, and you don't have to study endless lists of prefixes, suffixes, or Greek and Latin roots. I've partitioned the book into 365 sets of words, so you can read a page a day and enlarge your vocabulary systematically. Each page or day contains five words that are somehow related to a single topic. Because success is often equated with money in our society, many of the topics in this book are business-related. However, there are other ways to be successful in life, and I give you a sampling of successful non-business language as well.

At the bottom of each page is a short list of words to also explore. These words are related to the topic of the day but are not defined on that page—and, in many cases, are not defined anywhere in the book. (The words that are defined elsewhere in the book appear in italics.) Think of these words as extra credit to learn on your own. Some are more eclectic or literary and wouldn't necessarily be used on a daily basis. However, they can reveal subtle nuances of meaning or can lend greater precision when discussing the topic of the day. I recommend looking up these words to also explore in *Webster's New World College Dictionary*.

Before you get started on the words themselves, you might want to look at the top 20 lists at the back of the book. These lists provide you with 20 key words for some of the most common situations, activities, or professions you will encounter in your quest for success. Although most of these words are listed in more detail in the body of the book, some are for you to also explore (indicated by an asterisk (*)). The top 20 lists function as quick-reference shortcuts to words you need to know quickly for the unexpected invitation to play golf with your boss or to a power lunch to negotiate a new contract.

Finally, an index appears in the back of the book. Because the 1,800 plus words in this book are presented topically and not alphabetically, you can use the index to find that one specific word you're looking for.

Abbreviations Used in This Book

You'll find the following abbreviations used to describe the parts of speech presented in this book:

adj.   adjective

adv.   adverb

n.   noun

vi.   intransitive verb

vt.   transitive verb

Direction

---

vision, *n.* A mental image or imaginative contemplation. Organizations are often driven by an overriding vision. This vision is translated into a specific mission, which is quantified by one or more goals or objectives. These goals or objectives are reached by implementing an overall strategy, which is executed via specific tactics. Organizations without a vision are perceived as rudderless or unfocused—even though most visions are so vague that they are both unquantifiable and unachievable.

> *My **vision** for this company is for it to be a global innovator in information technology.*

---

mission, *n.* The overall purpose of a business or organization. A mission is more specific than a vision.

> *The **mission** of this company is to solve the networking problems of large- and medium-sized organizations.*

goal, *n.* The specific end or objective that a business or organization strives to attain, specific to its mission. A goal is quantifiable.

> *Our **goal** is to double our market share within five years.*

strategy, *n.* A plan of action to achieve the goals of a business or organization. Strategies describe how to meet goals and objectives.

> *Our **strategy** is to increase the value of our products while holding the line on pricing.*

tactic, *n.* The method used to implement an organization's strategy. Tactics are the details of a larger strategy.

> *Our primary **tactic** is to reduce manufacturing costs by sourcing key components overseas.*

 Also Explore: objective, modus operand.

Underpinnings

---

culture, *n.* The ideas, customs, skills, arts, and so on of a group or organization that are transferred, communicated, or passed along. An organization's culture exists independent of its stated goals and mission, formed by the behavior and attitudes of its key members.

> *Donating to local charities was part of the company's* ***culture,*** *borne from the charitable activities of its founder.*

---

climate, *n.* Any prevailing conditions affecting the life, activity, etc. of an organization.

> *Due to the new management team, there was a* ***climate*** *of change in the organization.*

atmosphere, *n.* General mood or social environment. The "feel" of the organization at any given moment.

> *After the announcement of the downsizing, the* ***atmosphere*** *was grim.*

environment, *n.* All the conditions, circumstances, and influences affecting an organization. Every facet of an organization—including the culture, the climate, and the atmosphere—contributes to the overall environment.

> *CompuTitan's work* ***environment*** *is conducive to long work hours.*

infrastructure, *n.* A substructure or underlying foundation—especially the basic installations and facilities on which the continuation and growth of an organization or community depend. Whereas a company's culture is somewhat ethereal, its infrastructure is purely physical.

> *Although the company had a culture that encouraged experimentation, the technological* ***infrastructure*** *was unable to support multiple new media projects simultaneously.*

 Also Explore: customs, facilities, ambience.

Indulgences

---

connoisseur, *n.* A person who has expert knowledge and keen discrimination in some field, especially in fine arts or in matters of taste. A connoisseur often has specific training or skills in his or her favored area.

> *Martha was a **connoisseur** of French cooking, having studied under a master chef in Paris.*

---

epicurean, *adj.* Fond of luxury and sensuous pleasure. Epicurean most often refers to refined taste in food and drink.

> *The dead comedian had been **epicurean** in his tastes, often indulging in the rarest of fine food and drink.*

gourmet, *n.* A person who is an excellent judge of fine food and drink. Although both epicures and connoisseurs are fond of fine food and drink, gourmets are often more critical in what they like.

> *Graham fancied himself a **gourmet,** so he frequented only the best restaurants in town.*

bon vivant, *n.* (bahn vee-vahnt) from the French. A person who enjoys good food and drink and other luxuries. Unlike a gourmet or connoisseur, a bon vivant is not necessarily a judge of fine food, just someone who enjoys it.

> *Club Trés Chic catered to **bon vivants** such as Randolph, who appreciated fine food and upscale surroundings.*

hedonist, *n.* One who practices the self-indulgent pursuit of pleasure as a way of life. A hedonist is more interested in quantity than quality and often indulges in pleasures beyond that of food and drink.

> *Stephen was an unabashed **hedonist,** indulging his urges with lavish meals and multiple sexual partners.*

 Also Explore: aesthete, *aficionado*, devotee, *dilettante*, gourmand.

Superiority

---

cachet, *n.* Distinction or prestige. Manufacturers of many high-priced products attempt to create a cachet around their brands, lending them an air of exclusivity that often commands a higher price in the marketplace.

> *Among the group of doctors, owning a Mercedes-Benz carried a certain* **cachet.**

---

prestigious, *adj.* Having or imparting the power to impress or influence because of success or wealth.

> *Dr. Morrow knew that receiving the* **prestigious** *Wellness Award would positively influence the board when it was time for his next review.*

distinguished, *adj.* A thing or person that is distinguished is not necessarily superior, just recognized or honored by others for some accomplishment.

> *The board welcomed the proposal submitted by the* **distinguished** *Dr. Morrow.*

distinctive, *adj.* Distinguishing from others; characteristic or unique. A thing or person that is distinctive is not necessarily superior or distinguished (honored), just different.

> *Dr. Morrow's Mercedes had a* **distinctive** *pattern on its leather upholstery.*

celebrated, *adj.* Much spoken of; famous or renowned. Celebrated differs from distinguished in that no formal honor is bestowed. Celebrated implies a widespread recognition, not necessarily for a specific accomplishment.

> *The* **celebrated** *author of several well-known novels was appearing at the local bookstore.*

 Also Explore: august, eminent, meritorious, nonpareil, notoriety, *sovereignty.*

Something Odd

anomaly, *n.* Departure from the regular arrangement, general rule, or usual method; something not expected. An anomaly is not necessarily something bad, just something unusual.

> *Sven's jet-black hair was an **anomaly** in a family of blonde Swedes.*

aberration, *n.* A deviation from the normal or typical; clearly out of the ordinary. Unlike an anomaly, an aberration is nearly always something that is undesired, awkward, or harmful.

> *The speeding ticket was an **aberration** on Beth's otherwise-perfect record.*

abnormality, *n.* A thing that is not normal. Often refers to a physical fault or malformation.

> *Sid's irregular heartbeat was an **abnormality** he'd had since birth.*

deviate, *n.* A person whose behavior diverges from what is considered normal in a group or for a society. Often used to connote some sort of sexual perversion.

> *Frank was labeled a **deviate** after he was accused of exposing himself to young boys.*

sordid, *adj.* Base or ignoble. Sordid often refers to behavior that is mean or tawdry.

> *After he was released from jail, Frank moved to a new town and tried to rise above his **sordid** past.*

Also Explore: *eccentric*, idiosyncrasy, maverick, nonconformist, unorthodox.

5

Beliefs (Positive)

---

optimist, *n.* One who has the tendency to take the most hopeful or cheerful view of matters or to expect the best outcome. Optimists are known for seeing a "half-full" glass.

> *Despite the latest opinion polls, Randolph remained an **optimist** regarding his candidate's ability to win the primary election.*

---

realist, *n.* One who has a tendency to face facts and be practical. An optimist looks on the bright side of things; a realist looks at things as they are, good or bad. Some optimists confuse realists with pessimists, especially if reality is less than bright.

> *Opinions aside, Michael tried to be a **realist** regarding his candidate's true chances in the fall election.*

pollyanna, *n.* Derived from the name of the young heroine of novels by Eleanor H. Porter (1868–1920). A pollyanna is an excessively or persistently optimistic person.

> *Roberta was such a **pollyanna** that she did not react to the crumbling situation until it was too late to rectify it.*

credulous, *adj.* Tending to believe too readily; easily convinced.

> ***Credulous** co-workers are prime targets for all kinds of practical jokes.*

confidence, *n.* Firm belief; trust or reliance. Where faith requires no proof, confidence is often based on evidence or past performance.

> *Based on the latest opinion polls, Richard had **confidence** that his candidate would sweep the primary election.*

 Also Explore: *credence*, dogmatic, expectation, gullible, *naïve*.

Beliefs (Negative)

pessimist, *n.* A person who expects misfortune or the worst outcome in any circumstances. Pessimists are known for seeing a "half-empty" glass.

> *Despite the upward marketplace trends, David was a **pessimist** about achieving his quarterly revenue plan.*

cynic, *n.* A person who believes that people are motivated in their actions only by selfishness, without sincerity. Where a pessimist expects the worst in any given situation, a cynic simply views other people negatively.

> *Ever a **cynic**, Marlon viewed the reverend's charitable activities with suspicion.*

skeptic, *n.* A person who habitually doubts or questions matters that are generally accepted. A cynic has predefined negative notions about things. A skeptic's opinions aren't predefined or negative; he or she simply questions everything.

> ***Skeptics** doubted whether ReallyBig Co. could execute the acquisition as planned.*

negativist, *n.* A person who ignores, resists, or opposes suggestions or orders from other people. Whereas a skeptic continually questions the status quo, a negativist continually resists the status quo.

> *Janet grew tired of her boss' being a **negativist**; he refused to even consider her plans to overhaul the department.*

denial, *n.* A state where one refuses to believe or accept a doctrine or what may be quite evident. A skeptic questions things but can accept an opposing view. Someone in denial doesn't question opposite views but refuses to accept them—no questions asked.

> *Upper management was in **denial** regarding the company's loss of market share; they blamed the numbers on poor reporting.*

 Also Explore: *agnostic*, defeatist, detractor, infidel, misanthrope.

7

Dedicated

committed, *adj.* Bound as by a promise. Committed implies a pledge or promise to do a certain thing; it is an intention rather than an existent state.

*Jim reaffirmed to his boss that he was **committed** to staying on the project through the end of the year.*

devoted, *adj.* Very loving, loyal, or faithful. Although being loyal implies an obligation, being devoted is more often altruistic.

*Even after 15 years of marriage, Beth and Paul remained **devoted** to each other.*

staunch, *adj.* Firm; steadfast; loyal. Implies such strong allegiance to one's principles or purposes as not to be turned aside by any cause.

*Bernard was a **staunch** defender of the members of his staff, even in the face of management criticism.*

obsessed, *adj.* Haunted by a persistent idea, desire, emotion, etc., especially one that cannot be reasoned away. Obsession is less rational and more emotional (and, taken to its extreme, psychotic) than commitment, loyalty, or devotion.

*Howard was **obsessed** with the notion that the market needed a third option, all facts to the contrary.*

addicted, *adj.* The condition of giving up oneself to some strong habit. Loyalty, devotion, and commitment are all matters of personal choice; one who is addicted has lost all choice in the matter.

*Jordan was **addicted** to the power that came with the office.*

Also Explore: *altruistic*, enamored, fidelity, infatuated, persistent.

The Past

nostalgia, *n.* A longing for something far away or long ago. Nostalgia is a positive reflection on past times that might not have been all positive.

> *Bryan felt a wave of **nostalgia** rush over him when he received the invitation to his high school reunion.*

yore, *n.* Time long past. Sometimes refers to ancient or mythological times but can also refer to any distant time.

> *In days of **yore**, giants walked the earth.*

halcyon, *adj.* Tranquil, happy, idyllic; usually with nostalgic references to earlier times. Often used in conjunction with the word *yore,* as in, "those halcyon days of yore."

> *The Christmas season always made Bonnie yearn for those **halcyon** days of her youth.*

antique, *n.* Anything from older times. Often used as a way to describe people, processes, or things that are perceived as out-of-date; can also be used to convey a nostalgic or financial value for something old and well-preserved.

> *Jones has been here so long that he's practically an **antique**.*

antiquated, *adj.* No longer used or useful. Antiquated implies something that is woefully out-of-date and no longer of value.

> *These procedures are so **antiquated** that they don't adequately deal with the problems we face today.*

Also Explore: curio, *idyllic*, obsolete, relic, superannuated.

Background

skill set, *n.* Familiar knowledge or dexterity in a given subject area or endeavor that comes with training and practice. A skill set is a combination of abilities and experience used to describe the basic proficiency one brings to a job or situation.

> *Gregory was looking for someone with a unique **skill set** to execute the new project—a combination of marketing, sales, and operational skills.*

savvy, *n.* Shrewdness or understanding; know-how. It refers to someone who is adept in a specific area due to a keen understanding or experience in that area.

> *Barbara's adept handling of the acquisition revealed her **savvy** in new business ventures.*

track record, *n.* The record of the performance of a person, organization, etc. as in some activity or on some issue. A track record is the measurement of how one has performed through a specific experience.

> *Mitch's **track record** in consumer marketing was checkered; there were few true successes and many outright failures.*

seasoning, *n.* Refers to the depth and richness of practical experience gained through time or seasons. Savvy can refer to an instant understanding whereas seasoning gives one understanding only through the passage of time.

> *Martha's ten years in the business gave her a **seasoning** no new college recruit could match.*

expertise, *n.* The skill, knowledge, judgment, and so on of an expert. Anyone can have skills or experience; only an expert at a given endeavor can have expertise.

> *Johnson relied on the lawyer's **expertise** in crafting the new contract.*

 Also Explore: *ability*, *discern*, proficiency, *repertoire*.

What You Have

ability, *n.* Skill or talent. Ability implies a strong competence in doing something or a sufficiency of strength, skill, and resources.

> *Jennifer amazed everyone with her **ability** to quickly turn a clever phrase, no matter what the situation.*

capability, *n.* A capacity for being used or developed. People have abilities; things have capabilities.

> *The new computer's **capabilities** were far beyond what the older machine could do.*

capacity, *n.* The ability to contain, absorb, or receive and hold. Capacity is a measurement of how much you can do.

> *The department had the **capacity** to process 200 resumés per day.*

faculty, *n.* Power or ability to do some particular thing; a special aptitude or skill. A faculty is a special ability, often innate.

> *Marcel's **faculty** for problem-solving was present at an early age.*

facility, *n.* A ready ability or skill; a dexterity or fluency at some endeavor. Facility refers to an ability that comes with special ease or quickness.

> *Rene's **facility** with languages enabled her to quickly master the necessary Japanese phrases when she was preparing for the Asian sales meeting.*

Also Explore: *aptitude,* dexterity, fluency.

11

School Days

sabbatical, *n.* A period of absence for study, rest, or travel, given at intervals to some college teachers, at full or partial salary. Some corporations extend sabbatical leave to their more tenured employees. Sabbaticals were originally given at seven-year intervals.

> *After achieving tenure in the spring, Professor Higgins was looking forward to his six-month **sabbatical.***

alma mater, *n.* The college or school that one attended.

> *Lana was proud to call Smallville College her **alma mater**; she graduated in 1985 with a degree in literature.*

campus, *n.* The grounds, sometimes including the buildings, of a school or college. Also used to describe the multiple-building facilities of some companies.

> *The **campus** had grown in the decade since Stan's graduation; there was a new science building, as well as an addition to the student union.*

alumnus, *n.* A person who has attended or is a graduate of a particular school, college, etc. Note that alumnus is singular; alumni, the plural form, is often misused to describe a single alumnus.

> *Clark was a distinguished **alumnus** of Metropolis University, as he was continually reminded by the mailings asking for donations to the alumni association.*

endowment, *n.* Any gift that provides an income for an institution or a person. An endowment is generally a gift of cash by a living alumnus, as contrasted with a bequest, which is a postmortem gift of property.

> *The university received a substantial **endowment** from John and Margaret Mitchell.*

 Also Explore: bequest, curriculum vitae, *tenure.*

Job Hunting

DAY 13

---

networking, *vi.* The developing of contacts or exchanging of information with others to further a career. Many job hunters find positions by networking with their contacts.

*Martha sensed it was time to change firms, so she stepped up her **networking** with other members of the Marketing Association.*

---

candidate, *n.* A person who seeks, or who has been proposed for, an office, an award, and so on. Candidate implies a seriously considered applicant—one having that foot in the proverbial door.

*Mark was one of five **candidates** for the open position at ReallyBig Co.*

resumé, *n.* A statement of a job applicant's previous employment experience, education, etc. Most companies winnow out potential new hires by comparing information submitted on a resumé.

*Rodney's **resumé** reflected his rapid progression through the ranks at his previous employer.*

reference, *n.* Another person who can offer employment information or a recommendation. Many companies check your references against your resumé.

*Martha asked Rodney if she could give his name as a **reference** when she interviewed at ReallyBig Co.*

interview, *n.* A face-to-face meeting to evaluate or question a job applicant. An interview is where your future employer sizes you up; you should also use an interview to learn more about the employer.

*Rodney's resumé was impressive, but he didn't leave a good impression at his initial **interview**.*

 Also Explore: *alliance*, audition, contact, credential, testimonial.

13

Pumping Up

motivate, *vt.* To incite or impel. Motivation is often created by use of a reward of some sort—or a punishment if one should fail.

> *The promise of a 20 percent bonus for success—and a 10 percent pay cut for failure—served to **motivate** the staff.*

inspire, *vt.* To have an animating effect upon or to influence to some creative or effective effort. Whereas motivation is often practical in nature, inspiration is more emotional or spiritual.

> *James was a natural leader, able to **inspire** his troops for the battle ahead.*

induce, *vt.* To lead on to some action, condition, belief, and so on. Induce implies an incentive or reward that persuades one to accomplish a certain task.

> *Randolph **induced** his staff with a promise of a free dinner to whoever finished first.*

encourage, *vt.* To give support to or to be favorable to; to help. Motivation and inspiration are relatively hands-off activities; encouragement often involves direct support of some kind.

> *Nancy **encouraged** Alan to apply for the open position.*

bolster, *vt.* To prop up, support, strengthen. Bolster implies an emotional encouragement.

> *Seeing that Maynard was getting demoralized, Susan tried to **bolster** his self-confidence.*

 Also Explore: actuate, foster, *impel*, *incentive*, *incite*.

Cheerful

effervescent, *adj.* Lively and high-spirited. A blithe personality is cheerful; an effervescent personality is sometimes referred to as "bubbly."

> *Suzy's **effervescent** personality helped to lift the spirits of the rest of the team.*

blithe, *adj.* Showing a gay, cheerful disposition. Blithe implies being carefree, happy, and lighthearted, sometimes to the point of lacking or showing a lack of due concern for any given situation.

> *Despite the potential downsizing, Martha remained a **blithe** spirit, unconcerned about how events might affect her future.*

buoyant, *adj.* Having a lightness or resilience of spirit. Buoyancy is often reflective of how one deals with despairing situations.

> *Even after receiving her second rejection letter, Martha remained **buoyant** about her chances of getting a new job.*

boisterous, *adj.* Noisy and lively; loud and exuberant. Boisterous behavior is not necessarily cheerful, just noisy.

> *The staff was **boisterous** when it heard the news of the big sale.*

bluster, *vi.* To speak or conduct oneself in a noisy, swaggering, or bullying manner. Although being boisterous is generally acceptable behavior, blustering behavior is negative and often obnoxious.

> *Mr. Big **blustered** through the cafeteria still shouting and waving his arms about angrily as he stormed from the meeting.*

 Also Explore: bubbly, ebullient, exuberant, irrepressible, vivacious.

High Potential

DAY 16

---

prodigy, *n.* A person so extraordinary as to inspire wonder. One who is a prodigy is wonderful and amazing due to a special or unusual talent.

*Williams was a **prodigy** with numbers; the speed at which he could perform calculations in his head was amazing.*

Wunderkind, *n.* (voonderkint) from the German "wonder child." A child prodigy. A prodigy can be of any age; a Wunderkind is always a child.

*Williams' six-year old son inherited his prodigious talents, making him a **Wunderkind** of the preschool set.*

genius, *n.* A person having great mental capacity and inventive ability, especially in some art, science, etc. All prodigies possess genius; not all geniuses are prodigies.

*Williams' solution to the Year 2000 problem was a stroke of **genius,** both original and effective.*

enfant terrible, *n.* (awn-fawn te-ree-ble) from the French. Anyone constantly vexing, startling, or embarrassing others by outraging conventional opinion or expectations. Wunderkinds are often enfant terribles; not all enfant terribles are Wunderkinds or even children.

*Williams' temperamental outbursts embarrassed his co-workers and pigeonholed him as an **enfant terrible.***

mogul, *n.* A powerful or important person, especially one with autocratic power, and it is not directly related to genius or talent.

*Williams left ReallyBig Co., founded his own software company, and soon became a **mogul** in the software industry.*

 Also Explore: *ability,* autocratic, inventive, magnate, mastermind.

All the Way

full-blown, *adj.* Fully grown or developed. An idea that is well thought-out is considered a full-blown idea. An idea that is not full-blown is sometimes half-baked.

> *The initial concept was only a sentence written on the back of a cocktail napkin, so Ray reworked it into a **full-blown** proposal.*

full-fledged, *adj.* Completely developed or trained; of full rank or status. Ideas become full-blown, not full-fledged; people become full-fledged after proper training or accomplishment.

> *After several months on the job, Samson considered himself a **full-fledged** representative of the firm.*

full-bodied, *adj.* Having a rich flavor and much strength; large or broad in body or substance. Ideas are full-blown, people are full-fledged, and things are full-bodied.

> *The brew had a **full-bodied** taste.*

fulfill, *vt.* To fill the requirements of or to satisfy (a condition) or answer (a purpose).

> *The proposal from the KJE agency **fulfilled** all the needs of the project.*

abundant, *adj.* Very plentiful; more than sufficient; ample. Because abundant refers to quantity rather than quality, a thing can be abundant yet still not fulfill a particular need.

> *There were an **abundant** number of resumés, although none were exactly what Henry was looking for.*

Also Explore: consummate, copious, half-baked, mature, sufficient.

Looks

style, *n.* Style is not content, only the way content appears; it is a mode of expressing or presenting yourself or your thoughts. Style can also be a manner that is deemed elegant, appropriate, and fashionable, especially in demeanor or dress.

> *The agency had a habit of emphasizing **style** over substance; Henry found their work content-free.*

superficial, *adj.* Concerned with and understanding only the easily apparent and obvious. Superficial is typically used in a negative fashion, referring to something or someone that is shallow or not profound. Style is superficial when compared to content.

> *Joseph had only a **superficial** understanding of the subject, so he couldn't hold his own in a heated debate.*

fashionable, *adj.* Following the current style. Fashion is often superficial and transient.

> *Lime-green pant suits were **fashionable** that year, even though Mary preferred a more conservative approach to her wardrobe.*

beauty, *n.* The quality attributed to whatever pleases or satisfies the senses or mind, as by line, color, form, or by behavior, attitude, etc. Beauty can be both superficial and fashionable because it is not self-defined, but defined, as the saying goes, by the beholder.

> *The new package had a certain **beauty** to it; target audiences were attracted to its pleasing color and design.*

mediagenic, *adj.* Attractive and appealing to viewers and readers of the news media. Mediagenic celebrities often define a society's view of beauty at any given time.

> *Mr. Xavier wanted someone more **mediagenic** as the spokesperson for the new product.*

 Also Explore: chic, cursory, elegance, photogenic.

Appealing

---

charismatic, *adj.* Of, having, or resulting from a special charm that inspires fascination or devotion. Leaders often possess charisma that inspires their followers. A person with charisma is charming.

> *Mr. Xavier had proven himself a **charismatic** leader; he was able to charm his way through any situation.*

---

alluring, *adj.* Highly attractive. If something is alluring, it is highly desirable; one wishes to possess a thing or person that is alluring.

> *The new convertible was **alluring;** all the guys on the bowling team were lusting after it.*

enticing, *vt.* That which attracts by offering hope of reward or pleasure. One is allured by the qualities of a thing itself; one is enticed by an end result related to a thing.

> *The prospect of making a million-dollar impact was **enticing** to Richard.*

tempting, *adj.* That which tries to induce or entice, especially to something immoral or sensually pleasurable. Temptation is enticement to do something that one probably shouldn't do.

> *Even though she knew it probably wouldn't be a long-term solution, Wanda found the job offer **tempting**.*

winsome, *adj.* Attractive in a sweet, engaging way; charming.

> *The young intern's **winsome** good looks made her a popular lunchtime companion for the men in the department.*

Also Explore: engaging, entrancing, fascination, *insinuate*.

Like

-phile, *n.* One that loves, likes, or is attracted to. Add *-phile* to the end of many words to denote a lover of the root word. Implies an intense feeling for the subject at hand, sometimes to the point of obsession.

> *Frank's love of high-fidelity music reproduction led to his becoming an **audiophile.***

---

desire, *n.* A wish or longing for something or someone; a craving.

> *Frank had a huge **desire** for a new subwoofer to add to his surround-sound setup.*

covet, *vt.* To want ardently (especially something that another person has); long for with envy. Coveting is more extreme than desiring.

> *Frank began to **covet** his neighbor's new home theater system.*

preference, *n.* Greater liking. Preference implies a priority order of things wanted.

> *Given a choice, Frank's **preference** was a DVD player instead of a VCR.*

fanatic, *n.* A person whose extreme zeal, piety, and so on goes beyond what is reasonable. The word fan comes from the word fanatic.

> *Once he got the new CD changer installed, Frank became a **fanatic;** within a month, he had purchased over a hundred compact discs.*

Also Explore: obsession, *zealot*, pedant, yearn.

Dislike

-phobe One who fears or hates. Add *-phobe* to the end of many words to denote one who fears the root word. Implies an intense feeling for the subject at hand, sometimes to the point of irrational hatred.

> *After being frightened by a spider as a child, Joyce became an **arachnophobe**.*

---

phobia, *n.* An irrational, excessive, and persistent fear of some particular thing or situation. One not only dislikes the object of a phobia; one has an unhealthy dread of that thing.

> *Her **phobia** led Joyce to schedule monthly appointments with an exterminator.*

abhor, *vt.* To shrink from in disgust, hatred, etc.; detest. Abhor implies an intense physical response to some object, situation, or person.

> *Joyce **abhorred** finding spider webs in her rose bushes.*

despise, *vt.* To regard with dislike or repugnance. Despise implies a strong emotional response toward that which one regards with contempt or aversion; compare with abhor, which is a more intense physical response.

> *The exterminator grew to **despise** Joyce's monthly appointment; she wouldn't let him leave until every corner of the house had been inspected.*

begrudge, *vt.* To regard with displeasure or disapproval. Begrudge is more passive than either despise or abhor; begrudge implies that you allow something to occur even though you don't like it.

> *Joyce did her best to manage her phobia and not **begrudge** her son an ant farm in his room.*

 Also Explore: aversion, contemn, loathe, neurosis, repugnance.

Ups and Downs

---

boom, *n.* A period of business prosperity, industrial expansion, etc. Boom and bust refer to the economy in general; bear and bull refer specifically to the stock market or to individual markets.

*Record-high housing starts contributed to the **boom** market in the fourth quarter.*

---

bust, *n.* A financial collapse; economic crash.

*The market was a **bust** after news of the impending international conflict.*

bear, *n.* An investor who believes that a stock or the market in general will decline. A bear market is an extended period of falling prices in the overall market.

*Mark turned **bearish** when he feared the market had topped out.*

bull, *n.* An investor who thinks the market or a specific security or industry will rise. A bull market is an extended period in which the market consistently rises.

*Mort was **bullish** on technology stocks, believing that more investors were due to jump on the bandwagon.*

slump, *n.* A decline in business activity, prices, and so on. Whereas a bust is a disastrous crash, a slump is a minor downturn.

*The market went into a **slump** when quarterly earnings were slightly below expectations.*

 Also Explore: collapse, downturn, expansion, *prosperity.*

Coming to an Agreement

DAY 23

---

arbitrate, *vt.* To decide a dispute. In collective bargaining negotiations, an arbitrator is named with the consent of both sides. An arbitrator is someone literally put in the middle of a dispute.

> *A special judge was appointed to **arbitrate** the long-running dispute between the company and the union.*

---

mediate, *vt.* To bring about by conciliation. Arbitration lets a neutral third party make an impartial decision; mediation requires both sides to make concessions.

> *Judge Randolph **mediated** an agreement that called for compromises from both the company and the union.*

ultimatum, *n.* A final offer or demand, especially by one of the parties engaged in negotiations, the rejection of which usually leads to a break in relations and unilateral action by the party issuing the ultimatum.

> *The union issued an **ultimatum:** Increase wages by 5 percent, or the workers go on strike.*

impasse, *n.* A situation offering no escape, a difficulty without solution, an argument where no agreement is possible, and so on; deadlock. An impasse often results when one party issues an ultimatum.

> *When the company stood fast against a pay increase, the situation was at an **impasse.***

compromise, *vt.* To settle or adjust by concessions on both sides. Compromise is often the only way to break an impasse in negotiations.

> *After long hours of negotiations, the company agreed to **compromise** with a 4 percent pay increase.*

 Also Explore: concession, conciliation, deadlock, *unilateral*, modus vivendi.

Religion

---

non-secular, *adj.* Of or relating to church and religion; sacred; religious. Do not confuse secular (relating to worldly things—not relating to religion) with non-secular. Public schools are secular schools; hymns are non-secular music.

> *The church choir put on a concert of **non-secular** Christmas music.*

---

agnostic, *n.* A person who believes that the human mind cannot know whether there is a God or an ultimate cause or anything beyond material phenomena. An agnostic questions the existence of God, heaven, and so on in the absence of material proof and in unwillingness to accept supernatural revelation.

> *Kevin was an **agnostic;** he simply saw no proof of the existence of a God.*

atheist, *n.* A person who believes that there is no God. Whereas an agnostic questions religious beliefs, an atheist rejects all religious beliefs and denies the existence of God.

> *The **atheist** coalition objected to the nativity scene in front of the school.*

sanctimonious, *adj.* Pretending to be very holy or pious; affecting righteousness. Sanctimonious implies insincerity.

> *William's **sanctimonious** posturing oozed of false sincerity.*

sacrilegious, *adj.* Guilty of violating what is consecrated to God or religion. Sacrilege can also be the desecration or disrespectful treatment of any person, place, thing, or idea held sacred.

> *To Brenda, taking the Lord's name in vain was **sacrilegious.***

Also Explore: consecrated, hypocritical, *pious*, *profane*, *skeptic.*

To Start With

---

assumption, *n.* Anything taken for granted or supposed to be a fact. Assumption implies taking something as the truth without actually checking to be sure.

> The **assumption** was that the payroll department could handle the change without major disruption, although Mary Lou feared otherwise.

---

presumption, *n.* The act of taking for granted; accepting as true, lacking proof to the contrary. A presumption differs from an assumption in that a presumption is usually made on the basis of probable evidence in its favor with an absence of proof to the contrary. A presumption is an assumption with some degree of fact checking.

> Based on their past performance, William committed his team to the project on the **presumption** that they could handle it.

postulate, *vt.* To assume without proof to be true, real, or necessary, especially as a basis for argument. Postulate implies the assumption of something as an underlying factor, often one that is incapable of proof.

> Without any proof to the contrary, Jamie **postulated** that the drop in sales was due to seasonal factors.

premise, *n.* A previous statement or assertion that serves as the basis for an argument. Premise implies the setting forth of a proposition on which a conclusion can be based.

> The entire proposal was based on the **premise** that men spent more time online than women.

conceit, *n.* An idea, thought, or concept. Many imaginary stories depend on a conceit to set the stage for an alternate reality or unrealistic situation.

> The story revolved around the **conceit** that astral projection was not only possible, but commonplace.

 Also Explore: *conceptual,* posit, stipulate, temerity.

Financial Instruments

stock, *n.* The capital invested in a company or corporation through the buying of shares, each of which entitles the buyer to a share in the ownerships, dividends, and voting rights.

> *The price of the company's* **stock** *rose in anticipation of strong quarterly earnings.*

bond, *n.* An interest-bearing certificate issued by a government or business, promising to pay the holder a specified sum on a written date. Both stocks and bonds are common ways of raising capital.

> *The* **bond** *market remained strong for the second consecutive week.*

mutual fund, *n.* A pool of money that is managed by an investment company. More precisely, a mutual fund is a company or corporation formed to invest in and manage a portfolio of stocks and bonds with the funds it obtains from its shareholders.

> *Randy didn't have enough money to create a diversified stock portfolio of his own, so he decided to invest in a* **mutual fund** *instead.*

IRA, *n.* Individual Retirement Account, a personal retirement plan whereby a limited amount of annual earned income may be saved or invested in specially designated accounts, deferring taxes on the earnings until retirement.

> *Helen contributed the maximum allowed amount to her* **IRA.**

401(k), *n.* A retirement plan, similar to an IRA, offered by for-profit companies for their employees. A 401(k) is employer sponsored and tax deferred and uses pretax contributions from an employee's regular compensation to invest for that employee.

> *ReallyBig Co. matched employee contributions to the* **401(k)** *plan up to a total of 10 percent of earnings.*

 Also Explore: *dividend,* portfolio, shareholder.

Stocks and Bonds

option, *n.* The right, but not the obligation, to buy or sell securities at a fixed price within a specified period. Exercising options involves speculating on the future price of stocks.

*First Financial began offering **options** on ReallyBig Co. stock.*

put, *n.* An option to sell a given quantity of stock, commodity, etc. at a specific price and within a specified period of time. A put is a particular type of option for selling stock in anticipation of, or to protect against, a decline in the price of the stock.

*Expecting a decline in ReallyBig Co. stock, Roger purchased 200 **put** options.*

call, *n.* An option to buy a given quantity of stock, commodity, and so on at a specified price and within a specified time. A call is a particular type of option for buying stock in expectation of a rise in the price of the stock.

*Wanting to ride the upward pricing trend in ReallyBig Co. stock, Mary Ann placed a **call** on 500 shares.*

short, *vt.* A sale of securities or commodities that the seller does not yet have but expects to cover later at a lower price. An investor "borrows" stock from a broker, sells it, and then eventually buys it back, repaying the broker with the new shares. If the stock declines in price, the investor realizes a profit; if the stock price increases, the investor loses money.

*Anticipating poor quarterly earnings, Harry decided to **short** ReallyBig Co.'s stock.*

dividend, *n.* A share of a company's earnings that are authorized by a company's board and paid to a particular class of shareholders, usually quarterly.

*ReallyBig Co. announced **dividends** of $0.25 per share.*

 Also Explore: earnings, futures, *proceeds.*

Social and Economic Systems

---

capitalism, n. The economic system in which all or most of the means of production and distribution are privately owned and operated for profit, originally under fully competitive conditions.

*After the fall of the Soviet Union, many former republics began to embrace the tenets of **capitalism**.*

---

socialism, n. Any economic system in which the means of production and distribution is owned and operated by the society, community, or government—as opposed to private individuals. Not to be confused with Socialism.

*Subsidized health care is one concept migrating into our culture from **socialism**.*

communism, n. Any economic theory or system based on the ownership of all property by the community as a whole. Socialism places the ownership of the means of production in the hands of the community; communism places the ownership of all property in the hands of the community. Not to be confused with Communism.

*Property ownership is one of the things the people would have to forgo in **communism**.*

libertarianism, n. A social doctrine based on full individual freedom of thought, expression, and action. Libertarians believe in minimized governmental control and interference.

*Abhorring government interference, Scott started leaning towards **libertarianism**.*

totalitarianism, n. A form of government in which one political party or group maintains complete control under a dictatorship and bans all others.

*Accustomed to a two-party system, Henry couldn't grasp how people could ever accept **totalitarianism**.*

 Also Explore: Socialism, Communism, autocracy.

Golf

par, *n.* The number of strokes established as the skillful score for any given hole or for the whole course. For example, a par three hole should be taken in three strokes.

> *After eight holes, Dave was one over **par**; his boss was two over.*

birdie, *n.* A score of one under par on any hole. Also note *eagle*, which is a score of two under par on any hole.

> *Dave needed a **birdie** on the next hole to shoot par on the front nine even though that would mean beating his boss.*

bogie, *n.* A score of one over par on any hole. A birdie is one stroke to the positive, and a bogie is one stroke to the negative.

> *Dave purposely hit a **bogie** on the last hole, finishing two over par for the front nine; fortunately, his boss parred the last hole, giving him a one-stroke lead over Dave.*

best-ball, *adj.* Designating a type of team competition for partners in which the lower score of either partner is recorded as the team score on each hole.

> *Because several players were relatively inexperienced, they decided to play **best-ball** at the annual company golf outing.*

dormie, *adj.* When scoring by the number of holes won, being ahead of an opponent by as many holes as are yet to be played.

> *Dave's team was **dormie** three and still lost the match.*

 Also Explore: fade, slice, stroke, tee.

Perks

---

flex time, *n.* A system allowing individual employees some flexibility in choosing the time, but not the number, of their working hours.

> *Marie appreciated the fact that working **flex-time** allowed her to start work early and be home by the time her children got out of school.*

---

relocation, *n.* To move to a new location. Many companies pay relocation costs for new employees moving from a different city.

> *ReallyBig Co. offered to pay **relocation** costs for the new hire from California.*

stock option, *n.* An option offered to an employee by a company to buy its stock for less than the market price at a specified date in time. Many companies offer their employees stock options as part of their overall compensation package.

> *Startup Inc. offered **stock options** as part of its compensation package.*

incentive, *n.* Something that stimulates one to take action, work harder, etc.; a stimulus or encouragement. An incentive is generally a "kicker" to one's base compensation, such as a monetary bonus or promise of time off for a job well done.

> *The promise of a week's paid vacation was an added **incentive** to finish the project ahead of schedule.*

outplacement, *n.* Assistance in finding a new job, provided to an employee, especially an executive, about to be fired. Not a perk per se, but a service often provided by companies downsizing their work forces.

> *Doug was offered **outplacement** services as part of his severance package.*

 Also Explore: *compensation*, fringe benefits, perquisite, *severance*.

Genetic Engineering

bioethics, *n.* The study of the ethical problems arising from scientific advances in biology and medicine. For example, the quandary surrounding the cloning of human beings is a bioethical dilemma.

> *The **bioethics** committee asked the question, "How do we know when it's right to administer genetic tests, and who should have access to the results of those tests?"*

biotechnology, *n.* The use of the data and techniques of engineering and technology for the study and solution of problems concerning living organisms. Also referred to as biotech.

> *CloneCo uses **biotechnology** to transfer useful genes from microbes to plants, creating crops that are resistant to herbicides.*

bioengineering, *n.* A science dealing with the application of engineering science and technology to problems of biology and medicine.

> *In Austria, the concern about **bioengineering** led the government to ban imports of gene-spliced crops.*

embryology, *n.* The branch of biology dealing with the formation and development of embryos.

> *The **embryology** department succeeded in cloning a tadpole from an embryo.*

genetics, *n.* The branch of biology that deals with heredity and variation in similar or related animals and plants. Can also refer to the genetic features or constitution of an individual, group, or kind.

> *There was a long-standing debate about whether homosexuality was caused by **genetics** or by environment.*

 Also Explore: *biological warfare, clone,* mutation.

Decorate and Elaborate

---

embellish, *vt.* To improve (an account or report) by adding details, often of a fictitious or imaginary kind; touch up. Embellish suggests the addition of something for effect.

> *Walter **embellished** the story by adding some colorful—but fictitious—details.*

---

adorn, *vt.* To add beauty, splendor, or distinction to. Adorn implies that something had beauty beforehand but has been made even more pleasing or attractive.

> *The Christmas tree was **adorned** with a beautiful glass angel at the top.*

ornament, *vt.* To furnish with anything serving to adorn or embellish; decorate; beautify. Ornament is used with reference to accessories that enhance the appearance of a thing. Unlike adorn, which implies a prior beauty, anything—even a previously ugly thing—can be ornamented.

> *Beatrice refused to **ornament** her office with personal effects; she preferred a sterile working environment.*

accentuate, *vt.* To emphasize; heighten the effect of. If the right parts of a story are accentuated, no embellishment may be necessary.

> *The President **accentuated** the positive impact of the latest legislation.*

accessorize, *vt.* To equip, decorate, supplement, and so on with accessories. Accessorizing something does not necessarily beautify it; it simply makes it more fully equipped.

> *Ralph **accessorized** his new SUV with running boards and a bicycle rack.*

 Also Explore: *augment*, elaborate, embroider, *enhance*.

Measurements

---

analysis, *n.* A separating or breaking up of any whole into its parts. Analysis implies an examination of the parts of things with the intent to find out their nature, proportion, function, interrelationship, etc.

> *Further **analysis** was necessary to determine why consumers weren't buying the new product.*

---

qualitative, *adj.* Analysis that involves aspects that cannot be directly measured. Qualitative analysis results in descriptions and opinions.

> ***Qualitative** analysis from the focus group indicated that the new package had little appeal for women.*

quantitative, *adj.* Capable of being measured. Quantitative analysis results in numbers that can be compared to other numbers.

> *A **quantitative** analysis of the research proved that women were 42 percent less likely than men to choose our product over that of the competition.*

anecdotal, *adj.* Evidence based on personal experience or reported observations unverified by controlled experiments. Anecdotal research has no quantitative component and is sometimes called mother-in-law research.

> *Based on Herm's personal observations, the **anecdotal** evidence indicated that the new product wasn't moving off the shelves.*

metric, *n.* Item of measurement. A metric is something that can be quantitatively measured.

> *A key **metric** for the success of the new product was its appeal to women in the 24–42 age group.*

 Also Explore: breakdown, dissection, objectivity, subjectivity.

Making Money

income, *n.* The money or other gain received, by a corporation from sales, investments, and operations. Income is not synonymous with cash. (Note that some firms prefer to use the word revenue instead of income.)

*ReallyBig Co. reported net **income** for the year of $200 million.*

profit, *n.* The sum remaining after all costs, direct and indirect, are deducted from the income of a business. (Note that some firms prefer to use the word earnings instead of profit.)

*After accounting for special items, ReallyBig Co.'s net **profit** was $22 million, or 11 percent.*

cash, *n.* Money that a company actually has, including money on deposit. Because corporate profit can include non-cash items such as depreciation, it is possible for a company to show a profit on paper but not have any cash on hand.

*Despite the acceptable profit numbers, ReallyBig Co. was hemorrhaging **cash.***

gross, *adj.* With no deductions; total; entire. Gross income includes revenues before returns, discounts, allowances, etc.; gross profit includes earnings before depreciation, adjustments, etc.

***Gross** revenues were higher than expected, due to strong sales in the Midwest.*

net, *adj.* Remaining after certain deductions have been made. Net income is the revenue after returns, cost of goods, and so on have been deducted; net profit is the earnings after depreciation, allowances, etc. have been deducted.

*Despite the stronger gross revenues, **net** revenues decreased due to high returns during the period.*

 Also Explore: allowance, *depreciation*, gain, *liquid*, receipts.

In Agreement

---

synchronous, *adj.* Happening at the same time; occurring together. Being in synch implies being aligned in some form or fashion.

> *The public relations department organized five **synchronous** events across the country, all timed to get coverage on the local 6:00 p.m. news.*

---

consonant, *adj.* In harmony or agreement. Consonant suggests a melodious, soothing agreement or an emotional or spiritual attunement.

> *Sherry's tastes in music were **consonant** with Michael's; she could count on him being pleased with the CD she bought him for his birthday.*

attune, *vt.* To bring into harmony or agreement.

> *Viewed as somewhat of an anachronism, Roger needed to better **attune** himself with the times.*

harmony, *n.* A combination of parts into a pleasing or orderly whole.

> *The workforce worked together in perfect **harmony;** not a single voice of dissent was heard.*

accord, *n.* Mutual agreement. Accord implies a formal agreement, as between countries.

> *The two companies reached an **accord** for the mutual use of the disputed trademark.*

 Also Explore: compliance, congruity, consensus, détente, rapport.

Workplace Injury

---

repetitive stress injury (RSI), *n.* An injury to the hands or wrists associated with any repetitive activity. RSI is also known as repetitive strain injury.

> *The benefits department began seeing more instances of **repetitive stress injury** on medical claim forms.*

---

carpal tunnel syndrome (CTS), *n.* A painful or numb condition of the wrist and hand resulting when tissues that form a tunnel-like passage in the wrist swell and pinch a nerve within the passage. CTS is a specific, severe, and debilitating form of RSI.

> *When her wrist began to ache after long hours at the keyboard, Margot began to wonder if she was suffering from **carpal tunnel syndrome.***

tendinitis, *n.* Inflammation of a tendon. These tendon inflammations usually occur before full-blown CTS.

> *The doctor diagnosed Margot as having **tendinitis.***

ergonomics, *n.* The science that seeks to adapt work or working conditions to fit the worker's body and make it safer and more comfortable.

> *In an effort to reduce the stress on her wrists, Margot invested in an **ergonomic** keyboard.*

lumbar, *adj.* The vertebrae, nerves, arteries, in the lower part of the back. Lumbar support is a chair backrest that supports the muscles of the lumbar region when sitting upright.

> *Margot's new office chair offered adjustable **lumbar** support, which helped to relieve her lower-back pain.*

 Also Explore: *chiropractor*, inflammation, vertebrae.

Alternative Medicine

holistic, *adj.* A system of medical thought that deals with the whole or integrated system rather than its parts.

> *Adherents of **holistic** medicine believe that there are four healing areas of energy and release in the body: mental, physical, emotional, and spiritual.*

homeopathy, *n.* A system of medical treatment based on the theory that certain diseases can be cured by small doses of drugs that in a healthy person would produce symptoms like those of the disease.

> *Dr. Benjamin, a practitioner of **homeopathy,** prescribed medicines based on the patient's idiosyncratic symptoms.*

allopathy *n.* The treatment of disease by remedies that produce effects different from or opposite to those produced by the disease. Today allopathy is sometimes loosely applied to the general practice of conventional medicine; but, in strict usage it refers only to treatment theory contrary to that of homeopathy.

> *Jeanine felt very fortunate that she found Dr. Singh, who had studied both **allopathy** and homeopathy.*

naturopathy, *n.* A system of treating diseases, largely employing natural agencies, such as fresh air and water, everyday foodstuffs, and herbs, and rejecting the use of drugs and medicines.

> *A practitioner of **naturopathy** told Carl that he could get rid of his warts by bandaging a sliver of onion to his finger.*

aromatherapy, *n.* The use of aromatic oils from herbs, flowers, and so on for their therapeutic effects when applied to the skin, as in massage, or when the scent is inhaled.

> *Adherents of **aromatherapy** believe that suffusing a room with lavender essence relieves the occupants from tension and anxiety.*

 Also Explore: acupuncture, aromatic, biofeedback.

Life Choices

cocooning, *vt*. The need to protect oneself from the harsh, unpredictable realities of the outside world; to pull a shell of safety around oneself or one's family; to isolate. Coined by trend spotter Faith Popcorn, cocooning is about insulation and avoidance, coziness, and control.

> *The Browns began **cocooning** by renting videos instead of going out to the movies. Within a few years, they decided to move out of the city to a more isolated house in the country.*

cloister, *vt*. To confine in a place where one may lead a secluded life. Cloistering is a form of cocooning without the defensive nature but with an even higher degree of isolation.

> *Wynton decided to **cloister** himself away from the hustle and bustle of the big city.*

nesting, *vt*. To settle in as in a nest. Nesting is typically what young families do while in the process of adding children.

> *After they'd been married a year, Jim and Mary began to **nest** in preparation for their upcoming brood.*

clanning, *vt*. Grouping together people on the basis of some commonality (blood relationships, special interests, political causes, shared tastes, and so on) in a "social cocoon."

> *Most of the marketing professionals in the community engaged in **clanning** by patronizing the same bar after work each night.*

streamlining, *vt*. To arrange or organize to gain simplicity and efficiency. Many families streamline their activities so they can lead less complex lives.

> *Dave and Margot decided to **streamline** their lives by cutting out most nonessential social activities.*

 Also Explore: circumscribe, *coterie*, immure, sequester.

Fooling Around

---

tinker, *vi.* To fuss or putter aimlessly or uselessly. More formally, to tinker can mean to mend or repair. Tinkering is not harmful, just generally aimless.

> *Ralph liked to relax by **tinkering** in his workshop on Saturday afternoons.*

---

meddle, *vi.* To concern oneself with or take part in other people's affairs without being asked or needed; interfere. Tinkering has no aim; meddling has purpose.

> *Justin liked to **meddle** in the projects of the other team.*

hamstring, *vt.* To lessen or destroy the effectiveness of. To hamstring is to affect the way something works.

> *Justin's meddling began to **hamstring** the team's effectiveness.*

impair, *vt.* To make worse, less, weaker, and so on; damage; reduce. Impairing does actual damage to a thing or person.

> *Ginger's vision was **impaired** by the crack in the windshield.*

erode, *vi.* To deteriorate, decay, or vanish. Impair implies breaking something; erode implies wearing down.

> *ReallyBig Co.'s profits had been **eroding** for the past six periods.*

 Also Explore: despoil, impede, interfere, putter, retard.

Beautiful People

glitterati, *n.* (glit-ter-ah-tee) a combination of glitter and literati. People who are wealthy, chic, famous, and so on. In today's society, glitterati are celebrities and inspire much media coverage.

*The National Tattler was filled with photos of the **glitterati** as they left the latest Hollywood hot spot.*

nouveau riche, *n.* (noo-vo-reesh) from the French (newly rich). A person who has only recently become rich: often connoting tasteless ostentation, lack of culture, etc. The nouveau riche often aspire to be glitterati.

*It was clear from their crude manners and affinity for polyester that the Stouffers were of the **nouveau riche.***

paparazzi, *n.* (pah-pah-raht-tsee) from paperasier (a scribbler or rummager in old papers). Photographers, especially freelance ones, who take candid shots, often in an intrusive manner, of celebrities for newspapers or magazines.

*The National Tattler paid handsomely for the best pictures from the **paparazzi.***

literati, *n.* (lit-eh-rah-tee) from the Latin litteratus (learned), scholarly or learned people. More usually, literati are the glitterati of the arts and letters scene.

*Professor Simonson longed to be considered one of the **literati** at the university; then he'd get respect from his peers!*

digerati, *n.* (dig-eh-rah-tee) from a combination of digital and literati. The digital version of literati; an elite class of netizens who are seen to be extremely knowledgeable, hip, or otherwise in-the-know regarding the digital revolution.

*The Web site trumpeted the new online column by one of the foremost **digerati.***

 Also Explore: chic, *elite*, *netizen*, illuminati, prima donna.

Journalism and the Media

---

sound bite, *n.* A brief, quotable remark or excerpt from a speech, suitable for use on TV or radio newscasts. The term is sometimes used in a dismissive fashion to imply superficiality.

> *The Senator's speech was reduced to a ten-second **sound bite** on the evening news.*

---

hard news, *n.* Hard news stories usually contain concrete information that describes things and actions, and there is no overt opinion from the reporter. Compare with soft news, which consists of lifestyle features, or analysis, which takes a broader, more opinionated view of a topic.

> *Channel 52 switched from a **hard news** format to a softer, more lifestyle-based format.*

tabloid, *n.* A newspaper, usually half the ordinary size, with many pictures and short, often sensational, news stories.

> *Thanks to the scoop about the movie star's love child, The National Tattler was the country's best-selling **tabloid** that week.*

zine, *n.* A cheaply printed magazine published irregularly by amateurs. Many zines (sometimes called e-zines) are Web-based.

> *The **zine's** editorial condemned the mayor's office for alleged racism in its hiring practices.*

advertorial, *n.* An advertisement that is styled to resemble the editorial or content of the medium in which it is placed. A television-based advertorial is called an infomercial.

> *Marie thought the **advertorial** was actual coverage of a new medical breakthrough.*

 Also Explore: fourth estate, yellow journalism.

Little White Lies

**DAY
42**

---

prevarication, *n.* An evasion of the truth. A prevarication is not necessarily a lie, just an avoidance of the truth.

> *Carly's **prevarication** about the accident to her father was shortly revealed for what it was by the insurance claim.*

---

deception, *n.* Something that misleads, as an illusion, or is meant to deceive, as a fraud. A deception isn't a lie or an avoidance, but rather something that draws attention away from the point at hand.

> *To keep Frank from finding out about the surprise party, Betty concocted an elaborate **deception**.*

ruse, *n.* A stratagem or trick. Like a deception, a ruse is not necessarily a lie; it is a trick, often designed to divert attention away from some point or scenario.

> *Although the planes and tanks looked real enough, it was all a **ruse** to trick the enemy into thinking the allies were invading elsewhere.*

mendacity, *n.* A lie; falsehood. A mendacity is a deliberate lie, no equivocation.

> *Carol realized that Robert was guilty of **mendacity** when she found the ticket stub in his shirt pocket.*

fabrication, *n.* A falsehood, false excuse, invention, etc. Fabrication implies an embellishment beyond that of a simple lie or mendacity.

> *The story was a complete—and elaborate—**fabrication**.*

 Also Explore: *artifice, embellish,* equivocation, *strategy.*

Secrets

nondisclosure, *n.* Not to reveal or make known. A person with access to confidential information often has to sign a nondisclosure agreement (NDA) that states he or she won't reveal said information.

> *Carl was kicked out of the program because he violated **nondisclosure** by revealing the details of the final version to the press.*

conceal, *vt.* To keep from another's knowledge; keep secret. Concealment implies a deliberate hiding.

> *Phyllis **concealed** her marital status when she filled out the claims form.*

clandestine, *adj.* Kept secret or hidden, especially for some illicit purpose. Clandestine implies a secret with an illicit motive.

> *Ned set up a **clandestine** meeting with the recruiter to discuss his jumping to the competition.*

illicit, *adj.* Not allowed by law, custom, rule, etc; unlawful and improper.

> *Bob's **illicit** behavior was discovered by his boss and got him dismissed from the team.*

private, *adj.* Not open to, intended for, or controlled by the public. Compare with public, which is known by, or open to the knowledge of, all or most people.

> *Discussion on the latest software was limited to a **private** mailing list.*

Also Explore: confidential, furtive, secluded, surreptitious.

Silent

reserved, *adj.* Self-restrained and withdrawn in speech and manner. Someone who is reserved keeps to themselves.

*Benjamin was **reserved** in his dealings with the company; he kept his motives well hidden.*

reticent, *adj.* Habitually silent or uncommunicative; disinclined to speak readily. Reticent implies a pattern of uncommunicative behavior.

*Everyone noticed that Dennis was **reticent** in crowds.*

taciturn, *adj.* Almost always silent; not liking to talk. Reticent is a disinclination to talk; taciturn is an actual dislike of talk.

*Alex was termed "the great stoneface" for his **taciturn** demeanor at management meetings.*

uncommunicative, *adj.* Tending to withhold information, opinions, feelings, and so on. Uncommunicative implies a deliberate withholding of information, not necessarily a dislike of talk.

*When he was accused of talking to a headhunter, Ned became **uncommunicative**.*

quiescent, *adj.* Quiet; still; inactive. Quiescent implies no motive or dislike of talk; it simply describes a quiet state.

*After executing three major acquisitions, ReallyBig Co. fell into a **quiescent** period, avoiding additional activities while it integrated the new additions to its portfolio.*

 Also Explore: *torpid*, cagey, evasive, discreet, leery.

Accuse

---

allude, *vt.* To refer in a casual or indirect way. An allusion is not a charge, only a reference. Something alluded to is hinted at.

> *In his own roundabout way, Melvin **alluded** to the difficulties he and other employees faced when dealing with the growing bureaucracy.*

---

imply, *vt.* To indicate indirectly or by allusion. Imply is stronger than allude.

> *Without saying so directly, Marvin **implied** that the human resources department was negligent in the matter.*

incriminate, *vt.* To involve in, or make appear guilty of, a crime or fault. Incriminate implies an appearance of wrongdoing, not a charge.

> *The circumstantial evidence was instrumental in **incriminating** Morley in the Chambers case.*

charge, *vt.* To accuse of wrongdoing. A charge is a formal accusation.

> *Robert was **charged** with stealing the portable computer from Melanie's office.*

arraign, *vt.* To bring before a court of law to hear and answer charges brought by police. Arraign implies a legal formality.

> *Maxwell was formally **arraigned** on theft charges.*

 Also Explore: *censure, impeach,* impute, *indict, litigate.*

Gangs

---

initiate, *vt.* To admit as a member into a fraternity, club, gang, etc., especially with a special or secret ceremony. Gang initiations often involve committing some action or crime.

> *When he was **initiated**, Waldo had to spray paint obscenities on the wall of the Biggie Mart.*

---

colors, *n.* Colored clothing (jackets, bandanas, and so on) that identifies the wearer as a member of a particular gang. Schools, sports teams, and businesses can also have colors.

> *When he was arrested, Waldo was wearing the **colors** of the 8th Street Boyz.*

graffiti, *n.* (gra-fee-tee) from the Italian (a scratch). Inscriptions, slogans, drawings, etc. scratched, scribbled, or drawn, often crudely, on a wall or other public surface. Note that graffiti is plural; graffito is singular.

> *Mr. Potter was forced to paint over the **graffiti** that was sprayed on the side of his building.*

posse, *n.* A body of persons associated with a specific leader.

> *After he was sprung from jail, Waldo hung with his **posse** in the Biggie Mart parking lot.*

turf, *n.* A neighborhood area regarded by a street gang as its own territory to be defended against other gangs.

> *The area from the Biggie Mart to the savings and loan was the 8th Street Boyz' **turf**.*

 Also Explore: *fraternity*, *cadre*, disciple, beat.

Turf Wars

territory, *n.* A sphere or province of action, existence, thought, and so on. Territory can refer to a physical area or an area of control or influence, such as a unit or division within a company or organization.

> *Even though he was only the national sales manager, Jones regarded all of marketing and sales as his **territory.***

territorial, *adj.* Behavior pattern exhibited by a person or animal defending its territory. Managers building an empire often start by being territorial.

> *Jones got **territorial** when the new VP tried to exert his authority.*

unit, *n.* An organized body of troops, airplanes, etc. forming a subdivision of a larger body. Departments within a larger organization are often perceived as individual units.

> *After consolidating his power in sales and marketing, Jones began to lust after control of the entire **unit.***

sovereignty, *n.* Supreme and independent political authority. Control-hungry heads of individual units often crave sovereignty from the central organization.

> *As part of his plan to take control of the local unit, Jones tried to maintain **sovereignty** from the central office.*

empire, *n.* An extensive social or economic organization under the control of a single person, family, or corporation. Once an individual unit achieves sovereignty, it is not unusual for the head of that unit to try to build an empire.

> *Jones' superiors soon realized that he was trying to build an **empire** of his own and handed him his walking papers.*

 Also Explore: domain, *mandate*, purview, scope.

Battle

---

blitzkrieg, *n.* (blits-krehg) from the German (lightning + war). Any sudden, overwhelming attack. A blitzkrieg is usually a large-scale offensive, intended to win a quick victory. Originally a word dealing with military maneuvers, blitzkrieg now can refer to maneuvers within a business environment.

*ReallyBig Co. planned to mount a **blitzkrieg** of promotional activity designed to surprise and stun its chief competitor.*

---

campaign, *n.* A series of organized, planned actions for a particular purpose.

*The advertising **campaign** was set to kick off in June.*

engagement, *n.* A conflict; battle. An engagement is part of a campaign.

*Ray regarded the initial ads as the first **engagement** in the campaign against NotSoBig Co.*

fray, *n.* A noisy quarrel or fight; brawl. Campaigns and engagements are organized; frays are not.

*Ray declined to join in the **fray** over which ad to run in the first month of the campaign.*

outflank, *vt.* To go around and beyond the side of an enemy. In more common parlance, when one outflanks an enemy, one outwits him.

*To ReallyBig Co.'s surprise, NotSoBig Co. **outflanked** it with a rebate promotion before the campaign even started.*

Also Explore: deploy, mèlée, skirmish, wage, coup de main.

Courtship

romance, vt. To seek to gain the favor of, as by flattery. One can romance someone solely to get on their good side; romancing does not necessarily lead to eventual engagement or possession. Be careful about using romance, seduce, and similar terms in a corporate environment because they have sexual overtones.

> *Dean was **romanced** by the director of accounting to take over the new finance department.*

seduce, vt. To persuade someone to do something disloyal, disobedient, etc. In the throes of passion, it is sometimes easy to mistake seduction for romance.

> *Overly leveraged with a high monthly mortgage, Don was easily **seduced** by the promise of a higher salary.*

tantalize, vt. To tease or disappoint by promising or showing something desirable and then withholding it. Tantalize differs from seduce in that the promise is never realized.

> *Dave **tantalized** the new recruit with stories of rapid promotions—promotions that, unfortunately, were not to come.*

passion, n. Extreme, compelling emotion; intense emotional drive or excitement. Although one can have passion for an activity, the word is more often used in conjunction with a sexual drive or desire.

> *Dan had a true **passion** for flying remote control airplanes.*

pander, vt. To provide the means of helping to satisfy the ignoble ambitions or desires, vices, etc. of another. A panderer is specifically a go-between in a sexual intrigue; a pimp. More generally pandering refers to an almost obsequious willingness to get what someone else wants whether it is illicit, of a sexual nature, or not.

> *Joel was told to **pander** to Tinycorp.'s biggest client in order to cinch the deal. He just hoped his boss didn't mean it literally.*

 Also Explore: *illicit,* woo, *solicit,* suit.

Movies

wide-screen, *adj.* A film made for projection on a screen much wider than it is high. Wide-screen films are edited for the narrower ratios of television screens through a pan-and-scan process.

> *The latest special effects extravaganza wasn't shot in **wide-screen** format; it lost much of its impact on the normal TV screen.*

letterboxed, *adj.* Recorded for playback on videotape, video discs, and so on by means of a format that preserves a wide-screen film image, using dark bands above and below the image.

> *Michael preferred to watch **letterboxed** movies on disc because he felt it preserved the original theatrical experience.*

DVD, *n.* digital versatile disk. A CD-ROM format capable of storing up to a maximum of 17G of data (enough for a full-length feature movie). It is expected to replace current CD-ROM drives, as well as VHS video tapes and laser disks.

> *Mark haunted the store day and night until Electrocorp's debut **DVD** player finally arrived.*

home theater, *n.* The goal of a home theater system is to reproduce the original theater viewing experience. Home theater systems comprise a large screen video monitor, five-speaker sound system, amplifier, surround sound decoder, and a high-quality video disc player or digital satellite system.

> *Michael's **home theater** system was optimized for his unique listening and viewing space.*

THX, *n.* THX is a performance criteria for movie theater sound systems developed by Lucasfilms that delivers superior audio reproduction. There is also a THX standard for home theater systems and video software.

> *Tammy drove all the way across town to see Return of the Jedi in **THX**.*

 Also Explore: *DSS,* pan-and-scan, laserdisc.

Opposites

---

bifurcate, *vt.* To divide into two parts or branches. Bifurcate implies something that was once one breaking into two.

> *On the subject of birth control in general, Bob and Janet were in complete agreement; their opinions, however, **bifurcated** on the issue of abortion.*

---

dichotomy, *n.* Division into two parts, groups, or classes, especially when these are sharply distinguished or opposed.

> *There was a **dichotomy** of opinion within the Smith family when it came to the subject of abortion; Bob was pro-choice, whereas Janet was pro-life.*

dialectic, *n.* The art or practice of examining opinions or ideas logically, often by the method of question and answer, to determine their validity.

> *The marriage counselor led Bob and Janet in a **dialectic** to better determine her views on the abortion issue.*

dialogue, *n.* Interchange and discussion of ideas, especially when open and frank, as in seeking mutual understanding or harmony. A dialectic is a question-and-answer session, whereas dialogue is a simple discussion.

> *Bob and Janet engaged in a heated **dialogue** on the pros and cons of abortion.*

diametric, *adj.* Designating an opposite, a contrary, a difference, and so on that is wholly so.

> *In the end, Bob and Janet's **diametric** positions on abortion doomed their marriage to failure.*

 Also Explore: antithesis, interchange, *intercourse,* obverse, polarity.

Too Much

redundant, *adj.* More than enough; overabundant or excessive. To be redundant, you have to go past the point where you should have stopped. Redundant implies that any new thing that could be done has already been done in some other fashion.

> *Bob found his weekly trade journal **redundant** now that he was getting the same information sooner on the Web.*

superfluous, *adj.* Not needed; unnecessary. Whereas redundancy implies that something was once necessary but is now in excess, superfluous implies that the thing was never necessary.

> *The dealer's free oil change offer for Bob's minivan was **superfluous** because he had sold the van three months prior.*

repetitious, *adj.* Characterized by repeating; a doing or saying again, or again and again, especially tiresome or boring repetition. Redundancy can involve adding up different things to excess; repetition involves the same thing repeated over and over.

> *Bob found his new job, which involved double-checking numbers for accounting, boring and **repetitious.***

verbose, *adj.* Using or containing too many words. Verbosity implies long-windedness.

> *Mr. Roberts had a reputation for being **verbose;** it took him three sentences to say what most people could say in one.*

prolix, *adj.* So wordy as to be tiresome. Prolixity is an extreme form of verbosity to the point of being annoying.

> *It was a **prolix** report with more detailed information than management cared to know.*

 Also Explore: garrulous, gratuitous, *irrelevant*, loquacious, verbiage.

A Small Bit

---

vestige, *n.* A trace; bit. Vestige implies a small bit left of something that once existed in a larger fashion or a faint mark or visible sign left by something that is lost, has perished, or is no longer present.

> *After years of working in the public relations department, Harris had only a vestige of his former idealism left.*

---

trace, *n.* A barely perceptible amount; very small quantity. Unlike vestige, trace does not imply any history.

> *There was a trace of sarcasm in Bob's reply.*

particle, *n.* An extremely small piece; tiny fragment. Whereas trace can refer to an amount, particle implies a (small) singular item.

> *Marcia found an insect particle in her creamed corn.*

picayune, *adj.* (pik-e-yoon) from the French picaillon (small coin). Trivial or petty; small or small-minded; stingy. Picayune implies a lack of importance rather than a degree of size.

> *Davidson's picayune contribution to the team caused the others to rank him as the least-important member.*

fragment, *n.* A part broken away from a whole; a broken piece. Fragment can also refer to the part that exists of a literary or other work left unfinished.

> *Donald gathered the fragments of his broken life and tried to start anew.*

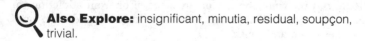

Also Explore: insignificant, minutia, residual, soupçon, trivial.

Habits

DAY 54

---

compulsion, *n.* An irresistible, repeated, irrational impulse to perform some act. An obsessive-compulsive neurosis is a neurosis characterized by compulsive ideas or irresistible urges, or both, and is often manifested in the ritualistic performance of certain acts.

*Don felt a **compulsion** to wash his hands at least once every hour.*

---

substance, *n.* Any addictive drug, including but not limited to opiates, depressants, stimulants, and hallucinogens. Addiction to or overuse of any substance is referred to as substance abuse.

*When Don's behavior became more erratic, Jennifer was afraid her husband was abusing a controlled **substance.***

twelve-step, *adj.* Designating or having to do with any of various programs that provide systematic support and guidance to individuals seeking to modify their behavior or outlook to control an addiction, compulsion, and so on. The name comes from the twelve guiding concepts forming part of the Alcoholics Anonymous program.

*Jennifer talked Don into attending a **twelve-step** program to kick his substance-abuse habit.*

sobriety, *n.* The state of being temperate or sparing in the use of alcoholic liquor.

*Jennifer had been living in a state of **sobriety** for more than five years.*

clean, *n.* Free from the use or presence of or from addiction to narcotics or other illicit drugs. When one kicks an addiction, one becomes clean and sober.

*After Don kicked his habit, he vowed to stay **clean** for the rest of his life.*

 Also Explore: addiction, inebriated, temperate.

Begging

pledge, *n.* Something promised, especially money to be contributed in regular payments. One often pledges a sum of money to be donated to a charity at some future time.

*Finally worn down by the endless membership drives, Beth **pledged** $20 to the local PBS station.*

handout, *n.* A gift of food, clothing, and so on, as to a beggar. Handout implies an informal gift, as opposed to the more formal donation, and often has a negative connotation. Few people with self-respect want a handout.

*Rosemarie deplored taking **handouts,** preferring to find a job that would keep her head above water.*

charity, *n.* A welfare institution, organization, or fund. Charities are often non-profit organizations that provide aid or assistance to the needy or to some worthwhile cause.

*Robert preferred to make anonymous donations to his favorite **charities.***

telethon, *n.* A campaign seeking support for a cause by pledged donations by telephone.

*Waldo volunteered to answer the phones during the Muscular Dystrophy **telethon.***

deduction, *n.* A sum or amount of money that is allowed as a deduction in computing income tax. Charitable contributions can often be allowed as deductions to lower the total tax owed.

*Robert was able to take his charitable contributions as **deductions** on his tax return.*

 Also Explore: *aid*, entreat, *petition*, supplicant.

Helping Hands

mentor, *n.* A wise advisor of a more junior employee. A mentor in a corporation is often an older, more experienced employee, one or more levels above the person mentored, but seldom in a direct management role; a mentor is often a manager in another department who informally takes the newer employee under his or her wing.

> *I'm lucky to have Mr. Seligman as my **mentor;** he can help me avoid the day-to-day politics in the accounting department.*

patron, *n.* A person who sponsors and supports some person or activity, usually financially.

> *Mrs. Gilbride had been a **patron** of the arts for 20 years, supporting both the chamber orchestra and the dance troupe.*

benefactor, *n.* A person who has given financial help to an individual or organization. A benefactor typically offers short-term help, whereas a patron's support is long-term.

> *Ron thanked his **benefactor** for helping him through a tough time.*

angel, *n.* A supporter who supplies money. In the business world, an angel is often a company that invests venture capital in smaller firms.

> *The startup was saved from insolvency by an **angel** from the West coast.*

white knight, *n.* A company that prevents an unfavorable takeover of another company, usually by means of a last-minute financial investment.

> *ReallyBig Co. acted as a **white knight** to thwart Large & Evil's hostile takeover of TinyCorp.*

 Also Explore: *advisor*, *advocate*, *consultant*, protégé, sponsor.

The Unsuccessful

poverty, _n._ The condition or quality of being poor. In the United States, the poverty level is set at a specific level of annual income for a given family size. For the year 1997, the U.S. Department of Health and Human Services defined the poverty level for a family of four as $16,050.

> _After being out of work for eight months, Rick and his family were getting dangerously close to living in **poverty.**_

illiterate, _adj._ Not knowing how to read or write. Illiterate implies a failure to conform to some standard of knowledge, especially an inability to read or write.

> _After admitting to his employer that he was **illiterate,** Thomas enrolled in a remedial reading course at the local high school._

ignorant, _adj._ Having little knowledge, education, or experience. Ignorant implies a lack of knowledge, either generally or on some particular subject.

> _Jan was **ignorant** of how the phone system worked at her new firm._

uneducated, _adj._ Not having gone through the process of formal schooling. Uneducated implies a lack of formal or systematic education, such as that acquired in schools.

> _Timothy possessed a brilliant but **uneducated** mind._

uncouth, _adj._ Uncultured; crude; boorish. A person of any income level, education level, or social class can be uncouth.

> _Bruce's **uncouth** behavior at the Spring Ball made headlines in the newspaper's society column._

 Also Explore: _destitute,_ indigent, low brow, _Philistine,_ troglodyte.

Doctors

---

optometrist, *n.* A doctor specializing in the care and treatment of the eyes. Optometrists deal with all aspects of vision, including measuring the eyes, measuring errors in refraction, and prescribing glasses or contact lenses to correct any defects.

> *After the **optometrist** changed her prescription, Brenda opted for contact lenses instead of glasses.*

---

ophthalmologist, *n.* A doctor specializing in the structure, functions, and diseases of the eye. Typically, an ophthalmologist deals with serious disorders of the eye, whereas an optometrist deals with issues regarding vision corrective devices.

> *Alice's optometrist recommended that she see an **ophthalmologist** to treat her cataracts.*

neurologist, *n.* A doctor specializing in disorders and diseases of the nervous system.

> *Dr. Benjamin recommended that Jamie see a **neurologist** for her pinched nerve.*

podiatrist, *n.* A doctor specializing in the care of the feet and especially with the treatment and prevention of foot disorders.

> *The **podiatrist** skillfully treated Ralph's ingrown toenail.*

chiropractor, *n.* One who practices the science and art of restoring and maintaining health, based on the theory that disease is caused by interference with nerve function, and employs manipulation of the body joints, especially of the spine, to restore normal nerve function.

> *Rhonda went to see a **chiropractor** about her bad back.*

 Also Explore: manipulation, refraction.

Impulsive

capricious, *adj.* Tending to change abruptly and without apparent reason. Capricious behavior is determined by chance or impulse or whim rather than necessity or reason; capricious behavior is sometimes seen as freakish.

*Paula thought it was **capricious** to fly to Rio for the weekend.*

whimsical, *adj.* Subject to sudden change. Whimsical implies a sudden fancy or humorous or light-hearted intent.

*Feeling **whimsical,** Karen recorded a humorous new message on her answering machine.*

erratic, *adj.* Having no fixed course or purpose; random; wandering. Erratic behavior is random, not impulsive, and often refers to one's mental or emotional instability.

*As she became more depressed, Patricia's behavior became more **erratic.***

precipitate, *adj.* Acting, happening, or done hastily or rashly; headstrong. Very sudden, unexpected, or abrupt.

*When she made an appointment to discuss his annual review, Doug's **precipitate** response of quitting on the spot surprised her.*

unpredictable, *adj.* Not able to say in advance what will happen.

*Debbie was so **unpredictable** that her own mother didn't know where she would be this weekend.*

Also Explore: fickle, inconstant, *irregular, mercurial, impetuous.*

High Society

---

elite, *n.* The group or part of a group selected or regarded as the finest, best, most distinguished, most powerful, etc. A group can be regarded as elite based on the amount of money they have, their pedigree, or the magnitude or type of their accomplishments.

> *George's prowess at marksmanship made him a potential member for the infantry **elite**.*

---

meritocracy, *n.* An intellectual elite, based on academic achievement. A system in which such an elite achieves special status, as in positions of leadership.

> *It's too bad that public service doesn't attract more candidates from the **meritocracy** of this country's colleges and universities.*

intelligentsia, *n.* The people regarded as, or regarding themselves as, the educated and enlightened class; collectively, the learned, intellectuals, or literati.

> *The novelist was regarded by the **intelligentsia** as somewhat of a hack—even though her book had been on the bestseller list for six weeks running.*

Brahmin, *n.* A cultured person from a long-established upper-class family. Brahmins are often regarded as haughty or conservative. Used in a pejorative sense by people who are not Brahmins, the term is equated to elitist, stuffed shirt, or even prig.

> *The dinner guests at the country club were dismayed when the guest speaker directly referred to his hosts as **Brahmins**.*

bon ton, *n.* from the French. In English it connotes stylishness, fine manners and in a general sense, fashionable society.

> *It is surprising how many high society people have no sense of **bon ton**.*

 Also Explore: aristocracy, haute couture, *literati,* panache, café society.

Affairs

---

dalliance, *n.* The act of flirting, toying, or trifling. Can also refer to the deliberate act of wasting time instead of working or a playful behavior intended to arouse sexual interest. Dalliance implies a short-term playing at love—not necessarily a sexual encounter.

> *Jennifer considered Steve just a casual **dalliance;** their dating was leading nowhere.*

---

extramarital, *adj.* Of or relating to sexual intercourse with someone other than one's spouse. An extramarital affair is typically more serious than a casual dalliance because it is by definition adultery.

> *When Maureen discovered Steve was having an **extramarital** affair with his secretary, she filed for divorce.*

corespondent, *n.* A person charged with having committed adultery with the wife or husband from whom a divorce is sought.

> *During Maureen's divorce proceedings, Jennifer was named as a **corespondent.***

indiscretion, *n.* Lack of good judgment; imprudence. Indiscretion can also refer to something told in confidence being made public. An indiscretion is not in and of itself improper; it is simply the result of unclear thinking.

> *Steve hoped everyone would forget about his **indiscretion** with Jennifer and let him get on with his work.*

impropriety, *n.* Improper action or behavior. An impropriety is wrong, whether or not it was thought out in advance.

> *Mr. Big knew that Steve was guilty of an **impropriety,** no matter what the circumstances, and gave him a severe reprimand.*

 Also Explore: adultery, entanglement, imprudent, liaison, philanderer.

Available . . . for a Price

prostitute, *vt*. To sell (oneself, one's artistic or moral integrity, etc.) for low or unworthy purposes. Prostitute implies gaining a material advantage at the cost of besmirching one's values or principles. One can prostitute one's body or one's values—and the exchange doesn't have to be a monetary one.

> *Robb felt like he was **prostituting** his values by taking a job with such a notorious polluter.*

venal, *adj*. Readily bribed or corrupted. Whereas prostitute implies a sale for a lowly purpose, venal simply implies a sale—for any purpose.

> *Senator Wilson's **venal** behavior made him a target for every lobbyist with a briefcase full of bills.*

bribe, *n*. Anything, especially money, given or promised to induce a person to do something illegal or wrong. Bribe implies to do something against one's will or better judgment.

> *The day after the judge accepted the **bribe**, he found grounds to dismiss the case.*

suborn, *vt*. To get or bring about through bribery or other illegal methods. Usually used to describe the method used to convince someone to commit perjury.

> *Robb's confession that the senior vice president of the company had **suborned** his testimony brought the case back to trial.*

graft, *n*. The act of taking advantage of one's position to gain money, property, and so on dishonestly, as in politics. Anything acquired by such illegal methods, as an illicit profit from government business.

> *The Senator's **graft** was revealed in the second trial, and it cost him his office.*

Also Explore: adulterate, *besmirch,* mercenary.

Outside Staff

---

outsource, *vt.* To acquire goods or services from nonstandard sources. Outsourced activities supplement or replace activities normally performed by in-house departments or units.

*The Kansas branch bypassed the central office and **outsourced** its payroll functions to a local firm.*

---

freelance, *vi.* When a writer, musician, artist, etc. who is not under contract for regular work sells his writings or services to individual buyers. A freelance supplier does not work on staff.

*Mackenzie liked the freedom from the corporate treadmill that **freelancing** provided.*

temporary, *n.* An employee hired for temporary service, especially an office worker. Temporaries (also known as temps) have no guarantees of long-term employment, no employment contracts, and no benefits; they essentially work on a day-to-day basis.

*Mr. Harrison needed a **temp** to fill in while his normal assistant was on vacation.*

contract, *vt.* To hire (a person, business, and so on) to perform under contract. A contract employee is similar to a temporary employee in that there is no ongoing obligation or benefits package; the difference is that a contract worker operates under the terms of a contract. Companies typically hire contract employees for more complex technical projects.

*The IS&T department decided to **contract** out the database project.*

moonlight, *vi.* To engage in the practice of holding a second regular job in addition to one's main job.

*To make both ends meet, Rodney was **moonlighting** as a clerk in a video store.*

 Also Explore: *benefits*, interim, provisional.

Fans

---

dilettante, *n.* A person who follows an art or science only for amusement and in a superficial way; dabbler. Dilettante refers to someone who appreciates art as distinguished from someone who creates it. The term is sometimes used disparagingly of one who dabbles superficially in the arts; dilettantes are less serious than hobbyists.

*Brenda's amateurish paintings and haphazard attendance branded her a **dilettante** to other members of the art club.*

---

enthusiast, *n.* A person full of intense or eager interest or fervor. An enthusiast is generally an observer—not necessarily a participant.

*Ken was an auto racing **enthusiast,** following all the NASCAR, CART, and Formula One races on television.*

hobbyist, *n.* One who engages in a favorite pastime or avocation. Unlike an enthusiast, a hobbyist is a participant.

*Andy was a model racing **hobbyist,** building his own models and attending club meetings once a month.*

avocation, *n.* Something one does in addition to a vocation or regular work and usually for pleasure. An avocation is a hobby.

*Accounting was Robert's vocation; writing romance novels was his **avocation.***

aficionado, *n.* A devoted follower of some sport, art, etc. An aficionado is a somewhat sophisticated fan.

*Randy was a comic book **aficionado** with a collection dating back to the mid-1960s; he even owned a near-mint copy of "Flash of Two Worlds."*

 Also Explore: dabbler, *fancier*, groupie, maniac, partisan.

Solo

lone wolf, *n.* One who prefers to be independent of others by living or working alone. A lone wolf holds corporate dictates and bureaucracies in disdain, choosing instead to make his or her own rules.

*A **lone wolf** in the corporate environment, Paul quit the company to work as a freelancer.*

rogue, *n.* A person or animal that wanders apart from the group and is fierce and wild. Lone wolves can be benign; rogues typically are harmful in some way.

*Williamson became a **rogue** and commandeered company resources for his skunkworks project.*

unique, *adj.* Highly unusual, extraordinary, rare, and so on. In a corporate environment, where uniformity is rewarded, uniqueness is not necessarily a valued property.

*Randolph's combination of hands-on experience and big-picture viewpoint was **unique** at the group level.*

eccentric, *adj.* Deviating from the norm, as in conduct; out of the ordinary; odd; unconventional. Whereas unique implies one-of-a-kind, eccentric goes beyond that to imply unusual or strange. Being eccentric is certainly not standard corporate behavior, but it is seldom harmful.

*Gibson's **eccentric** behavior went far beyond wearing bow ties and listening to Al Jolson records.*

eclectic, *adj.* Selecting from various systems, doctrines, or sources. Eccentrics and eclectics are often confused. Eclectics aren't necessarily odd; they just have widely varying influences.

*His CD collection reflected his **eclectic** tastes, covering everything from Nanci Griffith to Culture Club.*

 Also Explore: autonomous, cosmopolitan, eremitic, skunkworks, solitary.

As You Know It

DAY 66

---

paradigm, *n.* An overall concept accepted by most people because of its effectiveness in explaining a complex process, idea, or set of data. A paradigm is the way that things are in a particular area; a paradigm shift is a major change in the way things are done and the way people think.

*The new technology was certain to introduce a **paradigm** shift to the entire industry.*

---

status quo, *n.* (stat-es-kwo) from the Latin (literally, "the state in which"). The existing state of affairs (at a particular time). The world as it exists today is the status quo.

*Marilyn was concerned that the new employee would disrupt the **status quo** and dislodge her as group leader.*

model, *n.* A preliminary representation of something, serving as the plan from which the final, usually larger, object is to be constructed.

*The process for creating the Mark V was to be used as a **model** for all subsequent new product launches.*

archetype, *n.* Applies to the original pattern that serves as the model for all later things of the same kind or to a typical or perfect example of a type.

*Wonderland, Inc. is the **archetype** of all amusement parks in the U.S.*

conventional, *adj.* Of, sanctioned by, or growing out of custom or usage. Something that is customary depends on or conforms to formal or accepted standards or rules.

*The new office was still **conventional** in its floorplan, despite the marble and chrome that made it appear avant-garde.*

 Also Explore: avant-garde, benchmark, *exemplar,* hidebound, orthodoxy.

Baseball

double play, *n.* A play in which two runners are put out on the same play. For example, a batted ball is hit on the ground to the shortstop, who throws to second base to put out the runner forced from first base; the second baseman then throws quickly to first base to put out the batter.

*The first two outs were a result of a **double play.***

squeeze play, *n.* A play in which a team, with a runner on third base, attempts to score that runner by means of a bunt.

*The Orioles tried for a **squeeze play,** but the runner was caught out at home.*

designated hitter (D.H.), *n.* A player who bats in place of the pitcher (in the American League only). The D.H. does not play in the field.

*The manager signaled for the **designated hitter** to bunt for a squeeze play.*

bullpen, *n.* The area beyond the outfield fence where relief pitchers wait and warm up. A staff or pool of employees (such as in-house artists or writers) is also commonly referred to as a bullpen.

*A new pitcher was called up from the **bullpen.***

RBI, *n.* Runs batted in; the number of runs scored as the result of a player's hit, not counting any home runs scored by the batter himself. A batter is credited with an RBI for each run scored as a result of his batted ball unless the batter grounds into a double play or the run is scored as a direct result of an error.

*When the runner scored after he singled to right field, Fernandez got the **RBI.***

 Also Explore: bunt, home run, outfield, relief pitcher, runner.

Uncertainty

Catch-22, *n.* from the novel *Catch-22* (1961) by Joseph Heller. A paradox in a law, regulation, or practice that makes one a victim of its provisions no matter what one does. In a Catch-22 situation, you're damned if you do and damned if you don't.

> *Yossarian was caught in a real **Catch-22**. If he testified against his boss, he'd surely be fired; if he didn't, he'd go to jail, which would also get him fired.*

ambivalent, *adj.* Having simultaneous conflicting feelings toward a person or thing. It implies being both attracted to and repulsed by something. If ambivalence persists, you may find yourself in a quandary.

> *Henry was **ambivalent** about the new benefits package; he liked the dental plan but found the HMO lacking.*

ambiguous, adj. Having two or more possible meanings. Ambivalence is a feeling one has towards something else; ambiguousness is a duality possessed by a thing or person.

> *The meaning of the directive was **ambiguous;** half the staff read it one way, and half read it the exact opposite way.*

dither, *vi.* To be nervously excited or confused. One who dithers often vacillates back and forth between two conflicting positions—often for a considerable amount of time.

> *Henry **dithered** over which course to take; the wrong decision could prove disastrous in the marketplace.*

quandary, *n.* A state of uncertainty; perplexing situation or position. A quandary is a situation—especially an unpleasant or trying one—from which extrication is difficult.

> *Martin was in a **quandary**. Should he stay at work and finish the project or attend his daughter's piano recital?*

 Also Explore: diffident, *vacillate*, apostasy, predicament, dilemma.

Make It Last

protract, *vt.* To draw out; lengthen in duration. Protract implies being drawn out needlessly or wearingly.

*The lawyers attempted to **protract** the negotiations in the hopes of wearing down the other side.*

prolong, *vt.* To lengthen or extend in time. Prolong suggests a continuation beyond the usual or expected time.

*It seemed to Bob that his dentist was **prolonging** the agony of filling the cavity.*

extend, *vt.* To make longer in time or space. Whereas prolong applies only to time, extend can apply to either temporal or physical lengthening.

*Mr. Huddleston decided to **extend** the store's hours during the holiday season.*

endure, *vi.* To continue in existence; last; remain. Endure implies a struggle against some form of hardship.

*Reed made it clear that the company would **endure** the market downturn.*

sustain, *vt.* To keep in existence; keep up; maintain. Sustain implies a continuum rather than an isolated struggle.

*The company's long-term goal was to **sustain** its market share lead.*

 Also Explore: accretion, continuum, duration, *persevere*, temporal.

Brainy

---

cerebral, *adj.* Of, appealing to, or conceived by the intellect rather than the emotions. A cerebral approach is an intellectual approach.

> *Jim's comments were too **cerebral** for the crowd; they wanted to hear some true emotion.*

---

profound, *adj.* Marked by intellectual depth.

> *Marjorie had a **profound** discussion with her philosophy professor.*

cogitate *vt.* To think seriously and deeply (about); mediate; consider. To cogitate is to think.

> *Renee needed some time alone to **cogitate** on what would be the best decision to make.*

coherent, *adj.* Capable of logical, intelligible speech, thought, etc.

> *Ted's arguments were **coherent** and persuasive.*

perspicacious, *adj.* Having keen judgment or understanding; acutely perceptive. To be perspicacious is to be shrewd, not necessarily smart.

> *John's **perspicacious** bargaining won some major concessions from the other side.*

Also Explore: *discern*, intellect, judicious, *mediate*, ponder.

Cancel

---

expunge, *vt*. To erase or remove completely; blot out or strike out; delete or cancel. Expunge implies a complete wiping out of something that previously existed.

*Trying to cover his steps, Robinson sought to **expunge** all evidence of his existence from the computer files.*

---

abrogate, *vt*. To cancel or repeal by authority. Abrogate implies an official cancellation.

*Hill **abrogated** Wiggins's authority to sign company checks.*

annul, *vt*. To make no longer binding under the law; cancel. Annul implies not just canceling something but also returning things to the state they were before.

*Deborah sought to have the agreement **annulled** based on nonperformance.*

---

abolish, *vt*. To do away with completely; put an end to; especially, to make (a law and so on) null and void. Abolish implies officially ending a formal directive.

*ReallyBig Co. **abolished** its formal dress code; employees could wear business casual clothes to work every day.*

invalidate, *vt*. To make null and void; to deprive of legal force. Invalidate implies depriving a formal directive of any impact.

*The new directive from the home office **invalidated** the local office's standing policy.*

 Also Explore: countermand, *eradicate,* nullify, repeal, *rescind.*

Dull

---

vapid, *adj.* Uninteresting; lifeless; dull; boring. Vapid applies to that which once had but has since lost significance, sprit, freshness, sharpness, zest, etc.

*The brightly colored canvases, once so exciting and cutting-edge, now appeared **vapid** and out-of-style.*

---

insipid, *adj.* Not exciting or interesting; dull; lifeless. Insipid implies a lack of taste or flavor and is, hence, figuratively applied to anything that is lifeless, dull, and so on.

*Marie was bored to tears by the the **insipid** small talk at the party.*

monotonous, *adj.* Having little or no variation or variety. Because of the lack of variety, monotony soon becomes tiresome.

*Passing papers back and forth across his desk every day soon grew **monotonous.***

tedious, *adj.* Long or verbose and wearisome. Tedious is tiresome because it is long; monotonous is tiresome because it is unvarying.

*After ten straight hours of testimony, Samuel found the expert witness **tedious** and unconvincing.*

tasteless, *adj.* Dull; uninteresting. Literally means without taste or flavor. Typically refers to food or drink. Not to be confused with the alternate definition of tasteless: lacking good taste or showing poor taste.

*The steak was **tasteless,** almost generic in its lack of flavor.*

 Also Explore: *banal,* incessant, *obtuse, pedestrian,* perfunctory.

Painkillers

NSAID, *n.* Nonsteroidal anti-inflammatory drug. NSAIDs share three therapeutic effects: They alleviate pain, suppress pathologically elevated body temperatures, and reduce inflammation. Although these products can be effective, prolonged usage at high dosage levels can trigger side effects ranging from mild to severe.

*Dr. Benjamin debated the use of **NSAIDs** to alleviate the long-term pain; he felt the side effects might be too severe for younger patients.*

analgesic, *n.* Any drug that reduces pain. NSAIDs such as aspirin and ibuprofen function as analgesics, as do various opiates and narcotics.

*An **analgesic** was prescribed to reduce Lyn's lower back pain.*

aspirin, *n.* A white, crystalline powder or tablet, acetylsalicylic acid ($CH_3COOC_6H_4COOH$), used for reducing fever, relieving headaches, and so on.

*Roberta took two **aspirin** for her headache.*

ibuprofen, *n.* A white powder or tablet ($C_{13}H_{18}O_2$) used for reducing fever and relieving pain, especially to treat arthritis. Ibuprofen is sold under brand names such as Advil and Motrin.

*Geoffrey found that **ibuprofen** was more effective than aspirin in relieving his arthritis pain.*

opiate, *n.* Any medicine containing opium or any of its derivatives and acting as a sedative and narcotic. Opiates are effective analgesics, although their addictive qualities have led to their status as controlled substances.

*During the war, Clint became addicted to **opiates** when he was recovering from shrapnel wounds.*

 Also Explore: alleviate, narcotic, psychotropic, sedative, therapeutic.

Puzzling

enigma, *n.* A perplexing, baffling, or seemingly inexplicable matter, person, and so on. Enigma is synonymous with riddle or puzzle and refers to a person or thing, as opposed to a state or behavior.

*Roy was an **enigma;** no one knew where he came from or where he went after work.*

baffling, *adj.* Confusing so as to keep from understanding or solving; puzzling. An enigma is baffling.

*Roy's behavior was **baffling;** he seemed to flaunt conventional methods for no apparent reason.*

mysterious, *adj.* Characterized by being unexplained, unknown, or kept secret. Mysterious implies a secret, as opposed to something that is simply confusing or difficult to understand.

*Roy's **mysterious** comings and goings caused his co-workers to speculate about the nature of his private life.*

inexplicable, *adj.* That which cannot be explained, understood, or accounted for. Inexplicable implies an element of surprise, as if one thought something could be explained and then it couldn't.

*The background check revealed the **inexplicable** fact that Roy seemed to have no official existence prior to his current job.*

abstruse, *adj.* Hard to understand; deep. Abstruse is not so much puzzling as it is difficult to understand; implies a depth of content that is not easily mastered.

*Roy attempted to explain that his records had been corrupted by a computer error, but the details were too **abstruse** for his co-workers to understand.*

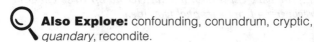

Also Explore: confounding, conundrum, cryptic, *quandary*, recondite.

Perfectly Clear

---

translucent, *adj.* Letting light pass but diffusing it so that objects on the other side cannot be clearly distinguished; particularly transparent, as frosted glass. Things that are translucent are not quite clear; one can partially see through them, but not clearly.

> *The design team decided to go with a **translucent** bottle so the color of the liquid could still be seen without drawing too much attention to the bottle's contents.*

---

transparent, *adj.* Transmitting light rays so that objects on the other side may be distinctly seen; capable of being seen through; neither opaque nor translucent. Things that are transparent are clear.

> *The **transparent** glass displayed all the imperfections of the contents within.*

pellucid, *adj.* Transparent or translucent; clear. Note the secondary definition of pellucid: easy to understand; clear and simple in style. Pellucid suggests the clearness of crystal.

> *James offered a **pellucid** explanation of the difficult-to-grasp situation.*

opaque, *adj.* Not letting light shine through; not transparent or translucent. Things that are opaque cannot be seen through.

> *The **opaque** glass in his office door protected Mr. Big from prying eyes.*

limpid, *adj.* Perfectly clear; transparent; not cloudy or turbid. Limpid implies a lack of cloudiness.

> *On this fine day the waters were **limpid,** free of their usual murkiness.*

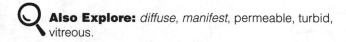 **Also Explore:** *diffuse, manifest,* permeable, turbid, vitreous.

Accounting

accrue, *vi.* To accumulate periodically as an increase. Businesses often plan ahead by creating *accruals* as reserves against future expenditures of a certain type.

> *Mary's savings account **accrued** more than a hundred dollars in interest last year.*

capitalize, *vt.* To set up expenditures as assets. Because capitalized assets can be written off over a long term and expenditures have to be accounted for immediately, businesses can show higher short-term profitability by capitalizing large assets—thus paying for them (on paper) over a longer period.

> *ReallyBig Co. decided to **capitalize** all their computer purchases so the expense would be spread over a number of years.*

amortize, *vt.* To write off expenditures by prorating over a fixed period. To amortize means to deduct capital expenses in small amounts over a period of time.

> *The purchase was **amortized** over a three-year period.*

depreciation, *n.* An expense recorded regularly on a company's books to reduce the value of a long-term tangible asset. Because it is a non-cash expense, it increases free cash flow while decreasing the amount of a company's reported earnings.

> *The company showed a loss on paper even though it had a positive cash flow, due to the effect of **depreciation.***

appreciate, *vt.* To raise the price or value of. Many types of assets appreciate over time.

> *Common wisdom is to buy those things that **appreciate** (such as land) and lease those that depreciate (such as automobiles).*

 Also Explore: *asset, cash flow,* expenditure, prorate, tangible.

Big Enough

---

material, *adj.* Important, essential, or pertinent to the matter under discussion. When something is material, it is big enough to make a difference to the situation at hand.

> *The difference in price was **material** and affected Jim's purchase decision.*

---

relevant, *adj.* Bearing upon or relating to the matter in hand; to the point. Relevant implies a close logical relationship with, and importance to, the matter under consideration. A thing can be relevant (pertinent) without being material (important enough to matter).

> *The judge found the argument **relevant** and allowed the line of questioning to continue.*

behemoth, *n.* Any animal or thing that is huge or very powerful.

> *With close to 40 percent market share, ReallyBig Co. was truly a **behemoth** in its industry.*

gargantuan, *adj.* Being large in size or appetite. A behemoth is, by definition, gargantuan.

> *Due to its size, ReallyBig Co. had **gargantuan** appetites; it used more than three tons of toilet paper and four truckloads of paper clips each year.*

robust, *adj.* Strongly built or based; muscular or sturdy. Unlike gargantuan, robust does not imply size—although it does imply health.

> *The new Web server was **robust;** the down time from crashes was minimal.*

 Also Explore: appreciable, germane, *incremental*, pertinent, prodigious.

Almost

figuratively, *adv.* Representing one concept in terms of another that may be thought of as analogous with it. In the phrase "screaming headlines," the word "screaming" is used figuratively.

> *Figuratively speaking, the new project was a black hole in terms of funding.*

literally, *adv.* In a literal manner or sense; specifically, word for word. Literally is the opposite of figuratively.

> *Robinson was literally at a loss for words; he couldn't think of a thing to say.*

virtually, *adv.* In effect, although not in fact. Virtually implies being almost but not quite something.

> *The twins were virtually identical, save for the length of their hair.*

practically, *adv.* For all practical purposes. Practically assumes an eventual connection when one does not exist yet.

> *With his boss hospitalized, Jones was practically manager of the entire department.*

allegedly, *adv.* So declared, but without proof or legal conviction. Allegedly implies a current or forthcoming formal accusation.

> *Crane had allegedly broken into the records room and stolen the confidential files.*

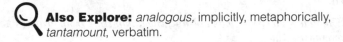 **Also Explore:** *analogous,* implicitly, metaphorically, *tantamount*, verbatim.

Edited

abridged, *adj.* Shortened by using fewer words but keeping the main contents; condensed. An edited version of a written work, usually to shorten an overly long work, yet retaining the sense of the original.

> *The magazine printed an **abridged** version of chapter four of his book.*

concise, *adj.* Brief and to the point; short and clear. A concise version of something is a shortened version that includes only the main points—but has not been summarized per se. For example, a concise edition might include only the lead sentences of key paragraphs.

> *Jonah was assigned the task of making a **concise** version of the 200-page report.*

summarize, *vt.* To present the substance of a general idea in brief form; state briefly. A summary retells an idea in different words—and at less length.

> *The first page **summarized** the key points in the report.*

expurgate, *vt.* To expunge objectionable material from; delete. An expurgated version of a thing has had parts removed to make it less objectionable.

> *An **expurgated** version of his memo was sent to outside vendors so as not to offend their sensibilities.*

censor, *vt.* To subject (a book, writer, and so on) to the removal of anything considered obscene, libelous, politically objectionable, etc. Censorship implies a larger agenda behind what is and is not permitted to be viewed by the public.

> *Whole sections of his book were **censored** by the committee at the public library.*

 Also Explore: cogent, epitomize, *expunge,* truncate.

Online Acronyms

BTW, by the way. Used to preface an aside.

> *BTW, here's what someone else said about your article.*

IMHO, in my humble opinion. Used to introduce the writer's opinion.

> *IMHO, this is the greatest work ever from this writing team.*

FYI, for your information. Used to introduce related material that may also be of interest.

> *FYI, here's my schedule for the next few days.*

LOL, laughing out loud. Used to indicate a positive reaction to something humorous. Related to ROFL (rolling on the floor laughing), an even stronger reaction to a humorous comment or situation.

> *LOL! That's the funniest thing I've read in ages.*

ASAP, as soon as possible. Used to indicate the immediacy of a response or action.

> *I'll get on that problem ASAP.*

 Also Explore: acronym, argot, jargon, slang.

In Other Words . . .

---

euphemism, *n.* The use of a word or phrase that is less direct but considered less distasteful and less offensive than another. Euphemism literally means "good word"; when you think the chosen word might be offensive to some, choose a euphemism instead.

> *Sensing a conservative audience, Randy substituted a* ***euphemism*** *for the word in question.*

---

paraphrase, *vt.* To reword the meaning expressed in something spoken or written. To paraphrase is not merely to substitute one word for another, but to reword an entire phrase or passage.

> *Samuel* ***paraphrased*** *a passage from the Bible in the preface to his book.*

restate, *vt.* To state again, especially in a different way. Restate implies that the first statement was misunderstood, thus necessitating the reiteration in different, probably better understood, words.

> *Samuel* ***restated*** *the question so it could be better understood.*

gloss, *vt.* To smooth over or cover up (an error, inadequacy, fault, etc.); make appear right by specious argument or by minimizing. To render a more brief or pleasant version of something spoken or written. Most often used with the word "over."

> *The district attorney* ***glossed*** *over the latest report on Megapolis' crime rate statistics.*

recapitulate, *vi.* To repeat briefly, as in an outline; to summarize.

> *To ensure that everyone understood what he'd said about the flu outbreak, Greg* ***recapitulated*** *his report by hitting the high points in plain, everyday English.*

 Also Explore: elucidate, hyperbole, reiterate, *simile.*

Off the Cuff

---

extemporaneous, *adj.* Made, done, or spoken without any formal preparation. Extemporaneous is most often used to describe a speech or performance that has received a small degree of preparation but has not been written out or memorized.

*Kristi gave an **extemporaneous** speech when she accepted the award for best project.*

---

impromptu, *adj.* Without preparation or advanced thought. Impromptu is applied to that which is spoken, made, or done on the spur of the moment to suit the occasion and stresses spontaneity. Although extemporaneous suggests a small degree of preparation, impromptu suggests no forethought.

*Sherry gave an **impromptu** performance when prompted at the party.*

vamp, *vt.* To invent; fabricate. Vamp implies a need to fill time.

*Ben **vamped** for five minutes before the opening act was ready to go on.*

improvise, *vt.* To compose music, or simultaneously compose and perform music, on the spur of the moment and without any preparation. When used with reference to things other than music, improvise suggests the ingenious use of whatever is at hand to fill an unforeseen and immediate need.

*Gail loved the sessions about **improvising** in her music class.*

ad lib, *vt.* To improvise words, gestures; not in a prepared speech, script, and so on; to extemporize.

*Dora lost her meeting notes and had to **ad lib** her way through the presentation.*

 Also Explore: *feign, impulsive,* offhand, spontaneous, unpremeditated.

Sex

DAY 83

---

erogenous, *adj.* Designating or of those areas of the body that are particularly sensitive to sexual stimulation. The most sexually sensitive parts of the body are called the erogenous zones.

> *Brett gently massaged Rhonda's* **erogenous** *zones.*

---

orgasm, *n.* The climax of sexual excitement, as in intercourse, normally accompanied in the male by ejaculation.

> *Brett's massaging slowly brought Rhonda to* **orgasm.**

cunnilingus, *n.* A sexual activity involving oral contact with the female genitals. Cunnilingus is oral sex with a female recipient.

> *Even though Brett was a good lover, Rhonda preferred* **cunnilingus** *to regular intercourse.*

fellatio, *n.* A sexual activity involving oral contact with the penis. Fellatio is oral sex with a male recipient.

> *Unlike Brett, Rhonda thought that* **fellatio** *was just an element of foreplay, not an end in itself.*

artificial insemination, *n.* The impregnation of a female by introducing semen taken from a male without sexual intercourse. The process involves placing semen into a woman's uterus by a means other than intercourse.

> *When Brett discovered he was sterile, he and Rhonda agreed to try* **artificial insemination** *from an anonymous sperm donor.*

 Also Explore: clitoris, ejaculation, penis, testicles, vagina.

Theories and Ideas

DAY 84

---

hypothesis, *n.* An unproved theory, proposition, supposition, etc. tentatively accepted to explain certain facts or to provide a basis for further investigation. Whereas theory implies considerable evidence has been gathered, hypothesis implies an inadequacy of evidence in support of only a tentative explanation.

> *Dr. Wan formed a working **hypothesis** that enabled him to begin preliminary testing.*

---

belief, *n.* Anything accepted as true, especially a creed, doctrine, or tenet. Theories and hypotheses are accepted to be speculative; beliefs are accepted (by believers, in any case) as universal truths.

> *There was a general **belief** that the two groups could not exist in close proximity.*

opinion, *n.* A belief not based on absolute certainty or positive knowledge but on what seems true, valid, or probable to one's own mind. Opinions are beliefs that are recognized as possibly not true or at least not universally true.

> *Dr. Wan's **opinion** was that, with careful preparation, the two groups could coexist.*

conviction, *n.* A strong belief. A conviction is stronger than an opinion because of the presence of satisfactory reasons or proof; sometimes conviction implies an earlier doubt.

> *After the first round of testing, Dr. Wan's **conviction** of the rightness of his proposal was strengthened.*

empirical, *adj.* Relying or based solely on experiment and observation rather than theory.

> *Dr. Wan's colleagues preferred to wait until **empirical** evidence was available before they committed to a full rollout.*

 Also Explore: doctrine, supposition, tenet, theorem.

What Came First

primary, *adj.* From which others are derived; fundamental; elemental or basic. Primary implies the first, from which others evolved or were derived.

> The **primary** goal of the trade show was to publicize the new product; the secondary goal was to obtain sales leads.

primordial, *adj.* First in time; existing at or from the beginning.

> The building blocks of life were present in the **primordial** ooze.

aboriginal, *adj.* Existing (in a place) from the beginning or from earliest days; first. Aboriginal implies habitation in a region.

> The **aboriginal** wildlife was slowly pushed out by the construction of new housing.

antediluvian, *adj.* Very old, old-fashioned, or primitive. Literally, antediluvian refers to anything dating from the time before the Biblical flood.

> Because Ralph had never heard of Snoop Doggy Dogg, Bibbo thought Ralph's tastes in music were positively **antediluvian.**

forebear, *n.* An ancestor. Do not confuse with the incorrect forebearer, which is not a real word.

> Mark's **forebears** all worked with their hands.

Also Explore: antecedent, indigenous, precursor, primeval, *progenitor.*

Proof

evidence, *n.* Something presented in a legal proceeding which bears on or establishes a point in question. In legal terms, evidence can be testimony, records, documents, material objects, or other things that prove the existence or nonexistence of a fact.

*Ally presented **evidence** showing that she was at the grocery store on the night in question.*

testimony, *n.* A declaration or statement made under oath or affirmation by a witness in a court to establish a fact. Do not confuse testimony, which is verbal, with evidence, which is physical.

*The witness's **testimony** corroborated Ally's claim.*

circumstantial, *adj.* Having to do with, or depending on, circumstances. Circumstantial testimony is not based on actual personal knowledge or observation of the facts in controversy.

*The only evidence tying her to the burglary was **circumstantial;** there were no witnesses to place her at the scene of the crime.*

hearsay, *n.* Something one has heard but does not know to be true; rumor; gossip. In legal terms, hearsay is second-hand testimony in which a witness can only repeat something that he or she heard someone else say.

*Ally's alleged plan to break into the store turned out to be **hearsay** on the part of her neighbors.*

inadmissible, *adj.* Not to be allowed, accepted, granted, or conceded. In legal terms, it refers to information that is so unreliable it cannot be admitted under the established rules of evidence.

*In the end, her neighbor's testimony was **inadmissible;** Mrs. Toomey couldn't vouch for her own whereabouts that evening.*

 Also Explore: corroboration, defamation, documentation, *presumption,* infer.

Opinions

intuition, *n.* The direct knowing or learning of something without the conscious use of reasoning; immediate understanding. Intuition implies an innate knowledge or sense or a suspicion that something might be the case.

> *Even after 20 years in the business, Jason still relied on his **intuition;** his gut was more accurate than any research he'd ever seen.*

conjecture, *n.* An inferring, theorizing, or predicting from incomplete or uncertain evidence; guesswork. Conjecture is an educated guess based on available facts.

> *The paper's editorial was full of **conjecture** based on an incomplete set of facts.*

opine, *vt.* To hold or express an opinion; think; suppose. Opine does not necessarily imply a lack of facts, simply the willingness to put forth an opinion. Now usually humorous.

> *Williamson **opined** that things weren't as good as they used to be in the old days.*

viewpoint, *n.* The mental position from which things are viewed and judged; point of view. One's point of view is more than just an opinion; it is related to one's sum knowledge and experience.

> *From the CFO's **viewpoint,** the company was in sound financial shape.*

sentiment, *n.* A complex combination of feelings and opinions as a basis for action or judgment; a general emotionalized attitude. A thought, opinion, judgment, or attitude, usually the result of careful consideration, but often colored with emotion. Often used in plural form.

> *Even after reviewing the facts of the crime, Cecilia's **sentiments** still were on the side of leniency for the accused.*

 Also Explore: cognition, predilection, surmise.

Inserting

interject, *vt.* To throw in between; insert or interpose. Interject implies a suddenness that could be perceived as rudeness.

> *With everyone talking at once, it was hard for Mary to **interject** her opinion.*

interpolate, *vt.* To alter, enlarge, or corrupt (a book or manuscript and so on) by putting in new words, subject matter, etc. Interpolate implies inserting new material in written communications.

> *The editor sensed a need to **interpolate** an introduction to make it more accessible to the masses.*

interrupt, *vt.* To break into or in upon (a discussion, train of thought, etc.). Interrupt implies intrusion.

> *Hastings was annoyed when Stephan rudely **interrupted** his coffee break.*

insinuate, *vt.* To introduce or work into gradually, indirectly, and artfully. Insinuate implies a gradual, nonintrusive insertion.

> *Graham gradually **insinuated** himself into Mr. Big's favor.*

intersperse, *vt.* To scatter among other things; put here and there or at intervals.

> *Laura **interspersed** cartoons amidst the text to break up the monotony.*

 Also Explore: imbue, infuse, instill, interpose, intrusion.

Details

specialist, *n.* A person who concentrates in a particular field of study, professional work, and so on. By dint of devoting increased attention to a specific area, specialists usually have a better grasp on details (in that area) than do generalists.

*The Year 2000 code fix required a COBOL **specialist**.*

generalist, *n.* An administrator, teacher, manager, etc., with broad general knowledge and experience in several disciplines or areas. A generalist is the opposite of a specialist.

*Jonathan was a marketing **generalist** with experience in everything from advertising to brand management.*

particulars, *n.* Details; items of information; points.

*After he took in the broad aspects of the job, Johnson filled him in on the **particulars**.*

minute, *adj.* (mi-nyoot) Of, characterized by, or attentive to tiny details; exact. Minute implies size or precision.

*Every action, no matter how **minute**, would be scrutinized by the watchdog committee.*

tangential, *adj.* Merely touching a subject, not dealing with it at length. A tangential approach does not dwell on details.

Robinson's decision making was tangential; he didn't realize how it would eventually impact the new project.

 **Also Explore:** convoluted, *exhaustive*, meticulous, *precise*.

Simple

---

prosaic, *adj.* Commonplace, dull, and ordinary; not particularly interesting. Often used to refer to prose rather than poetry because prosaic implies heavy, flat, and unimaginative.

> *Burns's outlook on life was practical to the point of being* ***prosaic.***

---

pedestrian, *adj.* Lacking interest or imagination. Pedestrian is mundane and trite and often connotes a lower class.

> *The writing was* ***pedestrian,*** *lacking impetus and imaginative characterization.*

mundane, *adj.* Commonplace, everyday, ordinary, and so on. Although often used as a close synonym of worldly, mundane especially stresses the commonplace or practical aspects of life.

> *Karen's life was too* ***mundane*** *to make an interesting autobiography.*

unsophisticated, *adj.* Artless; simple; not complex. Unsophisticated implies a desirable simplicity, a frankness or straightforwardness that suggests the simplicity of a child.

> *Even though Clint was relatively* ***unsophisticated,*** *his naïveté was refreshing to the society crowd.*

vacuous, *adj.* Having or showing lack of intelligence, interest, or thought; stupid; senseless. Vacuous implies being empty and devoid of meaning or importance.

> *Marilyn fit the stereotype of a* ***vacuous*** *blonde, attractive but empty-headed.*

 Also Explore: *banal*, *inane*, ingenuous, quotidian, *trite*.

Clear

manifest, *adj.* Apparent to the senses or to the mind. Manifest applies especially to that which can be perceived by the senses (especially sight) and implies something that is obvious to the understanding, apparent to the mind, or easily apprehensible.

> *John's situation was **manifest** to those around him; it was only a matter of weeks before he would get the axe.*

apparent, *adj.* Readily understood or perceived. Apparent suggests the use of deductive reasoning.

> *Based on his group's poor performance, it was **apparent** that he would take the fall when the downsizing began.*

evident, *adj.* Easy to see or perceive; clear; plain. Evident implies the existence of external signs.

> *His disappointment was **evident;** his shoulders drooped and he looked downcast.*

obvious, *adj.* Easy to see or understand; plain. Obvious refers to that which is so noticeable or obtrusive that no one can fail to perceive it.

> *It was **obvious** even to the newbies in the department that John was on his way out.*

palpable, *adj.* Easily perceived by the senses; audible, recognizable, perceptible, noticeable, and so on. Palpable applies especially to that which can be perceived through some sense other than that of sight.

> *As he walked into the meeting with Mr. Big, John's fear was **palpable.***

 Also Explore: blatant, *material*, obtrusive, patent, substantiate.

Workable

---

viable, *adj.* Workable and likely to survive or to have real meaning, pertinence, etc. In the business world, viability implies ongoing profitability.

> *After three years of losses, the new unit was on the verge of being a **viable** business.*

---

feasible, *adj.* Within reason; likely. Feasible implies the most likely and realistic outcome.

> *Given the facts of the case, Murray had the most **feasible** explanation for what might have happened.*

practicable, *adj.* Something that can be done or put into practice. Applies to that which can readily be affected under the prevailing conditions or by the means available.

> *The plan appeared immediately **practicable** to the board of directors.*

doable, *adj.* That can be done. Doable does not imply probability or improbability, only capability.

> *Given the group's light workload, the new project was eminently **doable.***

pragmatic, *adj.* Concerned with actual practice, everyday affairs, and so on, not with theory or speculation; practical.

> *Being **pragmatic,** Julie was concerned about the ability to hit that aggressive target.*

Also Explore: conceivable, *plausible*, potential, probable, utilitarian.

Not Workable

---

untenable, *adj.* That cannot be held, defended, or maintained. Untenable implies being put into a position or situation that, for one or more reasons, is unworkable. Typically, this happens when one is asked to perform conflicting duties; by definition, succeeding at one will cause failure at the other.

> *Terrence found himself in the **untenable** position of trying to increase both sales and profitability in an increasingly competitive market.*

---

nonproductive, *adj.* Not resulting in the production of the goods sought or the realization of the effects expected. Nonproductive is an after-the-fact realization of a lack of success.

> *As it turned out, most of the meetings held by the group were **nonproductive**.*

nonstarter, *n.* An expected occurrence, project, etc. that fails to materialize; a worthless idea. Nonproductive implies a lack of success; nonstarter implies not even getting off the ground.

> *The new product was a total **nonstarter**; it didn't make a dent against the competition.*

unavailing, *adj.* Ineffectual, pointless, without results, fruitless; to be of no use, help, worth, or advantage (to), as in accomplishing an end. Implies a sense of helplessness or an inability to fix something.

> *All contingency plans were **unavailing**; nothing could restore the politician's reputation.*

ineffectual, *adj.* Not producing, or unable to produce, the desired effect.

> *The new airbags proved **ineffectual** for shorter drivers.*

Also Explore: abortive, bootless, *Catch-22, dubious, quixotic.*

Software Testing

---

alpha, *adj.* The first stage of software testing, typically confined to a small group of internal or professional testers. Alpha testing usually involves testing not only the stability of the software, but also the usability of new features.

> *The product development team released the prototype to a small group of **alpha** testers.*

---

beta, *adj.* The second and final stage of software testing, typically expanded beyond the alpha test to a larger—although still private—group of testers. Beta testing is primarily concerned with ensuring the stability of the software with different software and hardware configurations.

> *The **beta** testing was proceeding as planned with the number of critical bugs decreasing each day.*

preview, *adj.* A preview release is a public release of a stable beta version with the twin goals of expanding the testing program (to a very large degree) and creating publicity for the upcoming final software release.

> *To gain more publicity for the upcoming release, the marketing department decided to release a **preview** version of the software outside the normal beta testing group.*

gold, *adj.* The final software version, with all testing completed, ready to be mass duplicated for commercial release to the general public.

> *When the last bug was killed, the software went **gold**.*

bug, *n.* A fault or error in a piece of software or hardware. Alpha and beta tests are designed to seek out software bugs, which can then be corrected before the final release of the software.

> *It was hard to tell if the unexpected behavior of the dialog box was a **bug** or an undocumented feature.*

 Also Explore: *crash,* glitch, stability, test, usability.

Disorders

attention deficit disorder (ADD), *n.* A disorder character-ized by poor sustained attention or persistence of effort to tasks, poor impulse control or delayed gratification, excessive activity that is not appropriate to the task at hand, trouble following rules, and trouble with filtering out distractions.

*Jimmy was diagnosed with **attention deficit disorder**, which explained his inability to concentrate in class.*

seasonal affective disorder (SAD), *n.* A mood disorder charac-terized by mental depression related to a certain season of the year—especially winter. SAD is related to the relative length of day and night.

*Sherry compensated for her **seasonal affective disorder** by using a special type of windowbox light.*

chronic fatigue syndrome (CFS), *n.* A syndrome characterized by severe fatigue, muscle aching, difficulty concentrating, and other symptoms.

*The doctors theorized that Brenda's lethargy could be a symp-tom of **chronic fatigue syndrome.***

anorexia nervosa, *n.* An eating disorder, chiefly in young women, characterized by aversion to food and obsession with weight loss, and manifested in self-induced starvation, excessive exercise, and so on.

*The young model was a classic case of **anorexia nervosa;** she wasted away to nothing.*

hypertension, *n.* Abnormally high blood pressure. Hypertension is one of the leading risk factors for heart attack and strokes.

*Doug's doctor told him that the best way to reduce his **hyper-tension** was to go on a strict diet.*

 Also Explore: complex, dysfunction, pathology, syndrome.

Bad Guys

adversary, *n.* A person who opposes or fights with another. An adversary is not necessarily an enemy, simply an opposing player. An adversarial relationship is one characterized by opposition, disagreement, and hostility.

*Roy's **adversary** was an overly political animal who tried to circumvent the system at every chance.*

antagonist, *n.* A person who opposes or competes with another. Antagonist implies ill feelings or making an enemy.

*Rudy became an **antagonist** when he deliberately recruited one of John's key managers.*

combatant, *n.* A person who engages in a fight, struggle, or conflict. A combatant is a fighter. Adversary and antagonist imply one-on-one conflicts; a combatant can be just one of many fighters in a mass conflict.

*There were numerous **combatants** in this segment of the market.*

opposition, *n.* Any person, group, or thing that opposes. The other side collectively is referred to as the opposition.

*Mary was labeled a traitor after she leaked information to the **opposition**.*

nemesis, *n.* Anyone or anything that seems to be the inevitable cause of a someone's downfall or defeat.

*Holmes was Moriarty's **nemesis,** appearing at the most inopportune moments to vex his schemes.*

 Also Explore: bète noire, janissary, litigant, villain.

Unfair Practices

---

protected class, *n.* Members of a group identified under Title VII of the Civil Rights Act of 1964, as amended, and Executive Order 11246. Members of a protected class are considered to be protected under operative equal opportunity and affirmative action legislation. Protected classes include minorities, disabled persons (including disabled veterans), older persons, and women.

*The human resources department warned management about dismissing any member of a **protected class.***

---

harassment, *n.* The act of troubling, worrying, or tormenting. Sexual harassment involves forcing unwanted sexual advances on a co-worker, often in implicit exchange for promotions and other advantages.

*After Mr. Big propositioned Maryann during a business trip, she sued ReallyBig Co. for sexual **harassment.***

affirmative action, *n.* A policy or program for correcting the effects of discrimination in the employment or education of members of certain groups, such as women, blacks, and so on.

*In the spirit of **affirmative action,** additional recruiting was done through minority newspapers and radio stations.*

nepotism, *n.* Favoritism shown to relatives, especially in appointment to desirable positions. Generally used to describe favoritism to friends and acqaintances too. This practice is revealed in the saying, "It's not what you know; it's who you know."

*The family-owned business operates by **nepotism.***

seniority, *n.* Status, priority, or precedence achieved by length of service in a given job. Seniority often brings with it special privileges, such as longer vacations, tenure, etc.

*Herb's **seniority** entitled him to an extra week of vacation and a special parking place.*

 Also Explore: *bias,* inequitable, *stereotype, tenure.*

Family

avuncular, *adj.* Having traits considered typical of uncles: jolly, indulgent, stodgy, and so on. Avuncular implies warmth and comfort; avuncular behavior is more commonly associated with older males.

*Walter Cronkite's **avuncular** demeanor endeared him to a generation of Americans.*

maternal, *adj.* Of, like, or characteristic of a mother or motherhood; motherly. Maternal implies nurturing.

*Molly treated her staff in a protecting, almost **maternal** fashion.*

paternal, *adj.* In a manner suggesting a father's relationship with his children. In a business environment, paternal implies special favors that a father would give his child.

*The employees believed that Mr. Big's **paternal** relationship with Gregory led to at least one undeserved promotion.*

sibling, *n.* One of two or more persons born of the same parents or, sometimes, having one parent in common. Brothers and sisters are siblings.

*The two remote locations were **siblings,** opened at the same time for the same reasons.*

brethren, *n.* Male fellows of the same race, church, profession, organization, etc. Brethren is typically used in religious connotations.

*Charles cherished his relationship with his **brethren** in the local marketing association.*

Also Explore: atavistic, *clanning,* congenital, *kindred,* nurturing.

Related To

perspective, *adj.* A specific point of view in understanding or judging things or events, especially one that shows them in their true relations to one another. Perspective implies a lack of bias or opinion.

> *Taken in **perspective**, the loss of the MacGregor account had no long-term ill effects.*

relative, *adj.* Related each to the other; dependent upon or referring to each other.

> *As the two companies grew, they kept their same positions **relative** to each other.*

similarity, *n.* Resemblance or likeness. Compares features that are nearly but not exactly the same or alike.

> *There was a **similarity** between the two firms in that they both were growing at exponential rates.*

comparative, *adj.* Estimated by comparison with something else.

> *In spite of its low profitability, the new firm was a **comparative** success, given the high failure rate within the industry.*

measure, *n.* The extent, dimensions, capacity, and so on of anything, especially as determined by a standard.

> *By any **measure**—revenues, profits, market share—the firm was a success.*

 Also Explore: *affinity*, allusive, correlative, vying.

Pretend

---

virtual reality, *n.* The computer-generated simulation of three-dimensional images of an environment or sequence of events that someone using special equipment may view, as on a video screen, and interact with in a seemingly physical way. Virtual reality differs from a standard computerized simulation in that it takes place in a 3D environment and lets the user interact with that environment in real time.

> *The new video game incorporated a 3D **virtual reality** environment.*

---

simulation, *n.* An imitation or counterfeit. In high-tech terms, a simulation involves the use of a computer to imitate a given physical process.

> *Robb was able to create a computer **simulation** of the manufacturing process.*

feign, *vt.* To make a false show of; imitate. Pretend and feign both imply a profession or display of what is false. The more literary feign sometimes suggests an elaborately contrived situation.

> *By putting an instant hotpack on her forehead, Marjorie was able to **feign** having a fever and avoid taking the math test that day.*

hoax, *n.* A trick or fraud, especially one meant as a practical joke.

> *The entire virus scare was a **hoax** perpetrated on the company by a disgruntled former employee.*

stunt, *n.* Something done for a thrill to attract attention. Whereas a hoax has some underlying intent, a stunt is done primarily for personal titillation.

> *The publicity **stunt** garnered attention from the local media.*

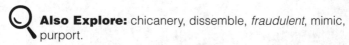

Also Explore: chicanery, dissemble, *fraudulent*, mimic, purport.

Versatile

protean, *adj.* Very changeable; readily taking on different shapes and forms. Protean implies the innate ability to assume multiple forms, to willingly and proactively change as circumstances dictate. Something or someone who is protean is more than flexible, veering toward chameleon-like.

*Willis gave a **protean** effort, assuming multiple roles within the group as conditions dictated.*

pliable, *adj.* Easily influenced or persuaded. Pliable implies that any change is reactionary.

*Barry was too **pliable**; he could be talked into just about anything.*

supple, *adj.* Adaptable, as to changes. Supple implies an ability to bend without breaking, to adapt rather than to change.

*Joan possessed a **supple** mind, continually adapting to the changing conditions around her.*

elastic, *adj.* Readily changed or changing to suit circumstances; adaptable. Elastic implies an ability to return to the original condition after being changed.

*Sue possessed an **elastic** temperament, which made it easier for her to deal with her mercurial manager.*

docile, *adj.* Easy to manage or discipline. Docile implies flexibility only in that being docile suggests a willingness to do anything to please.

*Barry was too **docile**; the other members of the department walked all over him.*

 Also Explore: adaptable, multifaceted, *reactionary*, submissive, tractable.

Working from Home

home office, *n.* An office or business run from one's home. As of 1997, more than 41 million Americans run businesses from their homes.

> *Paula set up an elaborate **home office** in her spare room, complete with computer, modem, and two-line telephone.*

self-employed, *adj.* Working for oneself, with direct control over work, services undertaken, and fees. Home offices can house either self-employed businesspeople or telecommuters.

> *Faced with the choice, Ralph decided he'd rather be **self-employed** than work for a large corporation.*

telecommuter, *n.* One who does work outside the office that traditionally has been done in the office. Telecommuters typically connect to the main office via their PCs.

> *Wally was a **telecommuter** two days a week, working out of his home office.*

teleconference, *n.* A conference of individuals in different locations by speakerphone, closed-circuit TV, Internet, or a personal computer. This is also known as a videoconference.

> *Paula and Wally participated in the **teleconference** from the comfort of their own homes.*

mobile computing, *n.* The use of various communications media with portable computers to meet the on-the-road computing and data needs of workers who don't have offices or who must be away from their offices. Telecommuters use mobile computing technologies to stay in touch with the main office, using a notebook or laptop PC and a modem connected to a normal telephone line.

> *Wally was a believer in **mobile computing**, taking his laptop with him whenever he traveled.*

 Also Explore: asynchronous communications, *modem,* telecommunications.

Government Acronyms

EEOC, Equal Employment Opportunity Commission. The EEOC's mission is to ensure equality of opportunity by vigorously enforcing federal legislation prohibiting discrimination in employment.

> *After several complaints from ex-employees, ReallyBig Co. faced an **EEOC** audit of its hiring practices.*

ADA, Americans with Disabilities Act. A U.S. law enacted in 1990, intended to remove barriers preventing qualified individuals with disabilities from enjoying equal opportunities.

> *Biggie Mart had to retrofit its restroom facilities to meet the provisions of the **ADA.***

DOJ, Department of Justice. The DOJ serves as counsel for all American citizens by enforcing the law in the public interest. The DOJ also conducts all suits in the Supreme Court in which the U.S. is concerned and represents the Government in legal matters.

> *The **DOJ** sought sanctions against ReallyBig Co. based on alleged monopolistic activity.*

DOE, Department of Energy. The DOE is concerned with U.S. energy policy. The DOE aims to foster a secure and reliable energy system that is environmentally and economically sustainable; to be a responsible steward of the nation's nuclear weapons; and to support continued U.S. leadership in science and technology.

> *The Springfield nuclear plant was under investigation by the **DOE.***

OSHA, Occupational Safety and Health Administration. OSHA's mission is to save lives, prevent injuries, and protect the health of America's workers in the workplace.

> ***OSHA** regulations mandated that each workstation be equipped with safety goggles and a fire extinguisher.*

 Also Explore: *bureaucracy, Congress,* EPA, litigation.

Needed

---

essential, *adj.* Absolutely necessary; requisite. Essential is applicable to that which constitutes the absolute essence or the fundamental nature of a thing and therefore must be present for the thing to exist, function, etc. Something that is essential is indispensable; it cannot be done without.

*Because profits are **essential** to the continued survival of a business, the future of NotSoBig Co. was in doubt.*

---

indispensable, *adj.* That which cannot be dispensed with or neglected. An indispensable person or thing cannot be done without if the specified or implied purpose is to be achieved.

*Due to his previous experience with COBOL programming, Sam was an **indispensable** part of the team dealing with the Year 2000 problem.*

exigency, *n.* A situation calling for immediate action or attention. Exigency implies an urgent need or emergency.

*NotSoBig Co.'s mounting losses created an **exigency** that had to be addressed immediately.*

core, *n.* The most important part of a matter, discussion, and so on; essence; pith.

*The **core** problem with the new product was that it cost too much to manufacture.*

key, *adj.* Controlling; important. Key is important, but not essential.

*In many companies, product manager is a **key** position.*

Also Explore: imperative, *intrinsic*, pivotal, quintessential, requisite.

Not Needed

---

extraneous, *adj.* Not truly or properly belonging; not essential. Extraneous may connote the possibility of integration of the external object into the thing to which it is added.

*Much to his boss's dismay, Pierce added an **extraneous** appendix to the group's final report.*

---

extrinsic, *adj.* Not really belonging to the thing with which it is connected; not inherent. Extrinsic refers to that which, coming from outside a thing, is not inherent to its real nature.

*The amendment was **extrinsic** to the bill to which it was attached, but helped forward the senator's own private agenda.*

inappropriate, *adj.* Not suitable, fitting, or proper. Inappropriate implies an ill fit, something not quite right for a specific purpose.

*Joan's behavior was totally **inappropriate** for the forum; she made many in the audience feel ill-at-ease.*

irrelevant, *adj.* Not pertinent; not to the point; not relating to the subject. Irrelevant implies no connection to the subject whatsoever.

*Hastings' **irrelevant** comment about pizza delivery elicited puzzled stares from those around the table discussing mutual funds.*

pleonastic, *adj.* The use of more words than are necessary for the expression of an idea; redundancy.

*Alan was annoyed that the professor's **pleonastic** explanation for the simple problem was taking so long.*

Also Explore: inapt, malapropos, noncompulsory, objectionable, *redundant.*

Wines

sauvignon blanc, *n.* A dry white wine made entirely or mainly from a white grape of Bordeaux. Sauvignon blanc is thought by many experts to be the perfect food wine in that it matches well with a vast array of dishes; it is also known as fumé blanc in California and Washington.

*Marissa ordered **sauvignon blanc** with her broiled sword-fish.*

chardonnay, *n.* A dry white wine. The chardonnay grape produces the world's greatest variety of white wines, including many of the finest white wines, both still and sparkling.

*Theodore offered his guests a glass of **chardonnay** before dinner.*

Chablis, *n.* A dry white Burgundy wine, often made in or near the town of Chablis, France. In America, also used as a generic term for common white table wines.

*Lynn committed a faux pas by having **Chablis** with her fillet mignon.*

merlot, *n.* A dark, dry red wine made from a red grape of Bordeaux. Merlot wines are often blended with Cabernet Sauvignon. Merlot wines tend to be lighter, with a little less intense varietal character than do Cabernet Sauvignon wines.

*Linda sipped a glass of **merlot** as she nibbled on a piece of gouda cheese.*

bouquet, *n.* The characteristic aroma of a wine or brandy. Bouquet refers to the smell or fragrance in wine that has its origins in the wine production or aging methods, as opposed to originating in the fruit itself.

*Diana savored the wine's **bouquet**.*

 Also Explore: Bordeaux, Cabernet Sauvignon, *faux pas*, fumé blanc.

Service Professionals

valet, *n.* An employee, such as of a hotel, who cleans or presses clothes or performs other personal services. Businesspeople on the road for long periods of time often find that using valet services helps maintain a certain level of personal upkeep. Valet parking is a service providing attendants who take, park, and later return vehicles to guests and customers of a restaurant or hotel.

> *Scott left his suit with the **valet** to be pressed.*

concierge, *n.* A member of the hotel staff who is responsible for serving guests miscellaneous needs, such as finding theater tickets, making dinner reservations, and so on.

> *Paul was impressed that the **concierge** was able to obtain four front-row tickets to the hottest Broadway play.*

maitre d', *n.* (mayt-er-dee) from the French (abbreviated from maitre d'hotel, "master of the house"). A headwaiter. In many cases, the major-domo of a restaurant's serving staff; the person responsible for taking reservations and assigning tables to guests.

> *The **maitre d'** seated Edward and his boss in a booth near the corner.*

porter, *n.* A person who carries luggage for hire or as an attendant at a railroad station, hotel, and so on. A bellhop or bellboy is more correctly referred to as a porter.

> *Christine tipped the **porter** a dollar a bag.*

gratuity, *n.* A gift of money to a waitress, porter, etc. for a service or favor; tip. A typical gratuity for most services is in the 15–20 percent range.

> *Ronald was so impressed with the service that he left a 20 percent **gratuity.***

 Also Explore: aide, Boston quarter, major-domo, proprietor, steward.

Letting Go

---

rightsize, *vt.* To cut staff, normally as part of a mass layoff. Rightsize is sometimes perceived (by management) to be less hard-hearted than the more descriptive downsize—as though cutting staff were a natural thing to do to get the company to the right size.

*The president decided to **rightsize** the company through a series of strategic layoffs.*

---

downsize, *vt.* To reduce the size of a company; to cut staff. Downsize is synonymous with the more politically correct rightsize.

*Johnson **downsized** his staff by ten percent to get expenses in line with expected revenues.*

terminate, *vt.* To dismiss from employment; fire. Unlike downsizing, termination is generally done one employee at a time.

*Because of Hastings's poor attendance record, Mr. Ringwald decided to **terminate** Hastings at the end of the month.*

attrition, *n.* Loss of personnel in an organization in the normal course of events, as by retirement. Forced attrition involves offering early retirement to more senior employees and small-or-no pay raises to poor performers in an attempt to force staff to quit rather than terminate them. Attrit is the informal verb form of attrition.

*Low unemployment rates caused higher-than-expected **attrition** because many low-wage employees left for better offers elsewhere.*

resign, *vi.* To give up an office, position of employment, etc., especially by formal notice. Resigning is quitting.

*Forced with a better offer elsewhere, Samuelson **resigned** his position at ReallyBig Co.*

 Also Explore: abdicate, *minimize*, oust, *outplacement*, *severance,* syncope.

Full of Yourself

---

pretentious, *adj.* Making claims, explicit or implicit, to some distinction, importance, dignity, or excellence. Pretentious implies creating an appearance of often undeserved importance or distinction; in other words, pretending to be something one is not.

> *It was **pretentious** of James to think he was calling the shots on the Burns project; his boss was not amused.*

---

ostentatious, *adj.* Putting on a showy display, as of wealth, knowledge, etc. Pretentious involves a claim; ostentatious involves a physical display or act.

> *Mrs. Williams **ostentatious** display of her new ring by waving her hand incessantly, annoyed everyone.*

affectation, *n.* Artificial behavior meant to impress others; mannerism for effect. Ostentatious behavior is typically an overall acting job; an affectation is more often a smaller display or a change in a specific mannerism.

> *Byron adopted the **affectation** of smoking a pipe to appear more mature.*

grandiose, *adj.* Seeming or trying to seem very important; pompous and showy. Grandiose implies taking normal behavior and making it larger.

> *Tutwiller made a **grandiose** entrance as he entered the boardroom for his presentation.*

vain, *adj.* Having or showing an excessively high regard for one's self, looks, possessions, ability, and so on; indulging in or resulting from personal vanity. Vain behavior is not necessarily making a false claim, just thinking a little too highly of oneself.

> *Suzanne was too **vain** to be caught bowling with the rest of the department.*

 Also Explore: *arrogant*, conceited, mannerism, narcissistic, pompous.

Crime

assault, *n.* An unlawful threat or unsuccessful attempt to do physical harm to another, causing a present fear of immediate harm. In legal terms, assault implies an unlawful offer or attempt with force to do a corporeal hurt to another person. The threat must place the person assaulted in reasonable apprehension of immediate offensive contact.

*June was **assaulted** as she walked home, but fortunately, she was able to run away before she came to any harm.*

battery, *n.* Any illegal beating or touching of another person, either directly or with an object. In legal terms, battery implies an intentional, unauthorized touching of other persons, their clothing, or effects, when that touching would be offensive to a person of ordinary sensibilities.

*Lawrence was arraigned on **battery** charges after the fight in the bar.*

homicide, *n.* Any killing of one human being by another. Murder and manslaughter are both homicide.

*The **homicide** squad was called in to investigate the body found in the alley.*

murder, *n.* The malicious or premeditated killing of one human being by another.

*Because he had deliberately plotted to kill his mother, Roland was arrested on the charge of **murder**.*

manslaughter, *n.* The killing of a human being by another, but without malice. Manslaughter may be voluntary, upon a sudden impulse, or involuntary, in the commission of some unlawful act.

*Alex had acted in self-defense, so the district attorney lowered the charge to **manslaughter**.*

 Also Explore: *bribe,* felony, malfeasance, *malicious,* premeditated.

Punishment

---

retribution, *n.* Punishment for evil done or reward for good done; requital. Retribution implies a payback—either positive or negative—for some previous action.

> *ReallyBig Co. demanded **retribution** for the trade secrets the former employees allegedly took to their new employer.*

---

retaliate, *vi.* To return like for like, especially to return evil for evil; pay back injury for injury. Retaliation implies a like response to a perceived wrong. An eye for an eye.

> *The President vowed to **retaliate** for any planes shot down over the gulf.*

revenge, *vt.* To take vengeance in behalf of a person, oneself, and so on; avenge. Revenge stresses the strong impulsion to action and the actual seeking of vengeance. Retribution can be done by a third party, such as a court; revenge is personal.

> *The dead girl's brother took **revenge** on the men suspected in her killing.*

censure, *n.* A condemnation of a person or an action as wrong; strong disapproval. Implies the expression of severe criticism or disapproval by a person in authority or in a position to pass judgment and is often made public.

> *The public **censure** of the Congresswoman's behavior by the ethics committee effectively killed her career in public service.*

reprimand, *n.* A severe or formal rebuke, especially by a person in authority. A reprimand involves no punishment, simply a stern talking to or scolding and usually remains relatively private.

> *Mr. Worthington **reprimanded** Johnson for surfing the Internet on company time.*

 Also Explore: admonition, berate, blackball, *castigate,* penance.

Computer Problems

spam, *n.* A mass posting of electronic messages, via the Internet, to bulletin boards, USENET newsgroups, or lists of e-mail addresses. Spam, which is the electronic equivalent of junk mail.

*Walter **spammed** over a hundred newsgroups with an advertisement for his latest get-rich-quick scheme.*

flame, *vt.* Posting an inflammatory electronic article or sending an inflammatory e-mail message. Flaming is a vitriolic personal attack on another individual.

*After Walter's spam, members of the newsgroups **flamed** his personal e-mail box complaining about the intrusion.*

crash, *vi.* To become inoperable because of a malfunction in the equipment or an error in the program.

*When his e-mail box got jammed with thousands of flames, Walter's entire system **crashed**.*

virus, *n.* An unauthorized, disruptive set of instructions placed in a computer program that either destroys data or leaves copies of itself in other programs and disks.

*One flamer was so incensed that he e-mailed Walter a program containing a **virus**.*

security, *n.* The state achieved by hardware, software, or data as a result of successful efforts to prevent damage, theft, or corruption. Computer security involves protecting personal computer systems from viruses, as well as protecting larger servers and networks against attack, interference, and espionage.

*Fortunately, the **security** on Walter's server was tight enough that it detected the virus before it could replicate itself.*

 Also Explore: *boot*, *firewall*, nonrepudiation, rave, Trojan horse.

Mobile Phones

cellular, *adj.* Cellular refers to a type of telecommunications system that connects the standard hardwired telephone system to a network of mobile phones. A cellular system comprises multiple small cells, each of which is equipped with a low-powered radio transmitter/receiver.

*David carried his **cellular** phone clipped to his belt in case anyone needed to reach him while he was walking the halls.*

roaming, *vt.* The ability to use a cellular phone outside its usual local service area. When you use your cellular phone while traveling, you are roaming.

*When he flew to New York, David was assessed a **roaming** fee for each call back to the office.*

standby, *adj.* The amount of time you can leave your fully charged cellular phone turned on before the phone will completely discharge the batteries.

*David's new phone could last for almost 24 hours on **standby**.*

handoff, *n.* The process by which a cellular phone conversation is transferred from one radio frequency in one cell to another radio frequency in another cell.

*During a drive to Chicago, David got disconnected during a **handoff** to a new cell.*

PCS, *n.* Personal Communications Services, a digital form of cellular communication. Digital PCS calls are clearer than normal analog cellular communications, although PCS is not currently available in all locations.

*The salesperson demonstrated the clearer call quality on the new **PCS** phone.*

 Also Explore: *analog,* cell, *digital*, telecommunications.

Lazy

---

indolent, *adj.* Disliking or avoiding work; idle; lazy. Indolent implies a true dislike of work. Indolent can be thought of as indulging in ease or being habitually idle. Indolence is characterized by mental and physical sluggishness, brought on by one's nature, intent, or both.

*Brad was so **indolent** he refused to even look for a job.*

---

sloth, *n.* Disinclination to work or exert oneself. Indolent implies a dislike of work; sloth implies a reluctance to expend energy for any reason.

*Jeffrey's **sloth** caused him to put a cooler next to the couch so he wouldn't have to walk to the kitchen to get a cold beer.*

dilatory, *adj.* Causing or tending to cause delay; meant to gain time or defer action to a future time. A person who is inclined to delay things; slow or late in doing things; procrastinator. Dilatory behavior can be intentional and strategic. Most often, however, it describes someone who dawdles while he works.

*Luanne couldn't be sure if Frank's **dilatory** behavior was intentional or just an irritating work habit.*

idle, *adj.* Not busy; inactive; not in use. Idle does not imply a reason for inactivity, but describes an inactive state.

*The entire department was **idle** during the holidays.*

inactive, *adj.* Not moving; not inclined to act; inert. Idle implies a lack of doing something; inactive implies a total lack of movement.

*Marcia received a call from her credit card company because her account had been **inactive** for 12 months.*

 Also Explore: *apathetic, enervate, inertia,* passive, *torpid.*

Average

mediocrity, _n._ The quality or state of being neither very good nor very bad; ordinary. Although mediocrity is defined as average or ordinary, it often has a negative connotation, especially when above-average performance is desired.

> _Mr. Drake expected top-notch performance from his troops, so Hawking's **mediocrity** was especially disappointing._

ordinary, _adj._ Customary; usual; regular; normal. Ordinary implies familiarity.

> _Lisa thought her home life was too **ordinary** to be interesting to the others._

adequate, _adj._ Good enough for what is required or needed; sufficient; barely satisfactory; acceptable but not remarkable. Adequate implies that there might be a better choice, but the current one will do.

> _Bennington found the agreement **adequate**, although he later commented that he could have cut an even better deal if he had wanted._

nondescript, _adj._ So lacking in recognizable character or qualities as to belong to no definite class or type; hard to classify or describe; not interesting; colorless; drab. Something or someone is nondescript when he is average or ordinary to such a degree that there is literally no way to describe him.

> _Murray's **nondescript** social life did not have even one extraordinary aspect. At parties, he was an incredible bore._

banal, _adj._ Dull or stale because of overuse; commonplace. Banality is defined by commonality and overuse, which ultimately suggests insincerity.

> _After weeks of the same **banal** compliments, Ralph was convinced that his work was not truly appreciated._

 Also Explore: acceptable, bourgeois, tolerable.

Upper Class

---

opulent, *adj.* Characterized by abundance or profusion; luxuriant. Whereas affluence applies to people, opulence can apply to either people or things.

*The executive's house was appointed in an **opulent** fashion.*

---

elegant, *adj.* Characterized by dignified richness and grace, as of design, dress, style, and so on; luxurious or opulent in a restrained, tasteful manner. One can be elegant without being affluent; richness is not the same as being rich.

*The gown was **elegant** and understated.*

affluent, *adj.* Wealthy; rich. Affluent implies an abundance of money and other possessions.

*Now that he was making over $100,000 a year, Jameson felt that he could easily afford to associate with the more **affluent** people in the city.*

patrician, *adj.* Originally, a member of Roman nobility (as opposed to plebeian). Today, "patrician" is used to describe any person of high social rank or haughty bearing; an aristocrat. The term is not generally negative, but it's not entirely positive.

*Breaking into the **patrician** society of Megapolis required more than just a lot of money; it required pedigree and a certain bearing before being accepted.*

aristocratic, *adj.* Like or characteristic of a person with the tastes, manners, beliefs, etc. of the upper class. Aristocratic can be used in either a positive sense (proud, distinguished, etc.) or an unfavorable sense (snobbish, haughty, etc.).

*Jennings appeared **aristocratic** in the eyes of his staff.*

 Also Explore: aloof, *Brahmin, haughty,* prosperous.

Lower Class

hoi polloi, *n.* (hoy-pe-loy) from the Greek (literally, "the many"). The common people; the masses. Hoi polloi is usually a patronizing or contemptuous term used by the upper crust to refer to those not in their social circles. Interestingly, the masses seldom view themselves as the hoi polloi; apparently, this is a designation that can only be perceived by someone of a higher class.

> *Oscar declined to associate with the **hoi polloi** in the lunch room, preferring to dine alone at his private club.*

Philistine, *n.* A person regarded as smugly narrow and conventional in views and tastes, lacking in and indifferent to cultural and aesthetic values.

> *Laura was a **philistine** when it came to literature; she was perfectly happy relaxing with the latest bodice buster.*

lowbrow, *n.* A person lacking or considered to lack highly cultivated, intellectual tastes. Often a term of contempt.

> *John's taste in beers—"lite" brew from a can!—was considered **lowbrow**.*

plebeian, *adj.* (plee-bee-en) from the Latin. Commonplace; ordinary. Plebeian does not necessarily imply a class distinction, simply a mode of behavior associated with the common people.

> *Niles wouldn't be caught dead shopping in such a **plebeian** mall; he preferred to frequent more upscale retailers.*

nonentity, *n.* A person of no importance, lacking meaningful identity or character.

> *In the eyes of the system, Jones was a **nonentity**—just a number, not a name.*

Also Explore: caste, patronizing, rank and file, riff raff, upper crust.

Overpowering

---

formidable, *adj.* Causing fear or dread; awe-inspiring in size, excellence, and so on. Formidable implies a force to be reckoned with; seriously challenging, able, and competent. A person or thing that is formidable will often excite fear or apprehension in others.

> *With his hefty war chest, Carver was a **formidable** opponent for the Senate race.*

---

imposing, *adj.* Making a strong impression because of great size, strength, dignity, etc. Imposing implies a fearful reaction to something that is big or of great ability.

> *At 6'5", Walter cut an **imposing** figure.*

menacing, *vt.* To threaten or be a danger (to). Menacing implies a threatening of harm or evil. One doesn't have to be imposing to be menacing, nor do all who are imposing exude menace.

> *Even though Tim was shorter than Walter, his devilish goatee and penetrating eyes made him appear more **menacing**.*

impressive, *adj.* Having or tending to have a strong effect on the mind or emotions; eliciting wonder or admiration. Something can be impressive for a number of reasons, not exclusively size or amount.

> *Holderman's credentials were **impressive**; Jensen had never hired a Harvard MBA before.*

majestic, *adj.* Very grand or dignified; lofty; stately. Majestic impresses with state and dignity, not with size.

> *The lobby of the new building was truly **majestic** with its sweeping arches and royal blue carpet.*

Also Explore: exorbitant, forbidding, illimitable, penetrating, unnerving.

Force Forward

compel, *vt.* To get or bring about by force. Compel implies forcing a conclusion to some action by physical means or threats. One can be compelled by either physical or moral force.

*After the browbeating from his boss, Bob was **compelled** to finish the report by the end of the week.*

impel, *vt.* To push, drive, or move forward; to force or urge. Impel implies an active force resulting in forward progress.

*Terrance **impelled** his staff to get the project in gear by threatening them with termination if they didn't.*

expedite, *vt.* To speed up or make easy the progress or action of; hasten. Expedite implies an unusual effort to get something done ahead of schedule.

*Hollingsworth told the HR department to **expedite** the paperwork on the new hire.*

adamant, *adj.* Not giving in or relenting; unyielding. Adamant implies an internal force that resists change or attack.

*Georgia was **adamant** about not using the color green on the new packaging.*

duress, *n.* The use of force or threats; compulsion.

*The confession was signed under **duress** after weeks of mental and physical torture.*

 Also Explore: actuate, *coerce*, *compulsion*, dispatch, *facilitate*.

Harmful

---

malevolent, *adj.* Wishing evil or harm to others; having or showing ill will. A malevolent person is not necessarily evil, just someone who wishes evil on others out of spite or malice.

*Rudy's **malevolent** threats disturbed his ex-girlfriend.*

---

pernicious, *adj.* Causing great injury, destruction, or ruin; fatal or deadly; [rare] wicked or evil. Pernicious applies to that which does great harm by insidiously undermining or weakening. The harm done by a pernicious person or action is usually not detectable until it is too late.

*Maryanne's continued **pernicious** gossip about Roger didn't seem to be affecting his career until it was repeated on the 6 o'clock evening news.*

malignant, *adj.* Having an evil influence; very harmful; causing or likely to cause death. Malignant implies an inevitability, that the situation cannot be reversed or cured.

*Hastings' very presence was **malignant;** whichever department he visited inevitably was targeted for downsizing.*

nefarious, *adj.* Very wicked; villainous. Nefarious implies both unlawful and evil.

*Jones was so desperate to succeed that he hatched a **nefarious** plot to sabotage his competitor's distribution system.*

anathema, *n.* A thing or person greatly detested. An anathema is not necessarily harmful, just something that is disliked to the point of being condemned.

*Borden had burned so many bridges behind him that he was an **anathema** within the company.*

 Also Explore: diabolic, iniquitous, insidious, *malicious,* noxious.

Harmless

placebo, *n.* A harmless, unmedicated preparation given as a medicine to a patient merely to humor him or used as a control in testing the efficacy of another, medicated substance. Placebo can refer to anything that a person might think has an effect, even if it is incapable of having that effect.

*Dr. Benjamin was surprised that Mrs. Miniver's headaches lessened after he gave her a **placebo;** there was no physical reason to see such an improvement.*

innocuous, *adj.* That does not injure or harm; not controversial, offensive, or stimulating; dull and uninspiring. Innocuous is sometimes used in a derogatory fashion to imply a person or thing that has no impact or is useless.

*Mr. Beevis was so **innocuous** as to be unnoticed at the office party.*

benign, *adj.* Doing little or no harm; not malignant; kindly. Benign can also refer to a non-malignant cancer.

*Fortunately, the effect of the new government regulation was **benign.***

ineffectual, *adj.* Not producing or not able to produce the desired effect. Something or someone who is ineffectual can actually cause harm by not being able to stop something bad from happening.

*Tony's entire team was **ineffectual** in stemming the flow of red ink.*

futile, *adj.* That which could not succeed; useless; vain. Futile is applied to that which fails completely of the desired end or is incapable of producing any result.

*In the end, all the internal efforts were **futile;** the competition was so entrenched that no new product could succeed.*

Also Explore: double-blind, *enervate*, flaccid, incapable, uninspiring.

Lots Of

plethora, *n.* The state of being too full; overabundance. Plethora implies an overwhelming amount, too many of a given thing. Think of plethora as extreme excess or an embarassment of riches.

> *Gordon was overwhelmed with a virtual **plethora** of options when he first took office; he didn't know where to start.*

cornucopia, *n.* An overflowing fullness; abundance. Whereas plethora implies too many, cornucopia implies a good—although large—amount of something desired.

> *Santa brought the boys a **cornucopia** of gifts.*

preponderance, *adj.* Greater in amount, weight, power, influence, importance, etc.; predominant. Preponderance implies a dominance due to volume or size.

> *The **preponderance** of evidence indicated that Bryce was guilty of the offense.*

prolific, *adj.* Turning out many products of the mind; fruitful; abounding. Prolific implies an above-average volume.

> *Asimov was a **prolific** writer, turning out a dozen books a year.*

profuse, *adj.* Giving or pouring forth freely; generous, often to excess. Profuse implies giving to the point of excess.

> *After the accident at the dinner party, Kim made **profuse** apologies to the hostess.*

Also Explore: *opulent*, replete, saturation, *superfluous*, unstinting.

Great Works

pièce de résistance, *n.* (pyes-de-ray-zees-tans) from the French (piece of resistance). The main item or event in a series. Pièce de résistance refers to the crowning achievement of a person or event.

*And now for the **pièce de résistance** of today's auction, the artist's most famous work.*

tour de force, *n.* (toor-de-fors) from the French (literally "feat of strength"). An unusually skillful or ingenious creation, production, or performance. Tour de force can sometimes refer to an action or object that is merely clever or spectacular.

*The new composition was a **tour de force,** using practically every instrument in the orchestra in unheard of ways.*

masterpiece, *n.* A thing made or done with masterly skill; great work of art or craftsmanship. Also used to refer to the most outstanding work made or done by a craftsman or creative artist. Masterpiece implies an irreplaceable and priceless quality.

*The figurine was a **masterpiece,** exquisitely detailed and extremely lifelike.*

objet d'art, *n.* (ob-zhay-dar) from the French (literally "object of art"). A relatively small value object of artistic value, as a figurine, vase, and so on.

*The **objet d'art** sat on the windowsill, the afternoon sunlight highlighting its masterful rendering.*

opus, *n.* A work; composition; especially any of the musical works of a composer numbered in order of composition or publication.

*The orchestra was to play Vayo's third **opus.***

 Also Explore: chef d'oeuvre, feat, pinnacle, showpiece.

Who Cares?

---

apathetic, *adj.* Not interested; unconcerned; feeling little or no emotion. Apathetic stresses an indifference or listlessness from which one cannot easily be stirred to feeling. Apathy is difficult to overcome because it is typically deep-rooted and connotes an extinction of passion, not simply a passing disinterest.

Due to a lack of real issues, the electorate was ***apathetic*** *about the upcoming election; voter turnout was expected to be at an all-time low.*

---

listless, *adj.* Having no interest in what is going on as a result of illness, weariness, dejection, etc.; spiritless; languid. Listless suggests a lack of interest due to a weak mental or physical state.

As the illness ravished her body, Mildred grew increasingly ***listless.***

unenthusiastic, *adj.* Not having or showing strong interest. Unenthusiastic does not imply a total lack of interest, just a lack of enthusiasm or zeal.

Robert was ***unenthusiastic*** *about the new bonus plan; it wasn't near as rich as the prior year plan.*

indifferent, *adj.* Having or showing no partiality, bias, or preference; neutral. Indifferent implies a neutrality, especially with reference to choice.

James remained ***indifferent*** *in the campaign; neither candidate appealed to him.*

impassive, *adj.* Not feeling or showing emotion; calm. Although impassive means not having or showing any pain or emotion, it does not necessarily connote an incapability of being affected.

He stood by ***impassively,*** *not betraying the anguish he felt by Beatrice's declaration that she was leaving him for another man.*

 Also Explore: detached, languid, nonchalant, *placid.*

Computer Jargon

FAQ, Frequently asked question; a compendium of common questions and accumulated lore. FAQs are usually prepared by an expert or group in a standard format and updated at regular intervals. Many FAQs are posted to USENET newsgroups to attempt to forestall newbies cluttering the group with redundant questions.

*The newbie got flamed because he posted a question to the group that was answered in the **FAQ**.*

surf, *vt.* To browse or sample a succession of Web pages on the Internet. Surfing implies a random browsing of the Web, moving from one point to another in no set order.

*Randolph spent the entire evening **surfing** the Web with nothing much to show from the effort.*

bulletproof, *adj.* A program or piece of code considered extremely robust; capable of correctly recovering from any imaginable exception condition. Bulletproof implies bug free.

*Joseph prided himself on his ability to write **bulletproof** code.*

Moore's Law, *n.* The prediction that the computing power of microprocessor chips will double every 18 months with proportional decreases in cost. First uttered by Intel co-founder Gordon Moore in 1964.

*Applying **Moore's Law,** one could expect to buy a much more powerful PC for $1000 next Christmas.*

Easter egg, *n.* A message, graphic, or sound effect emitted by a program in response to some undocumented set of commands or keystrokes, intended as a joke or to display program credits.

*When the right sequence of keystrokes was executed, the **Easter egg** displayed a scrolling list of the program's development team.*

Also Explore: fault tolerance, hyperlinks, *newbie*, robust, *USENET*.

Breaking Up

divorce, *n.* Legal and formal dissolution of a marriage. Grounds for a divorce differ from state to state; many states allow no-fault divorces, where no grounds need to be asserted other than incompatibility or irreconcilable differences, whereas other states require the plaintiff to prove grounds such as adultery, abandonment, or mental cruelty.

*The marriage had deteriorated to such a point that Randy and Mary agreed to seek a **divorce**.*

separation, *n.* An arrangement by which a man and wife live apart by agreement or by court degree. Typically, a legal separation is the first step toward obtaining a divorce.

*They agreed to a trial **separation** period of six months.*

reconcile, *vt.* To make friendly again or win over to a friendly attitude; to settle (a quarrel or dispute) or compose (a difference).

*Despite attempts to **reconcile,** their differences were too great and they decided to finalize the divorce.*

settlement, *n.* The conveyance or disposition of property for the benefit of a person or persons. During divorce proceedings, a couple will agree on a settlement that provides for the disposition of all shared property, custody of children, and payment of alimony.

*Randy agreed to a **settlement** that let Mary have custody of the children.*

alimony, *n.* A monetary allowance that a court orders paid to a person by that person's spouse or former spouse after a legal separation or divorce or while legal action on this is pending.

*As part of the settlement, Randy had to pay Mary $2000 a month in **alimony**.*

 Also Explore: annulment, disposition, dissolution, estrangement, irreconcilable.

Coming Together

partnership, *n.* An association of two or more individuals who carry on a continuing business for profit as co-owners. Under the law, a partnership is regarded as a group of individuals rather than as a single entity.

> *John and Joe decided to invest in the franchise as a limited **partnership**.*

acquisition, *n.* A business or part of a business taken over or bought by another company. An acquisition can include the purchase of just the assets of another firm or the ongoing operations.

> *ReallyBig Co. announced the **acquisition** of NewCo Corp.*

hostile takeover, *n.* The acquisition of a corporation against the wishes of its management. If successful, the management team of the acquired company is normally—and forcibly—downsized.

> *ReallyBig Co. attempted a **hostile takeover** of Independo Inc., whose management team looked for a white knight to rescue it from the unwanted advance.*

merger, *n.* A combining of two or more companies, corporations, and so on into one, such as by issuing stock of the controlling corporation to replace the greater part of that of the other.

> *Little Corp. and Medium Corp. agreed to a **merger** that would make the combined firm the third largest in the industry.*

joint venture, *n.* A business arrangement made by two or more companies. Typically, the funding and resources for a joint venture are supplied as appropriate by the companies involved.

> *The **joint venture** between Ultimate Inc. and Penultimate Corp. was doomed from the start because both firms were engaged in a power struggle.*

 Also Explore: affiliation, alignment, consolidation, incorporation, leveraged buyout.

The Past

memoir, *n.* An autobiography, especially one that is objective and anecdotal in emphasis rather than inward and subjective. A memoir can also be a report or record of important events based on the writer's personal observation or knowledge. Unlike a diary, a memoir is usually written with the hope of being read by others.

*Mike began writing his **memoirs,** starting with his remembrances of his high school days.*

autobiography, *n.* The story of one's own life written or dictated by oneself. An autobiography is one's own history written by oneself; a biography is one's history written by someone else.

*The celebrity's **autobiography** was much less objective than the biography written by a dispassionate third party.*

reminisce, *vi.* To think, talk, or write about remembered events or experiences.

*While they were having dinner, Mike and Sherry began to **reminisce** about their days in college.*

memento, *n.* Anything serving as a reminder or warning; a souvenir. Typically a memento is an object that carries a fond personal remembrance of some past time.

*Sherry kept Mike's keepsake ring as a **memento** of their time together.*

memorabilia, *n.* Things worth remembering or recording, such as a collection of anecdotes, accounts, items, etc., especially about one subject or event. A memento is a single thing; memorabilia is a collection of things.

*Mike collected musical **memorabilia,** especially vintage instruments and sheet music.*

 Also Explore: *anecdotal,* annals, commemorate, memorialize, souvenir.

Mother Earth

Gaia, *n.* (gay-eh) from Greek mythology. A goddess who is the personification of the Earth; the mother of nature and the protector of life. (Also Gaea.) The Gaia hypothesis expands on this idea to propose that the entire range of living matter on Earth can be regarded as constituting a single living entity.

> *Dr. Watson adhered to the* **Gaia** *hypothesis and believed that eliminating the tropical rainforests would have impact.*

---

greenhouse effect, *n.* Solar shortwave radiation easily penetrates to the planet where it is reradiated into the atmosphere as warmer, larger long waves that are readily absorbed by carbon dioxide, water vapor, and so on, thus trapping heat.

> *The banning of fluorocarbons was necessary to reduce the* **greenhouse effect.**

global warming, *n.* A slight but continuing increase in the temperature of the lower atmosphere, usually attributed to the greenhouse effect.

> **Global warming** *was thought to lead to extremes in weather—longer droughts, colder winters, and more hurricanes.*

Biodegradable, *adj.* Capable of being readily decomposed by microbial action. In biodegradable substances, the natural processes of decay lead to the eventual release of nutrients that are recycled by the ecosystem.

> *The new hamburger container was completely* **biodegradable;** *it disintigrated when exposed to the elements.*

terrain, *n.* Ground or a tract of ground, especially with regard to its natural or topographical features or fitness for some use.

> *The hilly* **terrain** *was perfect for the corporate hideaway.*

Also Explore: *ecology, environment,* lithosphere, terra firma, topography.

129

Working Together

alliance, *n.* A close association for a common objective, such as nations, political parties, etc. Alliance refers to any association entered into for mutual benefit and implies a formality such as a treaty or agreement. Alliances are common in high-technology industries, where multiple technologies from multiple companies often must be combined to offer a complete solution to the marketplace.

*The two companies formed an **alliance** to lobby Congress for regulatory reforms.*

collaboration, *n.* A working together, especially in some literary, artistic, or scientific undertaking. An alliance is a formal association; a collaboration is typically informal.

*Jordan and Alan worked on the project as a **collaboration** between their two teams.*

affiliate, *n.* An officially related individual or organization; member. Affiliate implies having joined some overriding organization, club, and so on.

*MarketCorp was an **affiliate** of the International Marketing Cooperative.*

colleague, *n.* A fellow worker in the same profession; associate. An affiliate has to formally belong to an organization; a colleague simply has to work at the same company or in the same profession.

*Even though they never ran into each other, Daniel and Michelle were **colleagues** at ReallyBig Co.*

cohort, *n.* An associate, colleague, or supporter; a conspirator or accomplice. Cohort implies a behind-the-scenes relationship.

*Despite his lack of experience, the mayor's **cohort** garnered the appointment.*

 Also Explore: ally, *patron, peer*, subsidiary.

Starting Your Computer

DAY
131

boot, *vt.* To load, such as from a disk, a program or instructions, such as for basic operation, into the memory of a computer; to turn on a computer. Boot comes from the older word *bootstrap*, which was the process of using a small initialization program bootstrap to load another program and to start an inactive computer.

*When his hard disk failed, Dean had to **boot** his computer from a floppy diskette.*

initialize, *vt.* To prepare hardware or software to perform a task. In some programs, initializing can be setting a counter or variable to zero before running a procedure.

*The software **initialized** the modem before accessing the telephone lines.*

log on, *vt.* Logging on is the process of establishing a connection with, or gaining access to, a computer system or peripheral device.

*Rudy had to **log on** to the network every time he booted up his computer.*

configure, *vt.* To assemble a selection of hardware, software, and peripheral equipment into a system and to adjust each of the parts so that they all work together.

*Samuel's system wasn't **configured** properly; his mouse kept freezing every time he used his modem.*

autoexec, *n.* A particular computer file (autoexec.bat) that is run automatically every time a computer is turned on. The autoexec file contains startup instructions for your computer.

*To fix the mouse and modem conflict, Samuel had to edit his **autoexec** file.*

 Also Explore: baud, *operating system,* parity, *peripheral,* read-only memory.

Safe Sex

---

protection, *n.* Devices or practices designed to reduce the risk of pregnancy or transmittal of sexually transmitted diseases (STDs) during sexual intercourse. Protection more often than not refers directly to condoms but can also include diaphragms, birth control pills, and other prophylactic devices.

*Margot refused to have sex without **protection**.*

---

safe sex, *n.* Sexual activity that does not involve the exchange of bodily fluids. Safe sex normally incorporates various practices, including the use of a condom, that reduce the risk of spreading STDs, especially AIDS. Don't confuse safe sex with sex with a male who is "safe"—that is, a male who has had a vasectomy.

*Ted engaged only in **safe sex** with a first-time partner.*

celibate, *n.* One who abstains from sexual intercourse. Celibacy is the only sure way to avoid STDs. In its strictest form, celibacy implies refraining from all types of sexual activity, including oral, anal, and vaginal sex.

*Don and Wilma decided to stay **celibate** until marriage.*

STD, *n.* Sexually transmitted disease; any infection that is acquired through sexual contact. STDs can include anything from nonspecific urethritis to the AIDS virus.

*Kenneth's doctor informed him that he had contracted an **STD**.*

bareback, *adv.* Sex without a condom. In an age of rampant STDs, bareback sex is the antithesis of safe sex.

*Louis liked to live dangerously, engaging in **bareback** sex with multiple partners.*

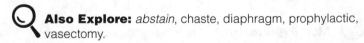

Also Explore: *abstain*, chaste, diaphragm, prophylactic, vasectomy.

Weddings

VOW, *n.* A solemn promise of love and fidelity. Although there are many different types of traditional marriage vows (based on religious practices and so on), it is becoming common for the bride and groom to create their own unique vows.

*Don and Wilma modified the traditional Catholic **vows** to make them more personal.*

betrothed, *adj.* Engaged to be married. Betrothed also refers to the person to whom one is engaged to be married.

*Mr. and Mrs. Harrington announced that their daughter Helen was **betrothed** to Marcus Greenspan.*

bridesmaid, *n.* One of the women who attend the bride at a wedding. The chief bridesmaid is the maid of honor.

*Cindy had been a **bridesmaid** in three different weddings that summer.*

nuptials, *n.* A wedding; marriage. More commonly, nuptials refers to the entire social event at which the ceremony of marriage is performed.

*Cindy helped Wilma prepare for the upcoming **nuptials;** they had to reserve a hall, find a band, and hire a caterer.*

reception, *n.* A social function, often formal, for the receiving of guests. The wedding reception is typically held immediately after the wedding ceremony and affords the opportunity for the guests to formally meet the new bride and groom.

*At the **reception** afterwards, the best man made a humorous toast to the new couple.*

Also Explore: connubial, engaged, espousal, fiancé, significant other.

Drinks

---

rocks, *n.* Ice cubes. On the rocks refers to any liquor or other alcoholic drink that is served over ice cubes. The opposite of on the rocks is straight, which is an alcoholic drink served without ice or chaser.

*Hubert preferred his bourbon on the **rocks**.*

---

shot, *n.* A drink of liquor. Specifically, a shot is a small straight drink, the size of a jigger (usually 1.5 fluid ounces). The small glass that a shot is served in is called a shot glass.

*The party really got wild when everyone started drinking **shots** of tequila.*

short, *vt.* When two sizes of drinks (coffee, espresso, liquor, etc.) are available, the smallest size. The larger size is called tall; if a third larger size is available, it is sometimes called grande.

*Rene ordered a **short** decaf espresso; Russell had a tall double mocha.*

twist, *n.* A sliver of peel from a lemon, lime, and so on twisted and added to a drink for flavor.

*Bob ordered a vodka martini with a **twist**.*

chaser, *n.* A mild drink, as water, ginger ale, or beer, taken after or with whiskey, rum, etc.

*Gene had a shot of whiskey with a beer **chaser**.*

Also Explore: boiler maker, jigger, zest, three fingers.

Rude

---

brusque, *adj.* Rough and abrupt in manner or speech. Brusque implies apparent rudeness, as evidenced by abruptness of speech or behavior. A brusque remark is characterized by preemptory shortness.

*Mary Ann's rejection of Dan's proposal was **brusque** and to top it off, she then slammed the door in his face.*

---

impertinent, *adj.* Having no connection with a given matter; irrelevant. Impertinent implies a forwardness of speech or action that is disrespectful and oversteps the bounds of propriety or courtesy.

*The young reporter's **impertinent** questions took the Senator aback.*

impudent, *adj.* Shamelessly bold or disrespectful. Impudent implies a shameless or brazen impertinence.

*Ricky's **impudent** behavior when he talked back to his math teacher earned him detention after school.*

arrogant, *adj.* Full of or due to unwarranted pride and self-importance; overbearing; haughty.

*The company's **arrogant** disregard for the regulations forced the EEOC to issue a warning.*

intrusive, *adj.* Forcing (oneself or one's thoughts) upon others without being asked or welcomed. Intrusive implies the forcing of oneself or something upon another without invitation, permission, or welcome.

*Selma found Ralph's incessant talking about his choice of candidate overly **intrusive,** especially during church services.*

 Also Explore: abrupt, brazen, curt, gauche, proprietary.

Put Downs

belittle, *vt.* To make seem little, less important, and so on; speak slightingly of; depreciate. Belittle is to lessen (something) in value by implying that it has less worth than is usually attributed to it and implies a contemptuous attitude in the speaker or writer. Interestingly, the word belittle was coined by Thomas Jefferson in 1780.

> *Jane **belittled** John's efforts on the Forbush project, saying he wasn't a significant contributor.*

pejorative, *adj.* Disparaging or derogatory. Pejorative implies making something appear worse than it actually is.

> *Randolph made a **pejorative** remark about Debbie's lack of social skills—which, truth be told, really weren't that bad.*

disparage, *vt.* To speak slightingly of; show disrespect for. To disparage is to attempt to lower in esteem, as by insinuation, invidious comparison, faint praise, etc.

> *Samuel's **disparaging** remarks damaged Sally's pride and reputation.*

deride, *vt.* To laugh at in contempt or scorn; make fun of; ridicule.

> *Michael's efforts in the negotiations were **derided** as being too little, too late.*

denounce, *vt.* To condemn strongly as evil.

> *The prosecutor **denounced** ReallyBig Co. as a flagrant polluter, insensitive to the needs of the environment and the community.*

Also Explore: *censure*, deprecate, derogatory, *insinuate*, invidious.

Motives

---

ulterior, *adj.* Further; more remote; especially, beyond what is expressed, implied, or evident; undisclosed. Ulterior implies something that is alternative, less visible or obvious, but is in fact the principal factor or reason.

> *Despite pristine appearances, Tony had an **ulterior** motive for pursuing the Hafnagel acquisition.*

---

concealed, *vt.* Kept from another's knowledge; kept secret.

> *Argent skillfully **concealed** his motives for wanting to do the Hafnagel acquisition; his colleagues had no idea that he stood to benefit personally when the acquisition was completed.*

suspect, *vi.* Viewed with suspicion; suspected. Suspect implies a belief that one is guilty of something specified, on little or no evidence.

> *Violet's motives were **suspect** ever since she revealed she used to be employed by their chief competitor.*

guile, *n.* Slyness and cunning in dealing with others; craftiness. Guile implies skill in deception and a wily or duplicitous nature.

> *Emma used **guile** to insinuate her way into Mr. McGiver's confidence.*

naïve, *adj.* Unaffectedly or sometimes foolishly simple; not suspicious. Naïve implies a genuine, innocent simplicity or lack of artificiality but sometimes connotes an almost foolish lack of worldly wisdom.

> *James' **naïve** belief in the kindness of others led him to pick up the two hitchhikers—who later robbed him and stole his car.*

 Also Explore: angle, cunning, duplicitous, rationale, wily.

Unfair Practices (Part 2)

discrimination, *n.* A showing of partiality or prejudice in treatment; specifically, action or policies directed against the welfare of minority groups. Any group can be discriminated against: blacks, Hispanics, women, senior citizens, and so on.

*The group of women filed a class action suit against ReallyBig Co. on grounds of sex **discrimination;** they claimed that the company had no women among its management ranks.*

prejudice, *n.* Suspicion, intolerance, or irrational hatred of other races, creeds, regions, occupations, etc. Prejudice implies a preconceived and unreasonable judgment or opinion, usually an unfavorable one marked as by suspicion, fear, or hatred.

*Sally was **prejudiced** against older employees; she thought that only younger people could effectively compete.*

stereotype, *n.* A fixed or conventional notion or conception, such as of a person, group, idea, etc., held by a number of people and allowing for no individuality, critical judgment, etc.

*Jack didn't fit the **stereotype** Susan had of a gay man; he was rugged, had a deep voice, and liked sports.*

typecast, *vt.* To cast (an actor) repeatedly in the same type of part or in the part of a character whose traits are very much like the actor's own. One does not have to be an actor to be typecast.

*Just because she was middle-aged, June felt she was **typecast** in housewife roles.*

ageism, *n.* Discrimination against people on the basis of age; specifically, discrimination against older people.

*Sally's hiring practices, based on her prejudice against older employees, smacked of **ageism.***

 Also Explore: *bias,* bigotry, intolerance, partiality.

Classifications of People

class, *n.* A number of people or things grouped together because of certain likenesses or common traits. Class implies a group of people considered as a unit according to economic, occupational, or social status, especially a social rank or caste.

*Despite his blue-collar background, Joe's current salary qualified him for membership in the upper **class.***

level, *n.* Position, elevation, or rank considered as one of the planes in a scale of values.

*With Lance leaving, Armstrong moved up a **level** in the pecking order.*

status, *n.* Position; rank; standing; particularly, high position; prestige, prominence in society. Status refers to one's position as determined by legal or customary precedent or by such arbitrary factors as age, parentage, training, wealth, and so on.

*George now had the symbols that reflected his new **status** in The City—a house on The Point, the yacht, and the SUV.*

demographics, *n.* The statistical characteristics of a population, especially as classified by age, sex, income, etc., for market research, sociological analysis, and so on.

*The **demographics** of the target consumer indicated a white male in his 40s, earning under $40,000 a year.*

psychographics, *n.* The study of the values, attitudes, etc. of a consumer population. Whereas demographics are concerned with the physical characteristics of people, psychographics are concerned with how people think and why they do what they do.

*The **psychographics** of the target consumer indicated someone frustrated with technology yet not a complete novice.*

 Also Explore: grade, income bracket, station, *stratum.*

Blend

adapt, *vt.* To adjust (oneself) to new or changed circumstances. Adapt implies a modifying to suit new conditions and suggests flexibility. The ability to adapt rapidly is a valued commodity in the business environment.

> *James rapidly **adapted** to the new environment at the satellite office, shedding his suits and braces for dockers and polo shirts.*

adopt, *vt.* To take up and use (an idea, a practice, etc.) as one's own. Adapt means to change oneself; adopt means to absorb something else (so as not to change oneself).

> *The organization eventually **adopted** the new casual dress code.*

coalesce, *vi.* To unite or merge into a single body, group, or mass. Coalesce does not imply adaptation or adoption; it is a merging rather than an absorption.

> *Gradually, a consensus of opinion began to **coalesce.***

amalgam, *n.* A combination or mixture; blend.

> *The new product was an **amalgam** of the best of the old product with the key features from the chief competitor.*

hybrid, *n.* Anything of mixed origin, unlike parts, and so on. Amalgam implies a smooth mixture; hybrid implies a grafting on of disparate parts.

> *ReallyBig Co. adopted a **hybrid** benefit plan for its most recent acquisition, adding necessary items from the corporate plan to the acquisition's existing program.*

 Also Explore: *affiliate*, fuse, *merger*, mingle, mutate.

Company Cultures

entrepreneurial, *adj.* An entrepreneurial culture is characterized by a high degree of risk taking, rapid speed of movement, and lack of a burdensome bureaucracy.

*NewCo's **entrepreneurial** culture allowed it to react quickly to marketplace changes.*

corporate, *adj.* A corporate culture is characterized by a managerial hierarchy, a lack of entrepreneurial spirit, and bureaucracy.

*As the company grew, the original culture was replaced by a **corporate** culture, complete with bureaucracy.*

bureaucracy, *n.* A bureaucratic culture is characterized by myriad regulations, inflexibility, and lack of individual accountability.

*The **bureaucracy** entangled the new group in so much red tape that Adamson spent half his day filling out paperwork.*

political, *adj.* A political environment is characterized by a striving for individual enrichment or advancement at the expense of the group or organization as a whole.

*The culture was overly **political** with much behind-the-scenes maneuvering and backstabbing.*

guerilla, *adj.* Any member of a small defensive force of irregular soldiers, usually volunteers, making surprise raids, especially behind the lines of an invading enemy army. In today's market "warfare," guerilla refers to a particularly aggressive entrepreneurial culture.

*At the very top of the Gigantico's management was a small, tight group of vice presidents who went out of their way to maintain a **guerilla** culture.*

 Also Explore: *accountability, capitalism,* financier.

Network Computing

LAN, *n.* Local area network; a computer network within a small area or within a common environment, such as one within a building or one connecting offices on separate floors. Whereas a LAN is local, a wide area network (WAN) is a network connecting disparate and far-flung locations.

*Greg's computer had to be connected to the corporate **LAN** so he could send and receive e-mail.*

client, *n.* A computer or computer program that uses the services of another computer or computer program. Client/server computing refers to computing that utilizes data and programs stored on a central server but accessed by individual client PCs or workstations.

*Each server could handle up to 100 **clients** simultaneously.*

server, *n.* A computer or computer program that shares its resources, such as printers and files, with other computers or computer programs over a network.

*A glitch in the **server** caused the entire network to go down for more than an hour.*

enterprise, *n.* A business venture or company. Enterprise computing is synonymous for client/server computing in large corporations.

*IS&T was charged with implementing Windows NT across the entire **enterprise.***

firewall, *n.* A firewall is a computer system that filters, for security reasons, traffic to and from a corporation's internal network. Firewalls are used to protect any networked server from damage (intentional or otherwise) by those who log in to it.

*The webmaster put up a **firewall** to protect the internal network from attacks originating on the Internet.*

 Also Explore: peer-to-peer, ring, and star networks, and wide area networks; *security.*

Mobile Computing

portable computer, *n.* Any computer that is capable of being transported. Most portable computers contain their own energy source in the form of rechargeable batteries.

> *Mandy preferred a **portable computer** to a desktop because she spent half of her time on the road.*

laptop, *n.* The largest form of portable computer. Laptop computers (sized to fit on a typical lap) are the most fully featured of all portable computers.

> *Simon's new **laptop** was as fully featured as his old desktop, with a large hard drive and the latest microprocessor.*

notebook, *n.* A smaller form of portable computer, typically with the dimensions of a paper notebook. Notebook computers are smaller and lighter than laptop computers although usually at the expense of features and performance.

> *Monica's new **notebook** fit comfortably in her briefcase.*

handheld, *n.* The smallest form of portable computer, capable of being held in one's hand or fitted into one's shirt pocket. Handheld computers often contain a small subset of the features found on larger notebook or laptop computers.

> *The **handheld** fit snugly in Roland's pocket and used a proprietary handwriting recognition system.*

PDA, *n.* Personal digital assistant, a form of handheld computer. PDAs are the smallest type of portable computer available; many PDAs use a form of handwriting recognition instead of keyboard input.

> *Greg used his **PDA** to keep track of his meetings and appointments.*

 Also Explore: NiCad, 3NiMH, and lithium ion batteries; *peripheral;* tranceiver.

Area

---

heartland, *n.* A geographically central area having crucial economic, political, or strategic importance. Heartland is often used to refer to rural areas of the U.S., particularly the Midwest, and is so-called because this region represents the "heart" of the country where mainstream or traditional values predominate.

> *The Senator knew he had to win the support of the **heartland** if he wanted to win the Presidential race.*

---

suburb, *n.* A district, especially a residential district, on or near the outskirts of a city and often a separately incorporated city or town. Multiple suburbs are often referred to collectively as suburbia.

> *ReallyBig Co. decided to relocate its corporate headquarters in the **suburbs,** avoiding big-city rent and traffic hassles.*

rural, *adj.* Of or characteristic of the country. Rural also refers to life on the farm or in the country as distinguished from life in the city.

> *Wal-Mart targeted **rural** areas, seeking to be the dominant retailer in smaller markets with fewer competitors.*

exurb, *n.* A region, generally semirural, beyond the suburbs of a city, inhabited largely by persons in the upper-income group.

> *Chip and Debbie decided to move to the **exurbs;** the long commute to work was worth it to have a bigger house with a lot of acreage.*

environs, *n.* The districts surrounding a town or city; suburbs or outskirts; surrounding area. At the center of the environs is an urban area; spreading outward, one finds suburban, then rural, then exurban areas.

> *FastMart had a dominant presence throughout the **environs** of Greater Philadelphia.*

 Also Explore: ghetto, *milieu*, outskirts, urban, vicinity.

Real Estate

escrow, *n.* A written agreement or something of value put in the care of a third party and not delivered until certain conditions are fulfilled. Homeowners typically have a monthly escrow payment held by the lender to pay for taxes, hazard insurance, mortgage insurance, lease payments, and other items as they become due.

> *Jack needed to put $1200 in* **escrow** *to cover taxes and insurance on his property.*

principal, *n.* The original amount (as in a loan) of the total due and payable at a certain date. The principal includes the total amount of debt, not including interest, and represents the face value of a note, mortgage, and so on.

> *The* **principal** *due on his house was $220,000.*

appraisal, *n.* An estimated value or price; especially, an expert valuation for taxation, tariff duty, sale, etc.

> *The* **appraisal** *showed that his house had appreciated by 20 percent since he purchased it.*

assessment, *n.* The act of setting the amount of tax. Assessment is the imposition of a tax, charge, or levy on a piece of property, usually according to established rates.

> *For tax* **assessment** *purposes, his property was valued at $200,000.*

point, *n.* An amount equal to one percent of a mortgage loan. Loan discount points are a one-time charge assessed at closing by the lender; by paying points, the borrower offers the lender up-front money to get a lower interest rate.

> *The current rate for a 30-year fixed-rate loan was 7.5 percent plus 2* **points.**

 Also Explore: estimation, imposition, levy, *mortgage,* tariff.

Lifestyles

---

yuppie, *n.* Young urban professional. Any young professional regarded as upscale, ambitious, materialistic, faddish, etc. Not to be confused with puppies (poor urban professionals), guppies (gay urban professionals), or buppies (black urban professionals).

After the downtown area was revitalized, it was overrun by ***yuppies*** *in SUVs.*

---

dink, *n.* Double income, no kids. Any couple (married or not) with both persons working and no dependent children. Dinks are highly desired consumers, with much disposable income.

TravelCo. decided to target ***dinks*** *for the new line of exotic luxury vacations because they had both high income and ample leisure time.*

moby, *n.* Mommy older, baby younger. A new population segment of women having babies later in life. Related to doby (daddy older, baby younger).

When Don called Melissa a ***moby,*** *he had to explain that he was referring to the fact she was pregnant at 35, not that she was getting too large.*

skippie, *n.* School kids with incomes and purchasing power. A growing population segment of younger, impressionable consumers.

Skippies *have a surprising amount of purchasing power, given their average age.*

woof, *n.* Well-off older folks. Any senior citizen with significant disposable income.

Recreational vehicle manufacturers counted ***woofs*** *as a significant part of their consumer base.*

 Also Explore: disposable income, faddish, materialistic, upscale.

Unchecked

---

rampant, *adj.* Spreading unchecked. Rampant implies a violent and uncontrollable action, manner, speech, and so on, characterized by rage and fury. Something that runs rampant is viewed to be almost unstoppable.

*The virus ran **rampant** over the entire computer network.*

---

pervasive, *adj.* Tending to be prevalent or spread throughout.

*Computitan's products were **pervasive** in most corporate environments.*

rife, *adj.* Frequently or commonly occurring; widespread; abundant; abounding.

*Gregory's report was **rife** with error.*

pandemic, *adj.* Prevalent over a whole area, country, etc.; universal; general. Pandemic often refers to a disease, epidemic over a large region.

*The new flu virus was **pandemic** in southeast Asia.*

omnivorous, *adj.* Eating any sort of food, especially both animal and vegetable food. Omnivorous implies taking in everything indiscriminately, such as with the intellect.

*Martin was an **omnivorous** reader; his library contained everything from trashy romance novels to serious dissertations on art and literature.*

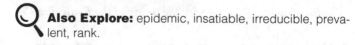
Also Explore: epidemic, insatiable, irreducible, prevalent, rank.

Gifts

---

subsidy, *n.* A grant of money; specifically, a grant of money from one government to another or a government grant to a private enterprise considered of benefit to the public. Subsidy implies a monetary grant from the government to subsidize some activity or operation. Most things that are subsidized cannot survive on their own means.

*The startup qualified for a government **subsidy**.*

---

grant, *n.* Something given, as property, a tract of land, an exclusive right or power, money from a fund, and so on. Grant implies a formal gift, according to legal procedure or by deed.

*The company made a **grant** of 200 new computers to the local school system.*

honorarium, *n.* A payment as to a professional person for services on which no fee is set or legally obtainable. Honorarium implies a payment when there should be no formal payments.

*The professor received an **honorarium** for his consulting services.*

aid, *n.* Help or assistance, especially financial help. Aid can be any form of assistance, not exclusively financial. Aid implies a need, which grant and honorarium do not.

*Marvin qualified for financial **aid** his first year at college.*

aegis, *n.* Sponsorship; auspices.

*The funding was given under the **aegis** of the ReallyBig Co.*

Also Explore: auspices, *endorse, endowment, patron,* stipend.

Furniture

baroque, *adj.* (be-rohk) from the French (imperfect pearl). Of, characteristic of or like a style of art and architecture characterized by much ornamentation and curved rather than straight lines. The baroque style originated in Italy and is noted for its bold curving forms.

*The **baroque** desk clashed with the more contemporary furnishings in the rest of the house.*

apron, *n.* A length of shaped and decorated wood found beneath the bottom framing of a chair seat or table top.

*Robert found the remote control behind the chair's **apron**.*

armoire, *n.* (ar-mwar) from the French (a chest for tools or arms). A large, usually ornate cupboard or clothespress. An armoire is a large mobile cupboard or wardrobe featuring doors and shelves for clothes storage.

*Sally placed her new suit in the **armoire**.*

brocade, *n.* A rich cloth with a raised design, such as of silk, velvet, gold, or silver, woven into it. Brocade implies the use of richly colored (sometimes metallic) threads that make a design stand out against a weave background.

*Meg's new chair featured a **brocade** with an ornate design.*

chaise, *n.* (shayz) from the French (literally, "chair"). A couchlike chair with a back support and a seat long enough to support outstretched legs. Typically, chaise is a style of furniture with an extending footrest; in a chaise style, the gap between the chair and footrest is covered by a pad.

*Ralph liked to relax at the end of the day in his favorite **chaise** lounge.*

 Also Explore: architecture, appointments, florid, *ornament*, wardrobe.

Slopes

---

curve, *n.* A curved line or similar graphic representation showing variations occurring or expected to occur in prices, business, conditions, group achievements, or other sets of data. Note that a straight line is a type of a curve—one with consistent variation.

*The graph of customer level followed the standard bell **curve**.*

---

steep, *adj.* Having a sharp rise or highly inclined slope. Steep suggests such sharpness of rise or slope as to make ascent or descent very difficult.

*The expense graph showed a **steep** slope, reflecting the rapid increase in fixed costs.*

flat, *adj.* Without variation; not fluctuating. A flat line is one where the data values remain constant across the axis.

*Due to the stagnating economy, the sales graph was **flat**.*

ceiling, *n.* The highest point of a set of data. Ceiling implies the highest something will go or the highest limit set. Carrying forth the architectural metaphor, note that ceilings can also be walls; when something has hit a ceiling, it is sometimes said to have "hit a wall."

*The CFO dictated an expense **ceiling** for the second half of the year.*

basement, *n.* The lowest point of a set of data. Basement (or floor) implies the lowest something will go or the lowest limit set.

*Fortunately, it looked like sales had hit the **basement** and were beginning to pick up again.*

 Also Explore: ascent, descent, graphic, incline, variation.

Steps

gradation, *n.* A gradual change by steps or stages from one condition, quality, and so on to another. Gradation implies a step, stage, or degree in a graded series or a transitional stage; it can also refer to a gradual shading of one tint, tone, or color into another.

*The package design incorporated a **gradation** from red to black.*

degree, *n.* Any of the successive steps or stages in a process or series; extent, amount, or relative intensity.

*There was only a small **degree** of change in the sample group.*

incremental, *adj.* A small amount of increase. Incremental implies no substantial change due to the increase.

*The new package design resulted in only **incremental** revenues.*

scalable, *adj.* That which can be increased or decreased according to a fixed ratio or proportion. Scalability implies an ease of making something larger or smaller by simply adding or subtracting simple units or subsets.

*The new process was totally **scalable;** to increase capacity, they only had to add extra modules.*

transition, *vt.* To pass from one condition, form stage, activity, place, etc. to another.

*We'll **transition** Gregory from the shipping department to the customer service department over a period of weeks.*

 Also Explore: proportion, ratio, subset, successive.

The Water of Life

aperitif, *n.* An alcoholic drink taken before a meal to stimulate the appetite. Any of certain wines flavored with herbs and other substances, used as a cocktail ingredient or drunk before meals.

> *While travelling in Europe, Todd grew accustomed to beginning his evening meal with an* **aperitif.**

liqueur, *n.* From the French with the stress on the second syllable. Any of certain strong, sweet, syrupy alcoholic liquors, variously flavored. A liqueur is generally offered as an after dinner drink.

> *Todd's dinner was then capped off by a delicious* **liqueur** *that was just as sweet as dessert.*

aqua vitae, *n.* From the Latin. Literally it means the "water of life." Historically it refers to a strong spirit distilled from wine and herbs. Today it is used more generally, and even fondly, in connection to all brandies and other strong liquor such as whiskey.

> *Upon his return to the United States, Todd's passion for ye olde* **aqua vitae** *returned in no time.*

whiskey, *n.* An angliciztion of the Irish *"usquebaugh"* or *water of life*. Whiskey is a strong alcoholic liquor distilled from the fermented mash of grain, especially of rye, wheat, corn, or barley. Other members of the whiskey family include Scotches and bourbons.

> *Soon he was quite the connoisseur of the* **whiskey** *family of drink.*

dram, *n.* A small drink of alcoholic liquor. Technically an apothecary weight of approximately ¹/₂ ounce. Usually used in connection with Scotches and other whiskies.

> *It was not unusual for Todd to spend $15 for a single* **dram** *of 25-year-old single malt scotch.*

 Also Explore: *cordial,* single malt, *brandy,* high ball, wassail.

Lead into Temptation

beguile, *vt.* To mislead by cheating or tricking; deceive. To deprive *of* or *out of* by deceit; cheat. To charm or delight. Beguile suggests the use of subtly alluring devices or wiles in enticing, deceiving or misleading prospects or leading someone on sexually.

> *Roger **beguiled** the venture capitalists with a show of wealth; they didn't know that everything was rented.*

inveigle, *vt.* To lead on with deception; entice or trick into doing or giving something, going somewhere, etc. Inveigle suggests the use of deception or cajolery in enticing someone.

> *John **inveigled** Ruth into working through her lunch hour by giving her two tickets to the show. She found out later that the show had long been cancelled.*

entice, *vt.* To attract by offering hope of reward or pleasure; tempt; allure. Entice implies a crafty or skillful attracting.

> *Gabe was able to **entice** JoAnn away from ReallyBig Co. with an additional week of vacation and a $1,000 signing bonus.*

bait, *vt.* To tease or goad, especially so as to provoke a reaction. Baiting can be done abusively or alluringly; what is important is eliciting a reaction from the subject without promising or giving them anything but words.

> *The attorneys continued to **bait** each other until the judge cited them both for contempt of court.*

ingratiate, *vt.* To make acceptable; especially, to bring oneself into another's favor or good graces by conscious effort. Often, however, ingratiate is used in the pejorative sense of brownnosing.

> *Walter tried desperately to **ingratiate** himself with his fiancee's parents.*

 Also Explore: siren song, *induce, suborn,* curry favor, *cajole.*

Special Groups

---

clique, *n.* A small, exclusive circle of people; snobbish or narrow. Clique refers to a small, highly exclusive group, often within a larger one, and implies snobbery, selfishness, or, sometimes, intrigue. A clique's behavior is clannish and exclusionary.

> *Jennifer was excluded from the **clique** because she lived in the wrong part of town.*

---

coterie, *n.* A close circle of friends who share a common interest or background. Coterie implies a small, intimate, somewhat select group of people associated for social or other reasons.

> *Marie was delighted when she was finally invited to be part of the literary **coterie.***

community, *n.* A group of people living together as a smaller social unit within a larger one and having interests, work, and so on in common. A community is generally inclusive rather than exclusive.

> *The gay **community** tended to support gay and lesbian-friendly businesses.*

niche, *n.* A place or position particularly suitable to the person or thing in it. Niche implies a particular role for an individual within a community or environment, based on behavior, position, experience, etc.

> *The convertible model occupied a small but attractive market **niche.***

fraternity, *n.* A group of men (or sometimes men and women) joined together by common interests, for fellowship, and so on; specifically, a Greek-letter college organization. A fraternity for women is called a sorority.

> *Matt and Ben decided to join a **fraternity** their second year at college.*

 Also Explore: exclusive, inclusive, *cadre,* salon, sorority.

Education

cum laude, *adj.* (koom lou-day) from the Latin. A phrase signifying above-average academic standing at the time of graduation from a college or university. There are three different cum laude categories: summa cum laude (highest), magna cum laude (second highest), and cum laude (third highest).

*Marcy studied hard and eventually graduated **cum laude** from the university.*

tenure, *n.* The status of holding one's position on a permanent basis, granted to teachers, civil service personnel, and so on, on the fulfillment of specified requirements. Typically, when a teacher is granted tenure, he or she is entitled to various protections (including job security) not afforded to less senior staff members.

*In one more year, Higgins will have **tenure**.*

prep school, *n.* (short for preparatory school). A private secondary school for preparing students to enter college. Because prep schools are outside the normal public education system, they are often exclusive and expensive.

*Chip wanted his daughter to go to an exclusive **prep school** to improve her chances of getting accepted to an Ivy League college.*

chair, *n.* A seat of authority or dignity. Chair (short for chairman or chairperson) implies an important or official position, such as a professorship or chairmanship.

*Professor Smith was named **chair** of the faculty committee.*

trustee, *n.* Any of a group or board of persons appointed to manage the affairs of an institution or organization. Typically, educational institutions are managed by a board of trustees.

*The **trustees** supported the tuition hikes.*

 Also Explore: *academic*, dean, faculty, inculcate, regent.

The Real Thing

bona fide, *adj.* In good faith; made or done without fraud or deceit. Bona fide implies genuine or real and is properly used when a question of good faith is involved. Something that is bona fide is unquestionably authentic.

> *Bobby received a **bona fide** offer to buy his entire collection of old comic books.*

veritable, *adj.* Being such truly or in fact. Veritable implies correspondence with the truth and connotes absolute affirmation.

> *Bobby's comic book collection was worth a **veritable** fortune, at least $100,000.*

authentic, *adj.* That is in fact as represented; genuine; real. Authentic implies reliability and trustworthiness, stressing that the thing considered is in agreement with fact or actuality.

> *Included in the collection was an **authentic** copy of Fantastic Four #1.*

legitimate, *adj.* Conforming to or abiding by law or custom; conforming to or in accordance with established rules, standards, principles.

> *Bobby took great care to ensure that the collector buying his books was a **legitimate** dealer.*

sanctioned, *adj.* The act of a recognized authority confirming or ratifying an action; authorized approval or permission. Sanctioned implies an official status with binding force.

> *In fact, the collector was a **sanctioned** member of the National Comic Book Dealer Association.*

Also Explore: canonize, indubitable, simon-pure, *unequivocal*, unimpeachable.

A Different Reality

---

spin, *n.* A particular emphasis or slant imparted to information to create a desired effect, such as a favorable public image for a politician. The word spin comes from the fact that the spin imparted to a ball in certain games affects its direction, bounce, and so on; thus, the spin imparted to information affects the way it is received.

> *Mr. Big wanted his public relations department to put a positive **spin** on the upcoming downsizing.*

---

hype, *n.* Extravagant or excessive promotion. Advertising slang for "hyperbole." To hype implies to promote in a sensational way.

> *The marketing department turned out its usual **hype** for the new product launch.*

rhetoric, *n.* Artificial eloquence; language that is showy and elaborate but largely empty of clear ideas or sincere emotion.

> *The chairman's speech was full of **rhetoric** but lacking in substance.*

flack, *n.* Press agent; a person whose business is to get publicity in the news media for a person or organization.

> *The reporter avoided meeting with the company's **flack,** preferring to search for hard news elsewhere in the organization.*

histrionic, *adj.* Of, or having the nature of, acting or actors. Speech or behavior characterized by overacting in a theatrical, artificial, and affected manner; melodramatic. Histrionics are often a calculated way to achieve a desired response in the usually shocked audience.

> *Mr. Murphy launched into a **histrionic** denial of his department's failures that left the board of directors unfazed. They were used to his melodrama.*

 Also Explore: blarney, bombast, fustian, slant, stentorian.

Philosophy

metaphysical, *adj.* Beyond the physical or material; incorporeal, supernatural, or transcendental. Metaphysics is the branch of philosophy that deals with first principles and seeks to explain the nature of being or reality (ontology) and of the origin and structure of the universe (cosmology). In common parlance, metaphysics can refer to any unnatural or nonphysical phenomena.

When no natural cause was found for the phenomena, Megan turned to **metaphysical** *explanations.*

ontology, *n.* The branch of metaphysics dealing with the nature of being, reality, or ultimate substance. Ontology also refers to the art of categorizing knowledge using the interrelations between concepts.

The Dewey Decimal System is one **ontology** *for classifying books and magazines in a library.*

phenomenology, *n.* The philosophical study of phenomena. Phenomenology is dedicated to describing the structures of experience as they present themselves to consciousness, without recourse to theory, deduction, or assumptions from other disciplines such as the natural sciences.

Jean Paul Sartre attempted to adapt Heidegger's **phenomenology** *to the philosophy of consciousness.*

being, *n.* The state or fact of existing or living; existence or life. Being is the act of existing.

For Jaspers, the purpose of existence is the realization of **being.**

reality, *n.* That which is real; existing objectively. Reality is existence itself.

Denying the **reality** *of the situation would be imprudent.*

 Also Explore: cosmology, epistemology, existentialism.

Inspect

---

examine, _vt._ To look at or into critically or methodically to find out the facts or condition of something or someone; investigate; inspect; inquire into. Examine suggests close observation or investigation to determine the condition, quality, validity, etc. of something. An examination is typically an in-depth or detailed activity.

> _Williams closely **examined** the document to determine which typewriter it came from._

---

scrutinize, _vt._ To look at very carefully; examine closely; inspect minutely. Scrutinize implies a looking over carefully and searchingly to observe the minutest details. Scrutinize implies more detail than examine.

> _Seligman **scrutinized** the balance sheet for errors._

survey, _vt._ To look at or consider, especially in a general or comprehensive way; view. Survey implies a larger, more comprehensive overview of a person or thing.

> _Mary Lou **surveyed** the staff to get their views on the situation._

scan, _vt._ To glance at quickly; consider hastily. Scan suggests a quick, rather superficial survey.

> _Miller **scanned** the data for the most important points._

surveillance, _n._ A close watch kept over someone, especially a suspect; constant observation of a place or process.

> _Winters instituted a round-the-clock **surveillance** of the loading dock to determine who was taking the excess stock._

Also Explore: audit, canvass, methodical, _minute_, reconnoiter.

Improper Behavior

unscrupulous, *adj.* Not restrained by ideas of right and wrong. Unscrupulous behavior is always unethical but not necessarily illegal; illegal behavior is always unscrupulous. Unscrupulous behavior is seldom condoned by respectable businesses and organizations; in most organizations, persons found engaging in unscrupulous behavior will likely be reprimanded or released from their position.

> *Daniel mistakenly thought that making the big sale justified his **unscrupulous** behavior; he was to find out later that the ends did not justify the means.*

mercurial, *adj.* Volatile, changeable, fickle. Mercurial behavior is not necessarily violent but is unpredictable and often inconsiderate of others; it often suggests a lack of mental or emotional stability.

> *Mr. Big's moods became increasingly **mercurial** during his divorce proceedings; no one knew what he would do next.*

indecorous, *adj.* Lacking decorum, propriety, good taste; unseemly.

> *Sullivan capped off his **indecorous** behavior at the awards dinner by asking the string quartet to play "Proud Mary."*

brutish, *adj.* Savage, gross, stupid, irrational. Brutish behavior often has a physical component.

> *His **brutish** behavior earned him no friends among his female co-workers.*

tempestuous, *adj.* Violent. Tempestuous behavior is not only violent, but also it is often unpredictable.

> *Their **tempestuous** relationship was both exciting and dangerous.*

 Also Explore: turbulent, *uncouth*, unethical, unprincipled, volatile.

Take Notice

vigilance, *n.* Staying watchful and alert to danger or trouble. Vigilance implies an active, keen watchfulness and connotes the immediate necessity for this.

> *Ray's constant **vigilance** over his clients' nest eggs made him the most highly sought-after broker in the whole firm.*

discern, *vt.* To perceive or recognize; make out clearly. Discern implies a making out or recognizing of something visually or mentally.

> *After many hours of examination, Peter was able to **discern** the error in the calculation.*

detect, *vt.* To catch or discover, as in a misdeed; to discover or manage to perceive (something hidden or not easily noticed). Detect implies a mental process.

> *When the numbers didn't add up, Julie **detected** that Benjamin was double-dipping with his expenses.*

conspicuous, *adj.* Conspicuous implies something important and expected to be present; hence, its absence is somewhat alarming and attention getting.

> *CompuTitan was **conspicuous** by its absence at the COMDEX trade show.*

salient, *adj.* Easily noticeable, demanding attention.

> *Among Dolan's most **salient** concerns was improving the firm's cash flow.*

Also Explore: ascertain, *evident*, mark, perceive, prominent.

Confusing

obfuscate, vt. To muddle; confuse; purposely make unclear or fuzzy. Obfuscate implies a deliberate attempt to cloud the truth. Someone who obfuscates makes every effort to muddle facts important to someone else's judgment or decision.

*Smithers attempted to **obfuscate** the situation to draw attention away from his actions.*

obscure, vt. To conceal from view; hide; make less conspicuous. Obscure applies to making something be perceived with difficulty.

*Linda made sure that the numbers in question were **obscured** on the copy she sent to corporate.*

bewilder, vt. To confuse hopelessly, as by something complicated or involved. Unlike obfuscate, bewilder does not imply any deliberation or ulterior motive.

*Jones was **bewildered** by the number of options available on the benefits enrollment form.*

Byzantine, adj. Characterized by complexity, deviousness, intrigue, etc. Byzantine refers to the government and politics of the Byzantine Empire (A.D. 395–1453) in southeast Europe and southwest Asia, which had an overly confusing, devious, and political culture.

*Mr. Hall concocted a **Byzantine** plot, full of twists and turns and unexpected intrigues.*

obtuse, adj. Slow to understand or perceive; dull or insensitive.

*Lawrence was convinced that his boss was **obtuse;** he didn't seem to understand the simplest proposals.*

Also Explore: befuddle, inscrutable, *intrigue*, perplex.

Technology Abbreviations and Acronyms

DAY 163

HDTV, *n.* High definition television, a new format for broadcasting digital rather than analog signals through the airwaves. HDTV will replace the 40-year-old NTSC standard with crisper, cinema-quality pictures, CD-quality sound, and five times the color information of today's televisions.

> *The salesman tried to convince Michael to upgrade to a **HDTV** monitor, even though there weren't many **HDTV** broadcasts.*

DSS, *n.* Digital satellite system; a broadcast reception system that uses a small dish antenna to receive digitally encoded audio and video signals broadcast from a low-powered satellite.

> *Michael added a **DSS** receiver to his home theater system because it had superior picture quality.*

GUI, *n.* Graphical user interface, a design for the part of a software program or operating system that interacts with the user and uses icons and other graphical elements to represent program features. The Apple Macintosh and Microsoft Windows operating environments are popular GUIs.

> *Marge found it difficult to transition from DOS to the Windows **GUI.***

Mb, *n.* Megabyte; a measurement of computer memory storage capacity equal to approximately 1 million bytes. Compare with Gb, which is one gigabyte (a thousand megabytes) of capacity.

> *Walter wanted at least 48**Mb** of RAM on his new PC.*

MHz, *n.* Megahertz; a unit of measurement equal to 1 million electrical vibrations or cycles per second. Commonly used to compare the speeds of computer processors or radio frequencies.

> *The latest Pentium II processor ran at 300**MHz.***

Also Explore: bitmap, *digital*, interface, *operating system,* processor.

Art Criticism

genre, *n.* (zhon-re) from the French (genus). A kind, or type, as of works of literature, art, and so on. In art, different genres include abstract art, post-impressionism, minimalism, etc. In literature, a genre is distinguished by subject, theme, or style, such as mystery, romance, science fiction, etc. In music, genre is the type of music, such as pop, country, rap, etc.

Rothbert chose to work in several ***genres,*** *including romanticism and abstract expressionism.*

milieu, *n.* (meel-yoo) from the French (literally, "middle"). Environment; especially a social or cultural setting.

After years of painting fantasy landscapes, he decided to embrace a different ***milieu*** *and paint realistic portraits.*

element, *n.* A component part or quality, often one that is basic or essential. Element, in its general use, is the broadest term for any of the basic, irreducible parts or principles of anything, concrete or abstract.

The key ***element*** *was the interplay between shadow and light.*

abstract, *adj.* Designating art abstracted from reality, in which designs or forms may be definite and geometric or fluid and amorphous. Abstract is a generic term that encompasses various nonrealistic contemporary schools of art.

Terrance preferred realism of the human figure to an ***abstract*** *representation.*

aesthetic, *n.* The underlying art and beauty of a thing.

The sculpture was an ***aesthetic*** *triumph.*

Also Explore: ambience, expressionism, impressionism, minimalism.

Right and Wrong

ethical, *adj.* Conforming to moral standards; conforming to the standards of conduct of a given profession or group. Ethical implies conformity with an elaborated, ideal code of moral principles, specifically with the code of a particular profession. Something can be unethical and still be legal.

*Morrison had **ethical** problems with the way ReallyBig Co. treated different accounts.*

moral, *adj.* Relating to, dealing with, or capable of making the distinction between right and wrong in conduct. Moral implies conformity with the generally accepted standards of goodness or rightness in conduct, character, or sexual conduct.

*Jeffrey had to make a **moral** judgment: Should he lie to his wife about where he was last night?*

legal, *adj.* In conformity with the positive rules of law; permitted by law. Legal implies literal connection or conformity with statute or common law or its administration.

*The company's behavior in pursuing the acquisition was questionable but **legal**.*

virtuous, *adj.* Having, or characterized by, moral virtue or righteousness. Virtuous implies a morally excellent character, connoting justice, integrity, and often chastity.

*The Prince was the most **virtuous** man in the kingdom, leading a pure and righteous life.*

situational ethics, *n.* A system of ethics according to which moral rules are not absolutely binding but may be modified in the light of specific situations.

*Applying **situational ethics,** Johnson would kill to protect his wife's life.*

 Also Explore: *indecorous*, *integrity*, laudable, scrupulous, statutory.

Out of Synch

dissonance, *n.* An inharmonious sound or combination of sounds. Dissonance also suggests any lack of harmony or agreement or an incongruity; a person opposing another or a group in opinion, temperament, and so on is said to be *dissonant.*

> *There was **dissonance** in the management ranks about the need to downsize staff.*

cacophony, *n.* Harsh, jarring sound. Cacophony implies a multitude of sounds (including those from musical instruments) speaking or playing at the same time.

> *The plant floor was a **cacophony** of different sounds and voices.*

babel, *n.* (bay-bel) A confusion of voices or languages. From the Biblical city of Babel. Babel implies multiple voices talking at the same time.

> *The meeting deteriorated to a state of **babel** with everyone trying to talk at the same time.*

havoc, *n.* Great destruction and devastation, as that resulting from hurricanes, wars, and so on.

> *The ice storm wreaked **havoc** on the company's delivery schedules.*

irregular, *adj.* Not straight or even; not uniform in shape, design, or proportion; uneven in occurrence or succession; variable or erratic. Irregular implies deviation from the customary or established rule, procedure, etc.

> *Choosing to pay the fine without dispute was highly **irregular.***

 Also Explore: *discordant,* incongruity, pandemonium, *synchronous,* tumultuous.

Music

tonality, *n.* In composition, the organization of tones around a central or pivotal tone or pitch class. Also refers to music based on the major-minor system. (Note that a tone is a sound that is distinct and identifiable by its regularity of vibration, or constant pitch, and that may be put into harmonic relation with other such sounds. In other words, a tone has pitch; noise doesn't.)

*Vayo employed a minor **tonality** for his third opus.*

chord, *n.* A combination of three or more tones sounded together in harmony.

*The song started with a B-flat major **chord.***

composition, *n.* A musical work; song. A composition is the basic melody, chords, and (if present) words to a piece of music. Composition also refers to the art of composing music.

*Vayo's latest **composition** was a suite in three movements.*

arrangement, *n.* Adaptation of a composition to other instruments or voices than those for which it was originally written or to the style of a certain band or orchestra; the composition as thus adapted. Don't confuse the arrangement (for a particular band or orchestra or choir) with the original composition.

*Sherry was responsible for the choir's **arrangement** of "Boogie Woogie Bugle Boy from Company B."*

voicing, *n.* The relationship of two or more instruments played together. Any given arrangement for two or more instruments contains voicings where the instruments play different notes from the same chord.

*It was an interesting **voicing**, an E-flat minor chord with the fifth in the bass.*

 Also Explore: intonation, modulation, *opus*, resonance, timbre.

Audio/Video

receiver, *n.* The component of an audio system that integrates an amplifier, preamplifier, and AM/FM tuner and controls functions for the entire audio system. Audio/video receivers also control functions for video devices in a home theater system.

*Mike bought a new audio / video **receiver** for his home theater system, complete with remote control and THX certification.*

amplifier, *n.* The component of an audio system that amplifies the selected signal and then sends it to the speakers. An integrated amplifier also contains a preamplifier that boosts the voltage of weak signals before they reach the input of the main amplifier; higher-end systems include a separate amp and preamp.

*The combination of a dedicated **amplifier** with a separate preamplifier produced the cleanest sound.*

tuner, *n.* The component of an audio system that receives AM and FM broadcast signals. Television sets also contain tuners that receive audio and video signals from broadcast, cable, and satellite sources.

*Because he bought a separate amp and preamp, he had to go with a stand-alone AM / FM **tuner,** as well.*

woofer, *n.* That component of a speaker system that produces low-frequency sounds. The woofer is the largest speaker in a speaker system enclosure. (A subwoofer is a nondirectional speaker that reproduces extremely low frequencies.)

*Mike decided to go with a small 10" **woofer** augmented with a separate subwoofer.*

tweeter, *n.* That component of a speaker system that produces high-frequency sounds. Most speakers contain a crossover to control the handoff of frequencies between the woofer and the tweeter.

*The **tweeters** were blown in his old speakers, impacting their ability to deliver the proper highs.*

 Also Explore: *compact disc,* component, *gain,* home theater, *modulation.*

Registered Pets

pedigree, *n.* A recorded or known line of descent, especially of a purebred animal. A pedigree is the written record of the animal's genealogy of three generations or more. A mutt (or mixed breed) by definition, has no pedigree.

> *The poodle came with a noted **pedigree**.*

breed, *n.* A group, or stock, of animals descended from common ancestors and having similar characteristics, especially such a group cultivated by humans.

> *The cat was a mixed **breed**. Near as anyone could tell, it was part Manx and part Siamese.*

purebred, *adj.* Belonging to a recognized breed with characteristics maintained through generations of unmixed descent. For example, the American Kennel Club defines a purebred dog as one whose parents belong to the same breed and are themselves of unmixed descent since recognition of the breed.

> *The kennel only sold **purebred** collies.*

throwback, *n.* Reversion to an earlier or more primitive type or condition. A return to a former state. An animal born of purebred parents that does not maintain the breed standard as set forth by a breed's governing body can be called a throwback.

> *In the litter of silver Schnauzer pups, the black and tan one was a conspicuous **throwback**.*

fancier, *n.* A person with a special interest in and knowledge of something, particularly of the breeding of plants or animals. A fancier is a person especially interested and active in some phase of the sport of purebred animal events.

> *After years of training, breeding, and showing Peruvian Pasos, Sean was considered one of the more expert horse **fanciers** to consult.*

 Also Explore: blooded, *enthusiast*, mongrel, regression.

Automobiles

SUV, Sport utility vehicle, a passenger vehicle similar to a station wagon but with the chassis of a small truck and, usually, four-wheel drive.

> *Jenny decided to replace the family's minivan with an **SUV**; it was trendier and performed better in bad weather.*

AWD, All-wheel drive, a automotive drive system that applies power to all four wheels of an automobile. Often confused with four-wheel drive (4WD), AWD applies power to all four wheels all the time.

> *The new SUV included **AWD**, which greatly improved handling in the snow.*

ABS, Anti-lock brake system, a computer-assisted system for emergency braking. Designed to prevent wheels from locking up or skidding, anti-lock brake systems feature sensors that detect the impending lockup of the brakes.

> *Although AWD improved traction, **ABS** was necessary to maximize braking on slick surfaces.*

horsepower, *n.* A unit for measuring the power of engines, equal to 33,000 foot-pounds per minute. Horsepower is a standard measurement used to determine how much effective power an engine produces based on torque and engine speed.

> *The Supra Twin Turbo generated 320 **horsepower**, making it best in its class.*

acceleration, *n.* The rate of change in the velocity of a moving body. In automotive terms, acceleration is about increasing speed and is normally measured against a standard.

> *The Supra's **acceleration** was 0-to-60 in 6.3 seconds.*

Also Explore: foot-pound, lockup, off-road, torque, velocity.

Journeys

trip, *n.* A traveling from one place to another; journey, especially a short one. A going to a place and returning. It is used generically as an equivalent for journey; but, journey generally implies travel of some length.

*Randy hoped that his **trip** to New York would be uneventful despite the reported weather conditions.*

jaunt, *n.* To take a short trip for pleasure. Jaunt is applied to a short, casual trip taken for pleasure or recreation.

*With airfares so low, it was possible for Carolyn to take a **jaunt** to Florida for the weekend.*

expedition, *n.* A sending forth or starting out on a journey, voyage, march, and so on for some definite purpose. Expedition can also refer to the journey itself or the people, ships, equipment, etc. on such a journey.

*The **expedition** of senior management to the opening of the flagship store at the Megamall was to ensure media coverage.*

pilgrimage, *n.* A journey made by a pilgrim, especially to a shrine or holy place. More generally, pilgrimage can refer to any long journey to a place of historical interest.

*An avid fan of westerns, Tom's **pilgrimage** across the flat, dusty plains to visit Cattleman City fulfilled a lifelong dream.*

itinerary, *n.* A detailed outline for a proposed journey. An itinerary is an agenda for a trip, usually including details of all transportation and lodging.

*Jim's **itinerary** included stops in London, Paris, Geneva, and Rome.*

 Also Explore: commute, excursion, junket, peregrination, sojourn.

Keeping in Touch Electronically

---

chat, *n.* A means of conversing one-on-one or in conference over the Internet with other online users. There are many types of Internet-based chat programs. A place where multiple users chat at the same time is called a chat room.

*Mandy stayed up until three in the morning visiting numerous **chat** rooms.*

---

conference, *n.* A formal meeting of a number of people for discussion or consultation. An electronic or virtual conference is an electronic meeting place on the Internet or on a commercial online service dedicated to a particular subject. Conferences are also referred to as newsgroups, bulletin boards, or echoes.

*Bob initiated an online **conference** on Internet censorship.*

e-mail, *n.* Electronic mail, messages typed or loaded into a computer and sent, by LAN or the Internet, to a receiving computer in a manner analogous to that provided by the postal service.

*When he checked his **e-mail,** Alan discovered he had more than 100 unread messages.*

voice mail, *n.* Voice mail is a computerized answering service that works similarly to a traditional answering machine, although typically with more and enhanced options.

*Perry hated people who left long **voice mail** messages.*

pager, *n.* Any electronic device that sends or receives an electronic signal, or beep, used to contact people for messages.

*When his wife was due to deliver, Joe carried a **pager** in case he got a call from the doctor.*

 Also Explore: domain, *LAN, lingua franca, USENET, virtual reality.*

Management

DAY 173

---

director, *n.* A person that directs or controls; the head of a project, bureau, school, etc., or a member of a board chosen to direct the affairs of a corporation or institution. A director is also a level of management above a manager but below a vice president. Depending on the company's overall structure, a director might be seen as middle management—and therefore ripe for downsizing if the need arises.

*John was named as the new **director** of marketing activities.*

---

board, *n.* A group or council of persons who manage or control a business, school system, and so on. Most publicly held corporations appoint a board of directors to oversee the management of the business; such boards meet periodically throughout the year.

*The **board** voted to withhold first quarter dividends.*

executive, *n.* Any person whose function is to administer or manage affairs, as of a corporation, school, etc. Executives are typically at a level above general management and receive benefits compensatory with their rank and responsibilities.

*Greg was recruited from ReallyBig Co. to be one of the company's key **executives.***

operator, *n.* A person who manages a business or part of a business. Operators have some sort of quantifiable responsibility, typically for revenue and profit functions.

*Bob had tried a staff position but preferred being an **operator** with financial responsibilities.*

manager, *n.* A person who manages a business, institution, etc.

*All **managers** had to complete their employee reviews by April 1.*

 Also Explore: *CEO*, comptroller, impresario, preside, *white-collar.*

Spy Games

espionage, *n.* The act of spying. In a business context, espionage refers to the use of spies in industry or commerce to learn the secrets of other companies. Industrial espionage appears to be an increasingly popular way to uncover competitive information.

> *The rival firm resorted to industrial **espionage** to find out what ReallyBig Co. had planned for the fall season.*

intelligence, *n.* The gathering of secret information, such as for military or police purposes. Intelligence is commonly used to refer to information of value in a business situation, publicly available or not.

> *Higby needed more **intelligence** on what his competitor had planned.*

intrigue, *n.* A secret or underhanded plot, scheme, or machination. Intrigue, implying intricate scheming, suggests furtive, underhanded maneuvering, often of an illicit nature.

> *Megan refused to be drawn into Bob's **intrigues;** she hated all the cloak and dagger activity.*

incognito, *adv.* With true identity unrevealed or disguised; under an assumed name, rank, and so on.

> *Rick checked into the hotel **incognito** so his tryst wouldn't be discovered.*

covert, *adj.* Concealed, hidden, disguised, or surreptitious.

> *Rodgers, who was in charge of **covert** operations, was responsible for tapping the phone lines of suspected employees.*

 Also Explore: *clandestine*, *collusion*, *illicit*, machination, reconnaissance.

Underhanded

---

connivance, *n.* Passive cooperation, as by consent or pretended ignorance, especially in wrongdoing. Connivance implies pretending not to see or look at something wrong or evil, thus giving tacit consent or cooperation.

> *Samantha's manager took part in the **connivance**, looking the other way while she changed the numbers on the time sheet.*

---

collusion, *n.* A secret agreement or conspiracy for fraudulent or illegal purpose.

> *The two firms engaged in **collusion** to fix prices.*

fraudulent, *adj.* Acting with deceit or trickery. In legal terms, fraud is described as an intentional perversion of truth; a deceitful practice or device resorted to with intent to deprive another of property or other right.

> *The real estate agent was charged with **fraudulent** activities after he pocketed the check meant for the appraisal firm.*

malicious, *adj.* Having, showing, or caused by active ill will; spiteful; intentionally mischievous or harmful.

> *Randolph **maliciously** jammed the wrong paper into the copier, knowing it would cause permanent damage.*

heinous, *adj.* (hay-nes) Outrageously evil or wicked; abominable.

> *Bundy's crime was so **heinous** that the prosecutor asked for the death penalty.*

 Also Explore: complicity, degenerate, fallacious, *intrigue*, *perverse*.

Hard to Manage

---

fractious, *adj.* Hard to manage. Fractious implies irritability. Fractious implies being stubborn and obstinate; a fractious person is quarrelsome and difficult.

*The boys from the group home were **fractious,** paying no attention to the leader's instructions.*

---

rebellious, *adj.* Resisting authority; engaged in rebellion. Rebellious implies opposition to any control, a degree of defiance, and being difficult to handle.

*As he entered adolescence, Dean became openly **rebellious** to his parents.*

insolent, *adj.* Boldly disrespectful in speech or behavior. Insolent implies defiant disrespect as displayed in openly insulting and contemptuous speech or behavior.

*Kevin's **insolent** behavior earned him a trip to the principal's office.*

unruly, *adj.* Hard to control, restrain, or keep in order; disorderly. Unruly implies a physical untidiness.

*Johnny had an **unruly** mop of hair on his head.*

defiant, *adj.* Openly or boldly resisting. Defiant implies an openly hostile attitude towards some dictate or expectation.

*Beth was **defiant** of the new antismoking regulations, openly lighting up in a public area.*

Also Explore: *impetuous,* insubordinate, profligate, *recalcitrant,* refractory.

176

Take Action

---

litigate, *vt.* To contest in a lawsuit. Litigation is the lawsuit itself, and a litigant is a party to a lawsuit. Someone who is litigious is one who is given to carrying on lawsuits, often of a frivolous nature.

*When a satisfactory agreement couldn't be worked out, the company decided to **litigate**.*

---

indict, *vt.* To charge with the commission of a crime; to make a formal accusation against someone on the basis of positive legal evidence. In legal terms, an indictment is an accusation of a criminal offense made by a grand jury.

*The real estate agent was **indicted** on four counts of fraud.*

impeach, *vt.* To challenge or discredit (a person's honor, reputation, etc.). In legal terms, impeachment is an attack on the credibility of a witness.

*The defense attorney tried to **impeach** the credibility of the key witness by showing that she had used drugs while she was in college.*

deposition, *n.* The testimony of a witness made under oath, but not in open court, and written down to be used when the case comes to trial. Witnesses are often called upon to give depositions prior to cases coming to trial.

*David completed a **deposition** in the Rawlings case.*

warrant, *n.* Authorization or sanction, as by a superior or the law. Most commonly, a warrant is a court order authorizing law enforcement officers to make an arrest or conduct a search.

*A **warrant** was issued for John's arrest on two counts of battery.*

 Also Explore: affidavit, *censure, impugn, sanctioned,* subpoena.

Domineering

dogmatic, *adj.* Doctrinal; asserted without proof; stating opinion in a positive or arrogant manner. Dogmatic suggests the attitude of a religious teacher in asserting certain doctrines as absolute truths not open to dispute.

*The professor was **dogmatic** in his assertions on the nature of being; he brooked no argument.*

imperious, *adj.* Arrogant; domineering. Imperious implies an insensitivity to the feelings of others.

*Kurt's **imperious** behavior alienated his underlings.*

haughty, *adj.* Having or showing great pride in oneself and disdain, contempt, or scorn for others. Haughty implies a pride behind the arrogance.

*The VP's wife was **haughty** with the staff, appearing as if she thought she was better than they were.*

dictatorial, *adj.* Autocratic; domineering. Dictatorial implies using domineering and sometimes irresponsible methods to rule without challenge.

*Leif's **dictatorial** methods made him a poor manager; he never let his staff figure out things on their own.*

tyrannical, *adj.* Arbitrary. A tyrant is a cruel, oppressive ruler. A dictator is simply domineering; a tyrant is both domineering and cruel.

*Walter's **tyrannical** methods drove several of his staff to request transfers.*

 Also Explore: despot, ex cathedra, fascist, supercilious, *totalitarianism.*

Talk Into

cajole, *vt.* To coax with flattery and insincere talk. Cajole implies the use of flattery to trick another into complying with a request. Cajole is somewhat synonymous with "sweet talk."

> *The used-car salesman tried to* **cajole** *Ralph into buying an extended warranty.*

convince, *vt.* To overcome the doubts of; persuade by argument or evidence; make feel sure. Convince implies no violence or threat and suggests eventual agreement of both parties.

> *The defense failed to* **convince** *the jury that the defendant was an innocent victim.*

champion, *vt.* To fight for; defend; support.

> *Molly* **championed** *the project to the senior management team.*

coerce, *vt.* To force or compel, such as by threats, to do something. Coerce implies force or threat of force.

> *By threatening to tell her boss about her long lunches, Simon* **coerced** *Terry to go on a date with him.*

compelling, *adj.* Irresistibly or keenly interesting, attractive, etc.

> *The team's presentation was so* **compelling** *that the board signed off on the expenditure on the spot.*

Also Explore: captivating, coax, *induce*, obsequious, wheedle.

Salary

---

compensation, *n.* Wages or payment for services . A compensation package includes the entirety of base salary, bonus, and benefits.

*Thompson's **compensation** was 10 percent below company average for that position.*

---

base, *n.* The basic rate of pay for a particular job exclusive of overtime pay, bonuses, and so on.

*Julie received a **base** of $50,000 plus a 10 percent bonus.*

bonus, *n.* A payment over and above salary given to an employee as an incentive or reward. Bonus refers to anything given over and above the regular wages.

*The **bonus** plan was based on the unit achieving planned profit numbers.*

benefits, *n.* Non-cash compensation. Benefits typically include medical coverage, retirement plans, etc.

*The **benefits** included both medical and dental coverage.*

noncompete, *n.* A contract between an employer and employee where the employee agrees not to go to work for a competing firm in the event of his or her leaving the company. A noncompete often compensates the employee with a one-time sum for signing the contract.

*Because of his **noncompete,** Jerry couldn't accept the job offer from the competing firm.*

Also Explore: emolument, *incentive*, kickback, remuneration.

Computer Technology

---

cyberspace, *n.* The nebulous "place" where humans interact over computer networks. Any or all of the following are part of cyberspace: virtual reality, the Internet, and the World Wide Web. The term was coined by science fiction writer William Gibson in the novel *Neuromancer.*

Johnny spent at least three hours each night playing interactive games in ***cyberspace.***

---

netizen, *n.* A person who uses a computer to communicate in public forums on other computers. Derived from the words network and citizen.

Concerned ***netizens*** *wrote their Congressmen about the proposed online censorship law.*

analog, *adj.* Designating or of electronic equipment, recordings, etc. in which the signal corresponds to a physical change, as sound to a groove in a phonograph record.

Carter clung to his ***analog*** *computer technology and cell phone despite the digital revolution going on around him.*

digital, *adj.* A term used to describe information that can be represented by a collection of bits, as opposed to the older analog technology.

Digital *technology led to more accurate recreation of video and audio images.*

webmaster, *n.* A person responsible for the development and maintenance of a World Wide Web server and some or all of the Web pages at a Web site.

The ***webmaster*** *turned off Web site access to suspected crackers.*

 Also Explore: cyberpunk, *internet, virtual reality,* webCrawler, web browser.

Believable

---

plausible, *adj.* Seemingly true, acceptable, etc. Plausible often implies distrust and applies to that which at first glance appears to be true, reasonable, valid, and so on but which may or may not be so, although there is no connotation of deliberate deception.

> *Beatrice made a **plausible** argument for why she couldn't have stolen the sugar cubes, although Stan wasn't sure he truly believed her.*

---

specious, *adj.* Seeming to be good, sound, correct, logical, and so on without really being so; plausible but not genuine. Specious applies to that which is superficially reasonable, valid, etc., but is actually not so, and it connotes intention to deceive.

> *Burt's logic about why he should get the raise was **specious**, raising Mr. Wetherby's suspicions.*

credible, *adj.* That can be believed; believable; reliable. Credible is used for that which is believable because it is supported by evidence, sound logic, etc.

> *Dawn gave a **credible** account of the accident.*

credence, *n.* Belief in the reports or testimony of others.

> *The appearance of a man in a black trench coat lent **credence** to the reports of an after-hours meeting.*

integrity, *n.* The quality or state of being of sound moral principle; uprightness, honesty, and sincerity.

> *Randolph's **integrity** was questioned when it was discovered he benefited personally from the Watson acquisition.*

 Also Explore: *ethical, moral,* ostensible, probity, valid.

Beyond Belief

---

paranormal, *adj.* Designating a psychic or mental phenomena outside the range of the normal. Paranormal is often used to describe anything that is unexplainable, unusual, or outside the range of normal experience or comprehension—and that can't be easily explained by other means.

*Jonathan's investigation into **paranormal** phenomena led some to call him a ghost chaser.*

UFO, Unidentified flying object; any number of unidentified objects or phenomena frequently reported, especially since 1947, to have been observed or tracked in the sky and variously explained as being atmospheric phenomena, hallucinations, misperceptions of actual objects, alien spacecraft, and so on.

*Were the lights in the sky a **UFO** or just a passing helicopter?*

OBE, Out-of-body experience; the feeling that the inner self or being of an individual separates from the physical body or shell and moves about at will. Some have equated OBEs with near-death experiences (NDEs).

*During her **OBE,** Kathleen felt her spirit rise above her body and was able to observe her body lying on the couch.*

apparition, *n.* Anything that appears unexpectedly or in an extraordinary way; especially, a strange figure appearing suddenly and thought to be a ghost.

*Alec and Ben saw an **apparition** at the window of the abandoned house.*

déjà vu, *n.* The feeling that one has had an experience or been in a place previously, although it is actually new to one.

*The sense of **déjà vu** was overpowering; he knew he had been in this house before, even though it was his first visit to this town.*

 Also Explore: *esoteric*, near-death experience, parapsychology, preternatural, transcendental.

Sure

---

unequivocal, *adj.* Not ambiguous; plain; clear. Unequivocal implies an unwavering stance on a given issue or in support of someone or something.

> *Adam was **unequivocal** on the matter of employee raises; no amount of discussion could cause him to change his mind.*

---

categorical, *adj.* Without qualifications or conditions; absolute; positive; direct; explicit: said of a statement, theory, and so on.

> *The senator **categorically** denied any impropriety.*

inevitable, *adj.* That which cannot be avoided or evaded; certain to happen. Implies a sense of fate or logical consequence.

> *Because the only restrooms were side-by-side, it was **inevitable** that Mark would see Cathy sooner or later.*

staunch, *adj.* Firm; loyal; faithful. Staunch can also imply strong or solidly made. Staunch implies such strong allegiance to one's principles or purposes as not to be turned aside by any cause.

> *Reggie was a **staunch** supporter of the casual Fridays initiative.*

assurance, *n.* The state of being assured; sureness; confidence; certainty. Something said or done to inspire confidence, such as a promise or guarantee. A belief in one's own abilities; self-confidence. Assurance suggests confidence, but not necessarily positiveness, usually in something that is yet to happen.

> *RealyBig Co. gave **assurances** to its employees that the hostile takeover of the company would not affect their livelihoods.*

 Also Explore: compulsory, impending, indisputable, *steadfast*, unwavering.

184

Not So Sure

DAY 185

---

jaundiced, _vt._ To make bitter or prejudiced through jealousy, envy, etc. Jaundice implies filled with resentment. One who is jaundiced is unreasonably and aggressively biased against someone or something.

> *Ever since he was passed over for a promotion, Simpson's opinion of management was **jaundiced**.*

---

dubious, _adj._ Causing doubt. Dubious infers rousing suspicion or shady.

> *He was a **dubious** character; no one knew exactly what his background was.*

filter, _vi._ To pass through or as if through a filter; to remove undesirable elements. Filter implies a selective telling of the facts to tell a modified version of a story.

> *Richardson **filtered** the story so it would be more palatable to his boss.*

vacillating, _adj._ Wavering or tending to waver in motion, opinion, and so on. Actively debating between various options.

> *The candidate's **vacillating** stance on affirmative action issues alienated his entire constituency, black and white.*

mutable, _adj._ Tending to frequent change; inconstant; fickle. Subject to mutation. Mutable refers more to a constant characteristic of going back and forth on issues. Something or someone who is mutable can be easily changed or swayed. It is not in his or her nature to hold on firmly to anything.

> *The governor was so **mutable** that his inside staffers referred to him secretly as "the chameleon."*

 Also Explore: abeyance, _bias_, _cynic_, problematic.

Write It Down

document, *vt.* To prove, as by reference to something printed, written, etc.

> *Frank* **documented** *the entire workflow process.*

ledger, *n.* In accounting, the book of final entry, used in a double-entry system, for according to the accounts to which they belong.

> *Traci double-checked all the entries in the* **ledger.**

white paper, *n.* An official government report, originally one bound in white paper. Any in-depth, authoritative report document, official statement, in-depth analysis, or in-depth account.

> *Ben spent the weekend preparing the* **white paper** *on the fight between the vice president and the reporter.*

correspondence, *n.* Communication by exchange of letters or the letters themselves once received or written. Correspondence can be generally used to indicate communication but specifically it refers to communication in writing.

> *The bank needed written* **correspondence** *before it would authorize the transfer.*

memorandum, *n.* A short note written to help remind you to do something. A record of events or observations, especially one for future use. An informal written communication from one department to another. In diplomacy, a summary or outline of a subject under discussion, reasons for or against some action, and so on. Informally referred to as a memo. Sometimes memos are all you need to document an action or lack thereof.

> *Bill started communicating with his co-workers by* **memo** *only. In this way, his instructions could not be misinterpreted.*

 Also Explore: billet-doux, copy, graphology, missive, paper trail.

Present It

---

chart, *n.* A group of facts about something, set up in the form of a diagram, table, etc. A chart presents data in either tabular or graphic form; a graph is graphic only. (In other words, all graphs are charts; not all charts are graphs.)

*Beth presented a **chart** showing the number of hours worked per employee.*

---

graph, *n.* A diagram, as a curve, broken line, series of bars, and so on, representing the successive changes in a variable quantity or quantities.

*Paul's **graph** illustrated how the workload had been increasing.*

plot, *vt.* To determine or mark the location of a point on a graph by means of coordinates.

*Ben **plotted** the coordinates on an x-y grid.*

pictograph, *n.* A diagram or graph using pictured objects to convey ideas, information, etc.; a graph that uses pictures in place of artificial graphic elements.

*Peter used a **pictograph** of stacks of coins instead of a normal bar chart.*

transparency, *n.* A piece of clear film, having a picture or writing that is visible when light shines through it or that can be projected on a screen. Transparencies are projected through the means of an overhead projector and are sometimes called foils.

*Jacob placed the **transparency** on the overhead projector.*

Also Explore: coordinate, diagram, *foil,* overhead projector, tabular.

Finances

---

cash flow, *n.* The pattern of receipts and expenditures of a company, government, and so on, resulting in the availability or nonavailability of cash. Cash flow is an indication of a company's financial strength and its ability to pay its bills.

*Even though it was showing profits on paper, the firm's **cash flow** wasn't enough to cover the weekly payroll.*

---

liquid, *adj.* The amount of a person's or firm's assets in cash or readily convertible to cash. The more assets in cash-convertible format, the more liquid one is.

*Jim had all his money tied up in long-term securities, so he wasn't **liquid** enough to make his quarterly insurance payment.*

float, *n.* The total value of checks or drafts in transit and not yet collected. One "works" the float by writing a check without sufficient funds in the bank, knowing that funds will be deposited before the check is cashed.

*Linda wrote $500 worth of checks, depending on the **float** to cover her temporary lack of funds.*

capital, *n.* The net worth of a business; amount by which the assets exceed the liabilities; the face value of all the stock issued or authorized by a corporation.

*The firm's **capital** was valued at $1.5 million.*

dilution, *n.* Regarding shares of ownership in a company, a decrease in the proportion of income to which each shareholder is entitled or a decrease in the percentage ownership of individual shareholders.

*Issuing more stock resulted in a **dilution** of the shares held by current investors.*

 Also Explore: *asset, depreciation,* pecuniary, realizable, revenue.

Management Acronyms

CEO, Chief executive officer, the highest executive officer of a company, organization, and so on. The CEO reports to the board of directors and has ultimate responsibility for the performance of a corporation.

*The **CEO** reported the quarterly results to the board.*

COO, Chief operating officer, the highest operating official of a company, organization, and so on. In companies with both CEOs and COOs, the CEO sets the strategic vision, whereas the COO is responsible for the day-to-day operations of the company.

*The **COO** instituted a headcount freeze.*

CFO, Chief financial officer, the highest financial official of a company, organization, and so on. The CFO is ultimately responsible for the financial reporting of a corporation.

*The **CFO** adjusted the balance sheet accruals to show a stronger profit for the period.*

CMO, Chief marketing officer, the highest marketing official of a company, organization, and so on. The CMO has ultimate authority for a corporation's marketing, brand management, and sales operations.

*The **CMO** laid out the branding strategy for the new product line.*

CTO, Chief technology officer, the highest technology official of a company, organization, and so on. The CTO is responsible for a company's technology strategy, as well as the operations of the MIS or IS&T departments.

*The **CTO** mandated the switch from UNIX-based servers to Windows NT.*

 Also Explore: *board*, old boys club, *strategy*, *vision*.

Steal

---

theft, *n.* The act or an instance of stealing. Theft is the general term and larceny is the legal term for the unlawful or felonious taking away of another's property without his or her consent and with the intention of depriving the person of it. Robberies and burglaries are both forms of theft.

*Martha reported the **theft** of important papers from her desk.*

---

robbery, *n.* The taking of personal property in the possession or immediate presence of another by the use of violence or intimidation. Robbery differs from theft in that it is done in the other's presence and accompanied by actual or threatened force.

*Jim lost $100 in the **robbery** but fortunately escaped without physical harm.*

burglary, *n.* The act of breaking into any building at any time to commit theft, some other felony, or a misdemeanor. In legal terms, the unlawful breaking into or entering of a building or dwelling with the intent to commit theft or other felony; often restricted to such an act accomplished at night.

*The **burglary** took place sometime after midnight; the burglars got away with ten PCs and a small amount of petty cash.*

appropriate, *vt.* To take improperly, as without permission. Appropriation is not necessarily theft because it can also involve borrowing without the owner's permission.

*Rifling through Marianne's purse, Herman **appropriated** the combination to the safe.*

abscond, *vi.* To go away hastily and secretly; run away and hide, especially in order to escape the law.

*Knowing the jig was up, Herman **absconded** with the company funds while the others were at the convention.*

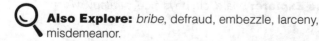 **Also Explore:** *bribe,* defraud, embezzle, larceny, misdemeanor.

Improper Behavior (Part 2)

---

incorrigible, *adj.* That which cannot be corrected, improved, or reformed, especially because it is firmly established as a habit or because of bad habits set in as a child. Incorrigible implies someone unlikely to change for the better or resisting improvement.

> *After his third arrest, the parole officer was convinced that Jimmy was **incorrigible** and should be put away for life.*

---

ruinous, *adj.* Very destructive or harmful; disastrous. Ruinous implies utter devastation and can refer to both physical and fiscal catastrophes.

> *El Niño had a **ruinous** effect on the local sardine fisheries.*

unbridled, *adj.* Not controlled or restrained. Unbridled implies actively pursuing something without thought to cost or consequence.

> *Terrence pursued the new account with **unbridled** enthusiasm.*

wanton, *adj.* Senseless, unprovoked, unjustifiable, or deliberately malicious. Wanton implies giving in to one's base desires and often refers to sexually loose or unrestrained behavior.

> *In spite of public appearances, Marvin was a **wanton** hedonist.*

scurrilous, *adj.* Using indecent or abusive language. Scurrilous behavior is verbal in nature.

> *Although his public image was squeaky clean, behind closed doors the Senator made **scurrilous** remarks and recited obscene limericks.*

Also Explore: *intractable,* licentious, *malicious,* rampant, ribald.

Foolish

---

fatuous, *adj.* Complacently stupid or foolish. Fatuous implies stupidity combined with smug complacency; a fatuous remark is completely idiotic.

*His **fatuous** remarks caused people to avoid him at the party.*

---

asinine, *adj.* Of or like an ass; especially having qualities regarded as characteristic of asses; stupid, silly, stubborn, and so on. Asinine implies stupidity mixed with obstinateness.

*He refused to stop his **asinine** behavior, further alienating his co-workers.*

inane, *adj.* Lacking sense or meaning; silly. Inane implies being foolish and not worthwhile.

*Everyone in the group thought the project was an **inane** waste of time.*

senseless, *adj.* Not having or showing good sense; stupid; foolish. Senseless implies having no real point or purpose or being meaningless.

*Tom's crude remark to the deceased's widow was **senseless**.*

simple, *adj.* Without guile or deceit; innocent. Simple does not necessarily imply foolishness or stupidity, simply that a person lacks sophistication.

*Doug was too **simple** to understand the machinations going on around him.*

 Also Explore: artless, complacent, *naïve,* sophomoric.

Mental Disorders

psychotic, *adj.* Having a major mental disorder in which the personality is seriously disorganized and contact with reality is usually impaired. Psychoses are of two sorts: functional, principally of the schizophrenic or manic-depressive type; and organic, characterized by a pathological organic condition such as brain damage or disease.

> *Lisa's behavior became increasing **psychotic;** at times, she was delusional and paranoid.*

neurotic, *adj.* Having one of various mental functional disorders characterized by anxiety, compulsions, phobias, and so on.

> *Don's **neurotic** behavior was manifested in a constant need to wash his hands.*

schizophrenic, *adj.* Having a major mental disorder of unknown cause characterized by a separation between the thought processes and the emotions, delusions and hallucinations, and a fragmentation of the personality.

> *In her **schizophrenic** delusions, Nicki thought she saw angels on every street corner.*

manic-depressive, *adj.* Having a psychosis characterized by alternating periods of "highs" (mania) and "lows" (depression).

> *Rick was borderline **manic-depressive,** and his staff never knew what kind of mood he'd be in.*

psychic, *adj.* Beyond natural or known physical processes; apparently sensitive to forces beyond the physical world. Do not confuse psychics with psychotics.

> *Maggie didn't have to be **psychic** to know that Don, Lisa, Rick, and Nicki were having severe emotional problems.*

Also Explore: bedlamite, *compulsion*, paranoid, pathologic, *phobia*.

Excess Baggage

encumbrance, *n.* Something that encumbers; obstruction; burden. In a very narrow and specific sense, it can refer to a dependent, especially a child. Legally, an encumbrance is a lien, charge, or claim attached to real property, such as a mortgage.

*Philip was eager to relieve himself of all **encumbrances** and begin again.*

accouterments, *n.* A personal outfit; clothes; dress. Historically, it refers to a soldier's equipment except clothes and weapons. Generically, it refers to equipment or gadgets.

*Kyle's Mercedes had all the expected **accouterments** of a luxury car.*

paraphernalia, *n.* Personal belongings. Any collection of articles, usually things used in some activity; equipment; apparatus; gear. Sometimes used in a pejorative sense to imply that all this gear is less than useful.

*Tim's old dirt biking equipment was just so much **paraphernalia** now with the improvements in plastics technologies.*

dunnage, *n.* A loose packing of any bulky material put around cargo for protection. Personal baggage or belongings.

*Karen despaired. How could anyone move in two days with so much **dunnage**?*

impedimenta, *n.* Things hindering progress, such as on a trip; encumbrances; especially baggage, supplies, or equipment, such as those carried along with an army.

*With all her **impedimenta**, JoAnn couldn't possibly make it to the other gate before her connecting flight left.*

 Also Explore: hinderance, *phobia, neurotic*, trappings.

Shared Feelings

empathy, *n.* The projection of one's own personality into the personality of another in order to understand the person better; ability to share in another's emotions, thoughts, or feelings. A person who is empathetic can feel the emotions (pain, happiness, and so on) of another.

> *Recently divorced herself, Paula felt* **empathy** *for June when she separated from Ward.*

sympathy, *n.* Pity or compassion felt for another's trouble, suffering, etc. Sympathy means to be sorry for another's pain; empathy means to literally or figuratively feel that pain.

> *The group expressed their* **sympathy** *for Dan when his father passed away.*

compatible, *adj.* Capable of living together or getting along well together; that which can work well together, get along well together, combine well, and so on.

> *Max and Maddie were so* **compatible** *they even used the same brand of toothpaste.*

congenial, *adj.* Having the same tastes and temperament. Congenial implies friendliness.

> *Bobbie's* **congenial** *personality helped her get along with the entire staff.*

kindred, *adj.* Of like nature; similar. An alternate definition refers to relationship by blood or marriage.

> *Ginger and Jack were* **kindred** *spirits, both growing up in small towns and finding themselves transplanted to the big city.*

 Also Explore: commiserate, compassion, concord, projection, simpatico.

Basic Computer Operation

operating system, *n.* Computer software that controls the low-level hardware operations and file management on a computer system. An operating system provides the link between the user and the hardware. Popular operating systems include Windows, Windows NT, DOS, MacOS, and UNIX.

*The IS&T department mandated that Windows NT be the **operating system** for all corporate desktops.*

DOS, Disk operating system. An operating system for IBM-compatible PCs. DOS uses a character-based interface (not a GUI) and has generally been replaced by Windows.

*Tom decided to upgrade his old computer from **DOS** to Windows but didn't have enough **RAM** to make it work.*

Windows, An operating system for IBM-compatible PCs that uses a graphical user interface (GUI). Created by Microsoft Corporation (and formally known as Microsoft Windows), Windows replaced DOS on most IBM-compatible PCs.

***Windows** crashed.*

UNIX, An operating system used on many Internet host systems.

*The webmaster relied on the bulletproof nature of **UNIX** for his Web servers.*

Macintosh, *n.* A type of computer made by Apple Corporation. The Macintosh—which is not IBM-compatible and cannot run DOS or Windows—was one of the first PCs to use a graphical user interface (GUI). (The first computer to use a GUI was the immediate predecessor to the Mac, the short-lived Apple Lisa.) The operating system for the Mac is known as the MacOS.

*The designers used **Macs** for all their creative work.*

Also Explore: API, *GUI*, multitasking, multithreading, shell.

Photography

aperture, *n.* The opening, or the diameter of the opening, in a camera, telescope, and so on through which light passes into the lens. The lens opening is expressed in what is called an f number (or f/stop), which is the number of times the diameter of the aperture divides into the focal length of the lens: f/2, f/4, etc. Aperture affects depth of field; the smaller the aperture, the greater the zone of sharpness.

*Melanie decreased the **aperture** to increase the depth of field.*

shutter speed, *n.* The length of time during which the camera shutter remains open. These speeds are expressed in seconds or fractions of a second: $\frac{1}{2}$, $\frac{1}{4}$, and so on. Each speed increment halves the amount of light.

*Dennis knew that a fast **shutter speed** was best for capturing fast-moving subjects, such as at sporting events.*

depth of field, *n.* The zone of sharpest focus in front of, behind, and around the subject on which the lens is focused.

*Ben attempted to increase the **depth of field** so that both the foreground and background were in focus.*

bracket, *vt.* To take a series of pictures of a subject using a range of exposures. In unfamiliar lighting conditions, this ensures that at least one image will be correctly exposed.

*Even though he was sure the first exposure was correct, Alec **bracketed** the shot just in case.*

SLR, *n.* Single lens reflex; a camera having a viewing system that allows the photographer to see the subject through the same lens that brings the image to the film.

*Mark decided to ditch his Polaroid and buy a good **SLR**.*

 Also Explore: exposure, focal length, lens, shutter.

Negatives

---

contrary, *adj.* Opposite in nature, order, direction, etc.; altogether different; inclined to oppose or disagree stubbornly. Contrary implies a habitual disinclination to accept orders, advice, etc.

*Brian's behavior was **contrary** to the norm; he tended to zig when everyone else zagged.*

---

antithetical, *adj.* Exactly opposite. Antithetical implies a contrast or opposition. Although contrary is simply opposed, antithetical is exactly the opposite thing or view; as an example, black is the antithesis of white.

*Wearing casual clothes to work was **antithetical** to what Kenneth was used to.*

down side, *n.* Drawback or disadvantage. Also used to refer to a downward trend or financial loss, such as on an investment.

*The plan had a $2 million **down side.***

adverse, *adj.* Unfavorable; harmful. Whereas a down side is not necessarily harmful (just undesirable), something that is adverse is harmful.

*Due to **adverse** weather conditions, the flight to Cleveland was cancelled.*

timorous, *adj.* Full of or subject to fear; timid.

*Sally was **timorous** around Mr. Big; she was afraid he'd fire her.*

 Also Explore: antagonistic, disinclination, *negativist*, *opposition*, unpropitious.

Positives

---

sanguine, *adj.* Cheerful and confident; optimistic; hopeful. Sanguine implies being positive despite obstacles or problems. A person who is sanguine possesses a positive attitude.

> *Despite her many problems, Ruth remained **sanguine** about her prospects.*

---

upswing, *n.* A swing, trend, or movement upward; an upward trend in business. Upswing implies a lasting or long-term trend.

> *The business started an **upswing** in the second quarter.*

uptick, *n.* An increase or upturn; rise. Upswing implies a larger increase than does uptick.

> *There was an **uptick** in sales during the second week, but it didn't sustain.*

up side, *n.* Unplanned benefit; potential.

> *The plan had a $2 million **up side**.*

uplifting, *adj.* Raised to a higher moral, social, or cultural level or condition.

> *The book about angels was both **uplifting** and enlightening.*

 Also Explore: *boom, optimist,* optimize, upturn.

Worth Doing

---

contribution margin, *n.* That part of the proceeds available to put toward the fixed costs of the business. Technically, contribution margin (also called CM) is the selling price less the variable cost.

*Hank approved any project that had a positive **contribution margin**.*

---

proceeds, *n.* The money or profit derived from a sale, business ventures, and so on.

*The **proceeds** from the charity drive helped pay down the center's debt.*

return, *n.* Yield, profit, or revenue, such as from labor, investments, etc. Whereas the proceeds are typically measured in absolute dollars, return is normally measured as a ratio of profit compared to cost or moneys invested.

*Jeff sought a **return** on his investment of 20 percent within 12 months.*

lucrative, *adj.* Producing wealth or profit; profitable.

*The new account proved quite **lucrative** for Carol; she was able to almost double her commissions.*

worthwhile, *adj.* Important or valuable enough to repay time or effort spent; of true value.

*As long as one of the children learned something, the time spent was **worthwhile**.*

 Also Explore: *fixed cost,* proceeds, *variable cost,* yield.

Sex (Non-Vanilla)

---

fetish, *n.* A focus on any nonsexual object, such as a foot or a glove, that abnormally excites erotic feelings. Fetishism implies obtaining sexual excitement primarily or exclusively from an inanimate object or a particular part of the body.

*Roger's foot **fetish** led him to collect literally hundreds of different women's shoes.*

---

b/d, Bondage and discipline. A sexual activity in which one person is bound while another engages in discipline activities, such as spanking and whipping.

*Sally's **b/d** fantasies involved being tied up while Roger paddled her with a flyswatter.*

d/s, Domination and submission. A sexual activity where sexual arousal is derived from acting out sexual fantasies in which one person dominates while the other submits.

*Roger preferred to be the master during their **d/s** play so he could treat Sally like a slave.*

s/m, Sadism and masochism; sadomasochism. A sexual activity often in a consensual, role-playing manner. Sadism is where a person derives sexual pleasure from inflicting pain on someone else; masochism is where an individual derives sexual pleasure from experiencing pain.

*Neither Roger nor Sally liked **s/m**; they weren't into pain.*

ménage à trois, *n.* (may-nazh-a-twa) from the French (household of three). Any ongoing sexual relationship involving three people, especially when they live together.

*Roger fantasized about a **ménage à trois** with Sally and her roommate.*

 Also Explore: consensual, debase, erotic, *perverse*, subjugation.

Weapons

WMD, Weapons of mass destruction, such as biological, chemical, or nuclear weapons. WMDs are capable of death and destruction on an almost unimaginable scale.

*The U.N. team suspected that the foreign government had several caches of **WMDs** hidden in safe houses.*

biological warfare, *n.* The deliberate use of disease-spreading microorganisms, toxins, viruses, etc. in warfare.

*The threat of **biological warfare** inspired officials to inoculate all troops against anthrax.*

chemical warfare, *n.* Warfare by means of chemicals and chemical devices such as poisonous gases, flame throwers, incendiary bombs, and smoke screens.

*Based on subsequent health problems experienced by some soldiers, it was possible that Iraq engaged in **chemical warfare** against U.S. troops in the Gulf War.*

nuclear warfare, *n.* Warfare by means of weapons that employ nuclear energy, such as atomic, hydrogen, or neutron bombs.

*Even with the collapse of the Soviet Union, the threat of **nuclear warfare** initiated by some terrorist group remained.*

nuclear winter, *n.* A hypothetical scenario following a major nuclear war in which the atmosphere will be clouded with smoke or dust for a long time, causing loss of sunlight and frigid temperatures. This is thought to be a threat to most life forms on the planet because accompanying high winds will carry the radioactive dust and smoke to many areas of the earth and destroy agriculture and food chains.

*Officials lived in fear of a **nuclear winter** resulting from even a tactical nuclear attack.*

 Also Explore: incendiary, microorganism, neutron, *tactic.*

Stick to It

persevere, *vi.* To continue in some effort or course of action in spite of difficulty, opposition, and so on; be steadfast in purpose, persist. To persevere is to maintain a purpose in spite of counter influences, opposition, or discouragement.

*In spite of the overwhelming odds, Chloe **persevered** in her pursuit of the world record.*

diligent, *adj.* Persevering and careful in work. Diligent implies a careful, steady, painstaking effort applied to some form of work.

*Curt was **diligent** in assembling the details necessary to move forward with the project.*

assiduous, *adj.* Done with constant and careful attention. Assiduous implies hardworking, active, and alert and emphasizes an almost fastidious attention to details.

*A less **assiduous** secretary would not have noticed that the wrong form had been submitted.*

discipline, *n.* Strict control to enforce obedience. Self-discipline is controlling oneself or one's desires, actions, habits, etc.

*The company needed **discipline** to sustain its market gains.*

tenacious, *adj.* Holding firmly; stubborn.

*Jordan was **tenacious** in holding on to his belief that the government would back down from its case.*

 Also Explore: industrious, *resolute*, *steadfast*, unremitting.

Market Control

monopoly, _n._ Exclusive control of a commodity or service in a given market, or control that makes possible the fixing of prices and the virtual elimination of free competition. Unregulated monopolies—especially those that engage in anticompetitive behavior—are not allowed under U.S. antitrust laws.

> _After the attempted hostile takeover of its largest competitor, CompuTitan was accused of trying to create a **monopoly** in desktop software._

duopoly, _n._ Control of a commodity or service in a given market by only two producers or suppliers.

> _The two largest competitors held an effective **duopoly** in the market._

oligopoly, _n._ Control of a commodity or service in a given market by a small number of companies or suppliers.

> _For years, the four firms were a de facto **oligopoly** with roughly equal shares of the market._

antitrust, _adj._ Designating or of federal laws, suits, and so on. Designed to prevent restraints on trade, as by business monopolies, cartels, etc. Antitrust practices are those that oppose or are intended to regulate business monopolies, such as trusts or cartels.

> _The government brought **antitrust** action against IBM in the 1960s, accusing the company of monopolistic practices._

anticompetitive, _adj._ Discouraging competition among businesses. Anticompetitive practices or activities work against the consumer by trying to eliminate free market competition.

> _The cartel engaged in **anticompetitive** practices designed to increase the price to consumers._

 Also Explore: _cartel, commodity,_ trust, unregulated.

Established

---

inveterate, *adj.* Firmly established over a long period; of long standing; deep-rooted. Inveterate implies dedication and permanence; something that persists or is long-established is inveterate.

*Herbert was an **inveterate** liar; no one ever believed a word he said.*

---

habitual, *adj.* Formed or acquired by continual use; customary.

*Jones had been **habitually** late for work for the past six months.*

traditional, *adj.* Handed down by predecessors or conforming to tradition, custom, or practice. Habitual implies long-standing use by an individual; traditional implies long-standing practice by a group or society.

*At ReallyBig Co., the **traditional** response to a mistake was to accept responsibility and move on to another topic.*

historical, *adj.* Established by history; not legendary or fictional but factual and real. Can also refer to showing the development or evolution of a thing in proper chronological order.

*The **historical** data indicated a lack of market acceptance for products in that price range.*

infrangible, *adj.* That cannot be broken or separated; that cannot be violated or infringed. Infrangible suggests an indelicacy of structure that is not easily broken and implies the connotation of liability if that thing were broken.

*The team members had been together so long that they were virtually **infrangible;** no one knew what would happen if they were to be broken up.*

 Also Explore: *endowment*, entrenched, *perpetual*, sanctioned.

205

Healthy Eating

healthful, *n.* Helping to produce, promote, or maintain health; salutary; wholesome. This is what we really mean to say when we say healthy eating. The adjective healthy describes having good health, being well or sound. We are healthy because what we are eating is healthful.

> *Patricia went out of her way to prepare **healthful** meals for her restaurant's health conscious diners.*

nutritive, *adj.* Having to do with nutrition, promoting nutrition; nutritious. Edible, wholesome. Nutritive is sometimes used to suggest healthy foods.

> *The **nutritive** value of the dinners on the menu made Winnie's restaurant a virtual haunt for world-class athletes.*

vegetarian, *n.* A person who eats no meat and sometimes no animal products at all, such as milk or eggs. A vegan is a vegetarian who eats no animal products at all.

> *Chloe had been a **vegetarian** for so long she forgot what the taste of red meat was like.*

dietetic *adj.* Of, relating to, or designed for a particular diet of food and drink.

> *The **dietetic** section in the grocery store had a wide selection of gluten-free breads for customers with allergies to wheat.*

diabetic *n.* A person who has diabetes. Not to be confused with diatetic. A person who has diabetes typically has an insulin deficiency. This requires a diet that minimizes the intake of sugars as well as salt, fats, and most other preservatives.

> *If we all ate as though we were **diabetic,** we'd be much healthier people.*

 Also Explore: *benign*, esculent, low-fat, sustentative.

Eco-Friendly

green, *adj.* Relating to or advocating ecological awareness, the preservation of natural resources, etc. Green implies an ecological focus and related political activity that borders on the zealous or fanatical.

*Chloe, ever an environmentalist, consistently supported **green** causes in the community.*

organic, *adj.* Grown with only animal or vegetable fertilizers, such as manure, bone meal, compost, and so on. Organic implies free from artificial additives.

*Chloe ate only **organic** foods, avoiding all preservatives.*

conservation, *n.* The official protection or management of natural resources.

*The community funded a **conservation** initiative for the local wetlands.*

reclamation, *n.* A reclaiming or being reclaimed; especially, the recovery of wasteland, desert, etc. by ditching, filling or irrigating. It also refers to the process or industry of obtaining useful materials from waste products. Ironically, the two definitions of reclamation are often at cross purposes regarding eco-friendly practices.

*When the mayor presented his proposal for **reclamation,** the green coalition was pleased when the Megapolis dump was designated as the main disposal point.*

ecology, *n.* The complex of relations between living organisms and their environment.

*Preserving the **ecology** of the wetlands was of utmost importance.*

 Also Explore: ecosystem, *environment*, habitat, husbandry, *recycling*.

Stir Up

foment, *vt.* To stir up trouble. Foment implies first eliciting and then bringing to full development and execution an action of serious consequence and suggests continued incitement over an extended period of time.

> *George's personal grudge against ReallyBig Co. led him to* **foment** *revolution among the factory workers.*

agitate, *vt.* To keep discussing so as to stir up interest in and support for a cause. Agitate implies using speeches and writing to stir up interest and support for actions that will produce changes.

> *The plan was to* **agitate** *the workers into forcing a union vote.*

rebel, *vi.* To resist any authority or controls.

> *Don* **rebelled** *against the directive from corporate headquarters, refusing to give a urine sample.*

revolt, *vi.* To refuse to submit to authority. Revolt is more extreme and organized than rebel.

> *The workers* **revolted** *when they heard the warehouse was being moved.*

anarchist, *n.* A person who believes in or advocates the theory that all forms of government interfere unjustly with individual liberty and should be replaced by the voluntary association of cooperative groups.

> *Levon was an* **anarchist,** *and he tried to bring the overthrow of the government through a series of mail bombs.*

 Also Explore: *advocate*, elicit, *incite*, instigate, mutiny.

Meals

---

cuisine, *n.* (kwee-zeen) from the French (to cook). The food prepared, such as at a restaurant. Sometimes refers to the style, type, or nationality of food prepared, as in low-fat cuisine or Italian cuisine.

> *Marty loved northern Italian **cuisine** and frequented the city's best Italian restaurants.*

---

appetizer, *n.* A small portion of a tasty food or a drink to stimulate the appetite at the beginning of a meal.

> *Melissa ordered escargot as an **appetizer.***

entrée, *n.* (ahn-tray) from the French (enter). The main course of a meal. In some countries, the entrée is a dish served before the main course or between the fish and meat courses.

> *Melissa's **entrée** was veal scaloppini.*

prix fixe, *n.* (pree-feks) from the French (fixed price). A meal that has a set price for the complete meal. Contrast with a la carte, referring to a separate price for each item on the menu.

> *Marty preferred the simplicity of a **prix fixe** menu.*

du jour, *adj.* (doo-zhoor) from the French (of the day). Available or offered on this day. Du jour refers to a particular part of the menu that changes daily.

> *Tomato bisque is today's soup **du jour.***

Also Explore: a la carte, course, *gourmet,* hors d'oeuvre, repast.

Different

---

esoteric, *adj.* Beyond the understanding or knowledge of most people. Esoteric implies something that is unique, specialized, and not widely understood.

> *His musical tastes were **esoteric,** running towards little-known folk artists such as Christine Lavin and Megon McDonough.*

---

exotic, *adj.* Strange or different in a way that is striking or fascinating; strangely beautiful and so on.

> *Michael loved **exotic** automobiles such as Ferraris and McLarens.*

dissimilar, *adj.* Not similar or alike; different.

> *Their tastes were so **dissimilar** they could never agree on a restaurant for dinner.*

discordant, *adj.* Not in accord; disagreeing; conflicting.

> *The group was becoming **discordant** as everyone's individual opinions came to the fore.*

mutation, *n.* A change, as in form, nature, qualities, etc. Mutation implies a sudden and unexpected change.

> *The virus went through a sudden **mutation** that made useless the previous antibiotic.*

 Also Explore: *dissonance*, divergent, *eccentric*, *eclectic*.

Similar

---

analogous, *adj.* Similar or comparable in certain respects. Analogous does not imply an exact match. The fact that it is usually paired with the word roughly emphasizes this.

> *Getting married is roughly **analogous** to jumping off a cliff.*

---

homogenous, *adj.* Having similarity in structure because of common descent. Homogenous implies overall similarities, for example, over an entire population.

> *The small island's inhabitants were remarkably **homogenous** in appearance. They had the same color hair, eyes, and general stature.*

interchangeable, *adj.* Usually something or someone that is so similar that they can be interchanged; more especially, they can be put or used in place of each other.

> *The temporaries' skills were so similar that the individuals were basically **interchangeable** without affecting the project.*

synonymous, *adj.* Of or having the nature of a synonym; equivalent or similar in meaning. Synonymous has the connotation of being identical.

> *At ReallyBig Co., being told you have an attitude problem was **synonymous** with being told you have 30 days to find another job.*

equivalent, *adj.* Equal in quantity, value, force, meaning, and so on. Implies of things that they amount to the same thing.

> *On her one-year anniversary with the company, Laura was given a four-day work week, which her boss thought was **equivalent** to the pay increase he couldn't afford because LittleTiny Co. was cash poor.*

 Also Explore: apposite, comparable, *invariable*, jibe, *kindred.*

Along With

supplement, *vt.* Add to in order to make up for a lack or deficiency. Supplement differs from augment in that the thing added to is initially lacking.

*Bob's eating habits were so poor he needed to **supplement** his diet with a daily multivitamin.*

augment, *vt.* To make greater, as in size, quantity, or strength; enlarge. Weak or small things can be supplemented; anything can be augmented.

*By **augmenting** the band with a horn section, Clive found the sound he was searching for.*

auxiliary, *adj.* Acting in a subsidiary, or subordinate, capacity. Whereas augment implies making something greater, auxiliary implies adding something extra.

*Horton added **auxiliary** staff over the holidays to handle the increased traffic.*

complement, *n.* That which completes or brings to perfection. Complementary implies making up what is lacking in one another. Don't confuse complement with compliment, which is something said in praise or flattery.

*Judy's way with words **complemented** Ralph's numerical skills.*

counterpart, *n.* A thing that, when added to another, completes or complements it. Counterpart can also refer to a person or thing that corresponds to or closely resembles another.

*Maurice needed to find the **counterpart** to the computer subroutine to complete the entire program.*

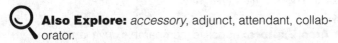 **Also Explore:** *accessory*, adjunct, attendant, collaborator.

Maddening

annoy, *vt.* To irritate, bother, or make somewhat angry, as by a repeated action, noise, etc. Annoy implies a temporary disturbance of mind caused by something that displeases one or tries one's patience.

> *Randy was **annoyed** when the phone rang while he was trying to find the error in the spreadsheet.*

irritate, *vt.* To excite to anger. Irritate suggests temporary superficial impatience in, constant annoyance in, or an outburst of anger from the person stirred to feeling. Irritate is more extreme than annoy.

> *As the phone continued to ring, Randy became more **irritated.***

exasperate, *vt.* To irritate or annoy very much; make angry. Exasperate implies intense irritation such as exhausts one's patience or makes one lose one's self-control. Exasperate is more extreme than irritate.

> *The combination of the phone ringing and his inability to find the spreadsheet error **exasperated** Randy.*

vex, *vt.* To give trouble to, especially in a petty or nagging way. Vex implies a more serious source of irritation and greater disturbance than exasperate, along with an often intense worry.

> *The source of the spreadsheet error **vexed** both Randy and his team.*

plague, *vt.* To harass; trouble; torment. Plague implies a constant vexation.

> *Over time, Randy realized that the spreadsheet was **plagued** with multiple errors.*

 Also Explore: *agitate*, exacerbate, irk, peeve, perturb.

Church

DAY 214

---

pious, *adj.* Having or showing religious devotion; zealous in the performance of religious obligations. Pious can also imply somone who is seemingly virtuous (but in a hypocritical fashion) or something that is sacred.

*Marcia was devoutly religious; she had a **pious** heart.*

---

covenant, *n.* A binding and solemn agreement to do or keep from doing a specified thing. In religious terms, an agreement among members of a church to defend and maintain its doctrines, polity, and faith.

*Marriage is a sacred **covenant** in the church.*

creed, *n.* A brief statement of religious belief; a confession of faith. More formally, a creed is a specific statement of this kind, accepted by a church.

*The congregation joined in reciting the Apostles' **creed**.*

benediction, *n.* A blessing. More formally, a benediction is an invocation of divine blessing, especially at the end of a religious service.

*The pastor ended the service with a **benediction**.*

denomination, *n.* A particular religious body within the Christian religion, with a specific name, organization, and so on. Lutheran and Presbyterian are two different types of denominations.

*Marjory decided to change churches and join the United Methodist **denomination**.*

 Also Explore: apostolic, devout, *dogmatic*, evangelical, sect.

Politics

---

conservative, *adj.* Tending to preserve established traditions or institutions and to resist or oppose any changes in these. Conservative politics are often referred to as right-wing politics.

*Barney's **conservative** policies made him the darling of the right-wing coalition.*

---

moderate, *adj.* Within reasonable limits; avoiding excesses or extremes. Moderate politics bridge the extremes of conservative and liberal and are sometimes referred to as middle of the road.

*Alan tried to set a **moderate** course, avoiding the extremes of either party.*

liberal, *adj.* Favoring political reform or progress tending toward democracy and personal freedom for the individual. Liberal politics are often referred to as left-wing politics.

*Miranda's **liberal** views put her at odds with her father, a dyed-in-the-wool Republican.*

radical, *adj.* Favoring fundamental or extreme change. Radical implies a change of the basic social or economic structure. Radicals can be either left-wing or right-wing.

*The right-wing **radical** group began picketing abortion clinics across the country.*

reactionary, *adj.* Advocating a movement back to a former or less advanced condition, stage, etc. Reactionaries often respond to the current situation by wanting to retreat to the way things were in the past.

*The coalition believed in **reactionary** politics; its response to an increase in violence in the media was to boycott all products of the Disney Corporation.*

 Also Explore: *anarchist,* fogy, fundamentalist, insurgent, seditious.

Sciences

---

physics, *n.* The science dealing with the properties, changes, interactions, etc. of matter and energy in which energy is considered to be continuous (classical physics) or discrete (quantum physics).

*The laws of **physics** dictated that the momentum of the object would continue even after it ceased accelerating—which explained why the car kept rolling when the brakes failed.*

---

mathematics, *n.* The group of sciences dealing with quantities, magnitudes, forms, and their relationships, attributes, etc., by the use of numbers and symbols.

*Frederick's **mathematics** skills helped to hone his ability to solve complex logic problems.*

biology, *n.* The science that deals with the origin, history, physical characteristics, life processes, habits, and so on of plants and animals. Biology is about living things and includes botany and zoology as subsets.

*The **biology** laboratory was filled with plants and animals of all shapes and sizes.*

astronomy, *n.* The science of the universe in which the stars, planets, etc. are studied, including their origins, evolution, composition, motions, relative positions, and sizes.

*The **astronomy** department planned to celebrate the anniversary of the launch of the Hubble space telescope.*

astrology, *n.* A pseudoscience based on the notion that the positions of the moon, sun, and stars affect human affairs and that one can foretell the future by studying their positions and interrelationships. Don't confuse astronomy with astrology.

*Samantha's **astrological** profile said Monday would be a good day to water her plants.*

 Also Explore: anthropology, chemistry, geology, sociology, zoology.

Indecent Behavior

ribald, *adj.* Characterized by coarse or vulgar joking or mocking; dealing with sex in a humorously earthy or direct way. Ribald definitely implies humor behind the vulgarity—even though ribald behavior is not appropriate in a corporate environment.

> *Mort told a **ribald** limerick, which offended the more puritanical members of the group.*

lewd, *adj.* Showing, or intended to excite, lust or sexual desire in an offensive way.

> *The prostitute's **lewd** behavior made her a target for the vice squad.*

profane, *adj.* Showing disrespect or contempt for sacred things;. Profane language (profanity) comprises "swear" words.

> *Bobby was sent to the principal's office for using **profane** language in class.*

perverse, *adj.* Deviating from what is considered right or good. Perverse sometimes implies the practice of various abnormal sexual activities.

> *Jim's **perverse** behavior included indulging in rubber and leather fetishes.*

scandalous, *adj.* Offensive to a sense of decency or shocking to the moral feelings of the community; shameful.

> *The schoolteacher's **scandalous** affair with the minister shocked the entire community.*

 Also Explore: blaspheme, lascivious, risqué, taboo, vulgar.

Online

Internet, *n.* An extensive computer network made up of thousands of other, smaller business, academic, and governmental networks. This "network of networks" allows users access to various types of services.

> ***Internet*** *access is essential in today's information society.*

intranet, *n.* A version of the Internet internal to a specific company or location. Although intranets often use the same networking technology as the Internet, they are different because the Internet is publicly controlled whereas an intranet is controlled privately.

> *ReallyBig Co. developed a corporate **intranet** so employees could access benefits information by using a Web browser.*

World Wide Web, *n.* A group of interconnected Internet sources providing access to images and sound in addition to text. The World Wide Web is a technology that allows users to travel through information (shown as pages) by clicking on hyperlinks that can point to any document anywhere on the Internet.

> *Many businesses are setting up e-commerce storefronts on the **World Wide Web.***

USENET, *n.* A group of interconnected Internet sources providing access to virtual community newsgroups that allow users to exchange electronic messages. A USENET newsgroup is analogous to a community bulletin board.

> *Jennifer subscribed to several **USENET** newsgroups specializing in Star Trek fan fiction.*

FTP, *n.* File transfer protocol. A protocol that allows for file transfers over the Internet.

> *Bob downloaded the files from an **FTP** site.*

 Also Explore: browser, extranet, *hypertext*, hypermedia, threaded newsreader.

Computer Programming

code, *n.* In a high-level programming language, the typed program instructions that programmers write before the program is compiled or interpreted into machine language.

Jason prided himself on his ability to write bulletproof **code,** *even though it put his projects months behind schedule.*

BASIC, *n.* Beginners All-purpose Symbolic Instruction Code, a simplified high-level programming language that utilizes common words and algebra.

He learned essential programming skills when he taught himself how to write simple programs in **BASIC.**

C, *n.* A high-level programming language widely used for professional programming and preferred by most major software publishers.

The main application was developed in **C.**

COBOL, *n.* Common Business Oriented Language, a high-level programming language specially designed for business applications. Released in 1964, COBOL is the most widely used programming language in corporate mainframe environments.

Most of the software with Year 2000 problems was written in **COBOL.**

assembly language, *n.* A low-level programming language in which each program statement corresponds to an instruction that the microprocessor can carry out. The resulting code is compact, operates quickly, and, when assembled, is more efficient than a compiled program.

Even though Jason did most of his coding in C, he still used **assembly language** *for some key subroutines.*

Also Explore: *bulletproof*, compiler, object-oriented, shareware, spaghetti code.

Accommodating

---

complaisant, *adj.* Willing to please. Complaisant implies yielding too easily to another's request or insistence and is often used in derogatory reference, implying a lack of strong will.

> *Hastings thought the store personnel were too **complaisant** when it came to customer returns; he couldn't believe they'd let customers return purchases without the original sales receipt.*

---

malleable, *adj.* Capable of being changed, molded, trained, and so on. Malleable implies yielding to required change or conformity.

> *Blake preferred to hire younger employees because she found them more **malleable** than set-in-their-ways older workers.*

compliant, *adj.* Acting in accordance. Compliant implies a willingness to adhere to a formal or informal rule or code of behavior.

> *The company was **compliant** with the agency's directives.*

amenable, *adj.* Able to be controlled or influenced. Amenable implies being controlled or influenced by another.

> *Quincy was **amenable** to his boss's suggestion that he work extra hours on Saturday.*

contrite, *adj.* Feeling remorse for having done wrong.

> *After the big project blew up in his face, Jefferson **contritely** accepted the blame.*

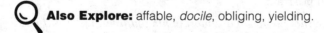

Also Explore: affable, *docile*, obliging, yielding.

Not Accommodating

recalcitrant, *adj.* Refusing to obey authority, custom, regulation; stubbornly defiant. A recalcitrant person is unlikely to be influenced by persuasion or inducement, particularly in matters relating to authority.

> *Don was **recalcitrant** when he was warned for smoking in the lunchroom; he lit up another cigarette as soon as the supervisor left the room.*

intractable, *adj.* Hard to manage; unruly or stubborn. Implies not easily yielding to influence.

> *For the leading project team, even the most **intractable** problems were eventually solved.*

petulant, *adj.* Impatient or irritable, especially over a petty annoyance.

> *Theodore became **petulant** when he found that someone had stolen his frozen dinner out of the company refrigerator.*

acrimonious, *adj.* Bitter and caustic in temper, manner, or speech.

> *Vance was **acrimonious** when he found out Howard had beat him out for the promotion.*

hostile, *adj.* Having or showing ill will; unfriendly.

> *Brenda accused ReallyBig Co. of having a **hostile** working environment after she was verbally accosted in the lunchroom.*

Also Explore: antisocial, caustic, *contrary*, irascible, rancorous.

Messing With

sabotage, *vt.* To injure or destroy by way of intentional destruction. Sabotage implies deliberate destruction to machines or other materials, or obstruction to a cause, movement, activity, effort, etc., by someone or some group opposed to the thing or activity.

*The union was suspected of **sabotaging** the new packing line in the warehouse.*

undermine, *vt.* To injure, weaken, or impair, especially by subtle, stealthy, or insidious means. Undermine implies inflicting damage in a subtle or covert fashion.

*Vance tried to **undermine** Howard's authority at every chance.*

thwart *vt.* To hinder, obstruct, frustrate, or defeat a person, plans, etc. Thwart means to frustrate by blocking (not necessarily in a covert way) someone or something moving toward some objective.

*The lack of proper tools **thwarted** Sam's ability to repair the copy machine before lunch.*

foil, *vt.* To keep from being successful; to frustrate. Foil means to throw off course so as to discourage further effort or make it of no avail. Foil has the connotation of creating a long lasting frustration of an effort or action such that it may not ever occur. Thwarting creates a more immediate and temporary frustration.

*Jonathan's cat **foiled** his dreams of wealth by shredding his winning lottery ticket into microscopic bits.*

intervene *vt.* To come between two or more things as an influence, in order to modify, settle, or hinder some action, argument.

*Martin felt he had to **intervene** in the conflict between Vance and Howard or the whole company would collapse.*

 Also Explore: *encumbrance*, impede, incapacitate, intercede, trammel.

222

Co-Workers

teammate, *n.* A fellow member on a team. Don't confuse team-mate with team player, who is one who subordinates personal aspirations and works in a coordinated effort with other members of a group, or team, in striving for a common goal. All team players are teammates; not all teammates are team players.

*Clyde depended on his **teammates** to pick up his slack when he had to work on another project for a week.*

peer, *n.* A person of the same rank, quality, or ability; an equal.

*Bob and Ray were **peers** in the organization and were compensated equally.*

accomplice, *n.* A person who knowingly participates with another in an unlawful act; partner in crime.

*Laura was an **accomplice** to Vance's plot to sabotage the packing line; she helped him gain entrance through the back door.*

accessory, *n.* A person who, although absent at the commission of a felony, aids or abets the accused before (or after) its commission.

*By supplying Vance with a stolen security card, she was an **accessory** to the crime that followed.*

confederate, *n.* A person, group, nation, or state united with another or others for a common purpose. A confederate is an ally.

*Johnson gathered his **confederates** before the big press conference announcing their new project.*

 Also Explore: abettor, ally, *cohort*, crony.

Out of It

disenfranchised, *adj.* Deprived of the rights of citizenship, especially of the right to vote. Disenfranchised (also used as disfranchised, without the "en" in the middle) can also refer to deprivation of any privilege, right, or power.

*Middle management felt **disenfranchised** when the CFO took away their check-signing privileges.*

disadvantaged, *adj.* Deprived of a decent standard of living, education, and so on by poverty and a lack of opportunity; underprivileged.

*Even though he grew up in a **disadvantaged** community, Ronald persevered and won a scholarship to the state university.*

displaced, *adj.* A person forced from his country, especially as a result of war, and left homeless elsewhere.

*There were hundreds of thousands of **displaced** persons after the war.*

disaffected, *adj.* Unfriendly, discontented, or disloyal, especially toward the government.

*Sam felt **disaffected** over the way he was being represented by his councilman.*

dispirited, *adj.* With spirits lowered; sad or discouraged. Someone who is dispirited is often depressed.

*After four consecutive quarters of losses, the management team was becoming **dispirited.***

 Also Explore: *apathetic*, challenged (politically correct), disinherited, itinerate, vagrant.

Fun

jovial, *adj.* Full of hearty, playful good humor. From the astrological notion that people born under the sign of Jupiter (Jovians) are joyful, genial, and gay.

*Louis was his usual **jovial** self, entertaining everyone at the table with amusing stories.*

gregarious, *adj.* Fond of the company of others. Gregarious is often misused to imply boisterous when in fact it is closer to sociable in meaning.

*Phil's **gregarious** nature made him a natural greeter for the company party.*

sociable, *adj.* Friendly or agreeable, especially in an easy, informal way. Sociable is characterized by pleasant, informal conversation and companionship.

*Linda was very **sociable,** flitting from table to table with light conversation.*

carouse, *vi.* To drink much alcoholic liquor, especially along with others having a noisy, merry time.

*Walter decided to go **carousing** with his buddies after the party ended.*

convivial, *adj.* Fond of eating, drinking, and good company.

*In spite of her reputation as a homebody, Joan was quite **convivial** when given the opportunity.*

Also Explore: amicable, *buoyant*, diversion, *congenial*, urbane.

Coffee

---

espresso, *n.* Italian coffee prepared in a special machine from finely ground coffee beans, through which steam under high pressure is forced. Espresso is made from a darker roast than regular coffee, resulting in less acid and less caffeine; a finer grind is required because of the special quick brewing process.

Uncle Bill couldn't start the day without a tall **espresso.**

---

cappuccino, *n.* Espresso coffee mixed with steamed milk and sometimes sprinkled with cinnamon or powdered chocolate. Cappuccino is created by ladling or pouring steamed milk over espresso and spooning the dense froth over the top. The basic proportion is $^1/_3$ espresso, $^1/_3$ steamed milk, and $^1/_3$ milk froth.

Mr. French was a connoisseur of espresso drinks and ordered a grande **cappuccino.**

latté, *n.* Espresso coffee mixed with steamed milk. A latté is made with the same ingredients as cappuccino, but in a latté, the milk is steamed, not frothed, and the proportion is $^1/_3$ espresso and $^2/_3$ steamed milk.

Sissy didn't like froth in her cup, so she ordered a short **latté.**

mocha, *n.* Espresso coffee mixed with chocolate, often with steamed milk added.

Jody liked chocolate, so he ordered a short **mocha.**

au lait, *adj.* With milk. Café au lait is coffee with an equal part of hot or scalded milk.

Buffy liked her coffee laced with milk, so she ordered café **au lait.**

 Also Explore: Arabica, demitasse, froth, Robusta, *short.*

Small Change

DAY 227

---

nuance, *n.* A slight or delicate variation in tone, color, meaning; shade of difference. Nuance implies a subtle meaning or refinement.

*The subtle **nuances** in her interpretation of the piece gave her performance an edge seldom found in her contemporaries.*

---

shade, *n.* A small difference or variation; a slight amount or degree; trace; touch; suggestion.

*He decided to tone down the rhetoric a **shade**.*

smidgen, *n.* A small amount; a bit. Shade refers to small differences; smidgen refers to small amounts.

*There was only a **smidgen** of truth in the newspaper article.*

nubbin, *n.* Anything small or undeveloped. Smidgen refers to small quantities of a thing; nubbin refers to small things.

*He picked at the **nubbin** of lint on the collar of his sweater.*

exiguous, *adj.* Scanty; little; small. Exiguous implies a lack of those qualities that give something richness, vigor, strength, etc.

*After the department was downsized, Paul was left with **exiguous** resources.*

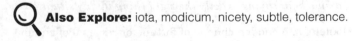 **Also Explore:** iota, modicum, nicety, subtle, tolerance.

Happy Accidents

serendipity, *n.* A seeming gift for finding something good accidentally. Serendipity implies a history of or knack for making pleasant discoveries by accident; serendipity is more than just a one-time occurrence.

*Maria was blessed with **serendipity;** the right thing always seemed to happen at the right time for her.*

fortuitous, *adj.* Happening by chance; bringing, or happening by, good luck. Fortuitous has more in common with accidental than it does with lucky.

*It was **fortuitous** that Marty ran into Marvin at the Quickie Mart; the two of them needed to share notes about the upcoming project.*

happenstance, *n.* By mere coincidence; a chance meeting having a beneficial outcome.

*It was only **happenstance** that Marla went to the department store the day that all winter clothing was marked down 40 percent.*

felicitous, *adj.* Used or expressed in a way suitable to the occasion. Felicitous implies good fortune or something happening at a good time.

*Morton was blessed with the gift of **felicitous** speech; he had a knack for saying exactly the right thing in any situation.*

peripeteia, *n.* A sudden change of fortune or reversal of circumstances. Peripeteia can be a change for the better or for the worse, as long as a change of some sort occurs.

*Jeff and Cindy experienced a run of **peripeteiac** fortune, beginning with the unexpected inheritance from her late aunt.*

Also Explore: auspicious, coincidence, *expedient*, kismet, opportune.

228

Economic Cycles

depression, *n.* A period marked by slackening of business activity, widespread unemployment, falling prices and wages, etc. The Great Depression was the period of economic depression that began in 1929 and lasted through most of the 1930s.

*Looking at the many warning signs, analysts thought that the economy was headed for a severe **depression.***

recession, *n.* A temporary falling off of business activity during a period when such activity has been generally increasing. A recession is less severe than a depression.

*In actuality, the business falloff resulted in a mild **recession.***

recovery, *n.* A return to economic health. A period of prosperity following a depression or recession.

*Following the recession was a period of economic **recovery.***

inflation, *n.* An increase in the amount of money and credit in relation to the supply of goods and services, resulting in an increase in the general price level, causing a decline in purchasing power.

*Workers worried about how an increase in the **inflation** rate would impact their standard of living.*

disinflation, *n.* A reduction of the general level of prices, designed to increase purchasing power but prevent deflation. Deflation is a lessening of the amount of money in circulation, resulting in a relatively sharp and sudden rise in its value and a fall in prices.

*Surprisingly, Moore's Law resulted in a gradual **disinflation** of technology-based goods and services.*

 Also Explore: *bear*, reflation, retrenchment, stagflation.

Health (Well)

---

salubrious, *adj.* Promoting health or welfare. Something that is salubrious is healthful.

*The diet recommended by Dr. Benjamin had a **salubrious** effect on Wanda's well-being.*

---

wellness, *n.* The condition of being healthy or sound, especially as the result of proper diet, exercise, and so on.

*Dr. Benjamin recommended a **wellness** program designed to promote overall health and fitness.*

wholesome, *adj.* Conducive to good health or well-being; tending to suggest health, soundness, or vigor. Also used to refer to things that improve the mind or character, as in a wholesome movie for children. Wholesome sometimes has a negative connotation as bland or uninteresting.

*The day care center purported to stage a variety of **wholesome** activities, although in actuality, it let the children watch cartoons all day long.*

salutary, adj. Promoting or conducive to health; healthful. Promoting or conducive to some good purpose; beneficial.

*Norma's proposal for a babysitting co-op among all the company's flex-time working mothers was a **salutary** idea.*

copacetic, *adj.* Good, excellent, fine. Copacetic is a term of broad scope and can refer to health, procedures, plans, etc. Anything that can go awry can be or remain copacetic.

*During the three-day conference, Diana phoned her store daily to see if everything was still **copacetic.***

 Also explore: constitution, *healthful*, *nutritive*, vigor.

Health (Not Well)

iatrogenic, *adj.* Caused by medical treatment. Iatrogenic refers to symptoms, ailments, or disorders induced by drugs or surgery or caused by diagnosis or treatment by a physician. When you exit a hospital in worse shape than when you went in, you're the victim of an iatrogenic situation—and a potential plaintiff in a malpractice case.

> *Bernie's respiratory infection was found to be **iatrogenic;** he picked it up while he was hospitalized for his kidney stones.*

malaise, *n.* A vague feeling of physical discomfort or uneasiness, such as early in an illness. Also used to refer to a vague awareness of moral or social decline.

> *The society was suffering from a moral **malaise**.*

indisposed, *adj.* Slightly ill or ailing.

> *Rachel's sinus drainage was making her feel **indisposed** so she went home early.*

fallow, *adj.* Pale-yellow; brownish-yellow.

> *As the disease progressed, Simon took on a **fallow** complexion.*

infirmity, *n.* Feebleness; weakness. Infirmity often denotes a frailty or ailment, such as from old age.

> *As he grew older, Melvin experienced a greater number of **infirmities**.*

 Also Explore: affliction, ailment, deficiency, *placebo.*

Clean

---

pristine, *adj.* Still pure. Pristine implies a natural state, free from the encroachment of modern society. Pristine means natural; virgin means untouched by man; unspoiled means existing in its original state.

*From a distance, the Rocky Mountains had a kind of **pristine** beauty.*

---

virgin, *adj.* Up to this time unused, unworked, undiscovered by man.

*There were thousands of acres of **virgin** forest less than a mile from his front door.*

unspoiled, *adj.* Not marred or impaired. Unspoiled implies something in its original condition.

*The new fallen snow was **unspoiled** by footprints.*

sanitary, *adj.* In a clean, healthy condition. Can infer a lack of emotional warmth.

*The operating room was completely **sanitary**.*

sterilized, *adj.* Free from living microorganisms, such as by subjecting to great heat or chemical action.

*The nurse **sterilized** the operating instruments.*

Also Explore: antiseptic, hygienic, pasteurized, uncorrupted, untrod.

Putting in Order

stratum, *n.* A horizontal layer or section of material, especially any of several lying one upon another. Stratum also refers to any of the socioeconomic groups of a society as determined by birth, income, education, and so on.

*The middle **stratum** was composed of workers earning $40,000 to $60,000 per year.*

stratify, *vt.* To form or arrange in layers or strata.

*Dean attempted to **stratify** the customer base in terms of income level.*

systematize, *vt.* To form into or arrange according to a set of facts, principles, rules, etc. Systematize implies a logical, pragmatic order.

*Kelly was charged with **systematizing** the month-end closing operation.*

taxonomy, *n.* The science of classification; laws and principles covering the classifying of objects.

*The formal naming of the newly discovered plant was a question of **taxonomy.***

nomenclature, *n.* The system or set of names used in a specific branch of learning or activity, as in biology or plants and animals, or for the parts of a particular mechanism.

*The first-year medical students needed to learn the **nomenclature** to better communicate with the staff physicians.*

Also Explore: *catalog,* codify, hierarchy, progression, succession.

Generations

soccer mom, *n.* A suburban woman with one or more children who play soccer. Soccer moms—typically married women in their 20s, 30s, or 40s—have become a distinct demographic group whose societal and political concerns revolve around their children and families and stress educational issues and family values.

> *The Senator realized that he had to win the* **soccer mom** *vote if he wanted to carry the heartland.*

baby boomer, *n.* A person born in the U.S. during the great increase in birthrate in the years following World War II. Boomers are the largest single generation in American history and have tended to define cultural tastes and habits for the larger society.

> *As the* **baby boomers** *began to age, the burden on the Social Security system increased.*

Generation X, *n.* The generation of persons born in the 1960s and 1970s, the children of the baby boomers.

> *Carolyn noticed that her* **Generation X** *staff had a different work ethic from that of the older baby boomers.*

tweener, *n.* A person born in the generation between the baby boomers and the Generation Xers. Don't confuse with tweenager, which refers to 9- to 14-year olds.

> *Mark was a* **tweener**—*too young to be a boomer but not quite part of the Gen X group.*

slacker, *n.* A person who shirks work or duty. Slackers are that subset of Gen Xers regarded as apathetic, and irresponsible.

> *Matt was a* **slacker,** *spending most of his time hanging out at the mall.*

 Also Explore: *apathetic, demographics, psychographics, sandwicher, tweenager.*

Music (Part 2)

---

tempo, *n.* The speed at which a musical composition is or is supposed to be performed. The tempo is indicated by such notations as allegro, andante, etc. or by reference to metronome timing (number of beats per minute).

*The conductor preferred to perform the second movement at a slightly faster **tempo** than normal.*

---

allegro, *adj.* Fast; faster than allegretto but not so fast as presto. The opposite of andante (slow).

*The waltz was to be performed **allegro** for a very fast dance.*

fortissimo, *adj.* Very loud; louder than forte. The opposite of pianissimo (very soft), which is softer than piano.

*The final passage, complete with tympani and cymbals, was performed **fortissimo.***

key, *n.* The main tonality of a composition. The key is based on a root note and can be either major or minor.

*Sherry transposed the song to the **key** of A-minor.*

coda, *n.* A more or less independent passage added to the end of a section or composition to reinforce the sense of conclusion.

*The maestro instructed the orchestra to start the rehearsal at the **coda** because it had previously perfected the main body of the piece.*

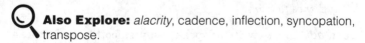 **Also Explore:** *alacrity,* cadence, inflection, syncopation, transpose.

Speaking

lexicon, *n.* The special vocabulary of a particular author, field of study, group, and so on. Most professions and hobbies tend to have their own special words (or common words with special meanings) that comprise their own unique lexicon. Many lexicons are filled with jargon and acronyms.

> *Although outsiders thought she was speaking in code, Beatrice was simply well-versed in the* **lexicon** *of accounting.*

vernacular, *n.* The common, everyday language of ordinary people in a particular locality. Also used to describe the shop talk or idiom of a profession or trade. Vernacular refers to the informal or colloquial variety of a language as distinguished from the formal or literary variety.

> *In the* **vernacular** *of the hotel trade, a cancelled reservation is a "no show."*

dialect, *n.* The form or variety of a spoken language peculiar to a region, community, social group, occupational group, and so on. Dialect refers to a form of language differing from the standard language in matters of pronunciation, syntax, etc.

> *In her travels, Frieda learned to quickly pick up the local* **dialect** *so as not to sound like an outsider.*

eloquent, *adj.* Having a vivid, forceful, fluent, graceful, and persuasive speaking style; vividly expressive.

> *Mitchell's* **eloquent** *farewell speech brought many in the audience to tears.*

fluent, *adj.* Able to write or speak easily, smoothly, and expressively. Often used to describe a facility to speak in a foreign tongue.

> *Henderson was* **fluent** *in both Japanese and Spanish.*

 Also Explore: articulate, colloquial, lingo, polyglot.

Writing

---

calligraphy, *n.* Literally means beautiful writing. Specifically it refers to beautiful handwriting, especially as an art; handwriting; penmanship. Calligraphy is done by hand only.

> *Carey's* **calligraphy** *business nearly quadruples in the spring, due to the huge demand for wedding invitations.*

---

wordsmith, *n.* A person, especially a professional writer, who uses language skillfully; a person who coins new words. A wordsmith connotes a person who is interested in language for its own sake and the words they use or develop are generally more eclectic and even eccentric than particularly useful.

> *Mark was told by his editor that he was quite a* **wordsmith;** *he wasn't quite sure it was a compliment.*

compendium, *n.* A summary or abstract containing the essential information in a brief form; concise but comprehensive treatise. Despite the sound of this word it does not refer to a large work.

> *Michael's desk encyclopedia was quite a handy* **compendium** *of facts and information.*

monograph, *n.* A book or long article, especially a scholarly one, on a single subject or a limited aspect of a subject.

> *Erik's* **monograph** *on the benefits of reintroducing wolves into the larger national parks was so convincing it managed to start legislation for their reintroduction to some select smaller parks.*

tome, *n.* A book, especially a large, scholarly, or ponderous one.

> *Susan was looking for some light summer reading; she didn't want to spend weeks poring over some slow-moving* **tome.**

Also Explore: *abridge,* exposition, lexicographer, *opus,* *treatise.*

Fakes

---

forgery, *n.* The act or legal offense of imitating or counterfeiting documents, signatures, works of art, and so on to deceive. In legal terms, the false making or material altering, with intent to defraud, of any writing that, if genuine, might be the foundation of a legal liability.

> *When it was revealed that the entire manuscript was a **forgery,** the agent who transacted the deal was forced to return the publisher's advance.*

---

counterfeit, *adj.* To make in imitation of something genuine to deceive or defraud; forged.

> *The ring was **counterfeit,** a poor imitation of the original.*

plagiarism, *n.* The act of taking an idea, plot, etc. from another and passing it off as one's own.

> *After he borrowed liberally from the subject's own autobiography, Kevin was accused of **plagiarism.***

ersatz, *adj.* Substitute or synthetic. Ersatz usually suggests inferior quality.

> *The **ersatz** diamonds didn't fool Cavandish; he knew the ring was a fake.*

reproduction, *n.* Copy, close imitation, duplication, and so on.

> *The painting on the wall was a **reproduction;** the original was the property of a museum in France.*

Also Explore: *facsimile*, piracy, pretense, simulacrum, synthetic.

Ruin

DAY
239

---

sully, *vt.* To soil, stain, tarnish, or besmirch, especially by disgracing. Sully implies casting aspersions on a person or institution.

> *The gossip about his relationship with the divorcee **sullied** the minister's reputation among his parishioners.*

---

besmirch, *vt.* To bring dishonor to.

> *The revelation that the general accepted bribes from a foreign country **besmirched** his hard-earned reputation for honesty.*

desecrate, *vt.* To take away the sacredness of; treat as not sacred.

> *The vandals **desecrated** the gravestones in the cemetery.*

eradicate, *vt.* To tear out by the roots; uproot; wipe out; destroy. Eradicate and extirpate both suggest the extinction or abolition of something. Eradicate connotes less violence and, often, the working of natural processes or a methodical plan.

> *Donald carefully and methodically **eradicated** every vestige of his ex-wife's presence in their once happy home.*

obliterate, *vt.* To blot out or wear away, leaving no traces; erase. Obliterate implies doing away with completely so that no trace is left.

> *The secretary **obliterated** all records pertaining to the affair so no one could trace the evidence back to her.*

 Also Explore: aspersions, efface, extirpate, *profane*.

Remove

---

expurgate, *vt.* To remove passages considered obscene or otherwise objectionable. To expurgate is to purify by removing objectionable matter; expurgate has censorous connotations.

> *The religious council suggested that several offensive passages be **expurgated** from the script.*

---

expunge, *vt.* To erase or remove completely; blot out or strike out; delete; cancel.

> *All details pertaining to the illegal operation were **expunged** from the record.*

extricate, *vt.* To set free; release or disentangle.

> *Marty found it hard to **extricate** himself from the group; they kept calling him and asking him to dinners and other functions.*

eviscerate, *vt.* To deprive of an essential part; take away the force and significance of.

> *The committee **eviscerated** the proposal, leaving nothing that would offend even one of its constituents.*

defenestrate, *vt.* Throw something out a window.

> *In a fit of anger, Warren climbed to the top floor and **defenestrated** the bowling trophy.*

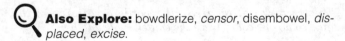 **Also Explore:** bowdlerize, *censor*, disembowel, *displaced*, *excise*.

Make it Easier

---

grease, *vt.* To influence by giving money to; bribe or tip. Grease can also refer to any activity that makes it easier to perform a subsequent activity.

*Harold **greased** the palms of the city council to get the zoning ordinance passed.*

---

bribe, *n.* Anything, especially money, given or promised to induce a person to do something illegal or wrong.

*Joan **bribed** the official $100 to dismiss the charges pending against her.*

lubricate, *vt.* To make slippery or smooth. One who is intoxicated is often referred to as lubricated.

*Al needed to **lubricate** the hinges to get rid of the annoying squeak.*

imbibe, *vt.* To drink, especially alcohol.

*Kenneth must have **imbibed** an entire fifth by himself.*

intoxicated, *vt.* Made drunk; stupefied; inebriated. When one imbibes too much, one becomes intoxicated.

*When Nicki became **intoxicated,** she got sleepy.*

 Also Explore: *carouse, graft, nepotism, quaff, suborn.*

Worldwide

---

import, *vt.* To bring goods from another country or countries, for purposes of sale. Compare to export, which is to carry or send goods to another country or countries. A country that has more exports than imports has a favorable balance of trade.

> *The U.S. **imported** virtually all its television sets from the Far East or Mexico.*

---

global, *adj.* Of, relating to, or including the whole earth; worldwide. Global implies a scope beyond domestic operations.

> *ReallyBig Co. sought to be a **global** force by acquiring the leading player in the European market.*

domestic, *adj.* Made or produced in the home country; native.

> *International Inc.'s **domestic** operations only contributed a third of its total worldwide revenues.*

multinational, *n.* A corporation with branches in a number of countries.

> *The two **multinationals** were both looking for local acquisitions in the Pacific Rim.*

internationalism, *n.* The principle or policy of international cooperation for the common good.

> *The Senator preached a policy of **internationalism,** believing that U.S. companies would benefit from the increased access to foreign markets.*

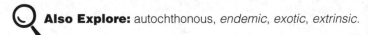 **Also Explore:** autochthonous, *endemic, exotic, extrinsic.*

Here, There, and Everywhere

ubiquitous, *adj.* Present, or seeming to be present, everywhere at the same time. Ubiquitous implies something so common it appears to be all places.

*The **ubiquitous** white minivans filled up the parking lot; each one contained a soccer mom and at least two tow-headed moppets.*

universal, *adj.* That which can be used for a great many or all kinds, forms, sizes, and so on; highly adaptable. Universal implies applicability to every case or individual, without exception, in the class, category, etc. concerned.

*The need for love is **universal;** the ability to love, less so.*

endemic, *adj.* Constantly present in a particular region.

*The labor shortage was **endemic** in Smallville.*

proximity, *n.* The state or quality of being near; nearness in space, time, and so on.

*Don's **proximity** to Mr. Big helped him gain frequent access to the corner office.*

venue, *n.* The scene or locale of a large gathering, such as for a sports event or rock concert.

*The promoter opted for a larger **venue** for the concert when the smaller hall sold out in less than an hour.*

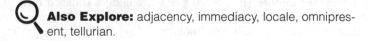

Also Explore: adjacency, immediacy, locale, omnipresent, tellurian.

New Technology

DAY 244

---

hypertext, *n.* Information stored in a computer and specially organized so that related items which are linked together can be readily accessed. Hypertext is the basis of the World Wide Web.

*Julie clicked on the **hypertext** link to jump to a list of related Web sites.*

---

interactive, *adj.* A continual exchange of information between the computer and its user.

*The computer-based tutorial was completely **interactive,** requiring active participation from the student.*

multimedia, *n.* A computer-based method of presenting information by using more than one medium of communication and emphasizing interactivity. A multimedia application might include images, sounds, video, and text in multiple fonts and styles.

*The edutainment software required a **multimedia** PC for optimal playback.*

new media, *n.* Digital or electronic publishing, such as on CD-ROM or online. Note: the definition of "new" is always changing, some sectors are already starting to regard CD-ROMs as "old media."

*The shift to **new media** publishing caught many newspapers by surprise.*

convergence, *n.* The act, fact, or condition of converging. Digital convergence implies the merging of various digital-based technologies, such as the computer, the Internet, digital telephones, into one all-encompassing technology.

*Many old media companies feared the coming digital **convergence.***

 Also Explore: *digital*, edutainment, hyperlinks, nodes, resolution.

Capacity

bandwidth, *n.* Attention span. A person with high bandwidth has a large attention span and can deal with multiple inputs simultaneously; this can also be referred to as multitasking. A person with low bandwidth can only deal with a few items at one time and thus has lower mental capacity.

*Bill thought his attorney had low **bandwidth;** she could only handle one train of thought at a time.*

acumen, *n.* Keenness and quickness in understanding and dealing with a situation; shrewdness.

*Robert spent years honing his business **acumen** so that he could react quickly to any possible situation.*

aptitude, *n.* A natural ability or talent; quickness to learn and understand.

*Florence's **aptitude** for numbers put her in good stead among the other members of the group.*

competence, *n.* Condition or quality of being well qualified, capable, or fit. One who is competent is not necessarily a star but can get by in most cases.

*Joan's **competence** at the task was barely enough to win her the job, given the high standards set by the rest of the staff.*

repertoire, *n.* (rep-er-twar) from the French (an inventory). The stock of special skills, devices, and techniques of a particular person or particular field of endeavor.

*Janet's marketing **repertoire** included copywriting, design, and market analysis.*

 Also Explore: *capacity*, *facility*, *genius*, multitasking.

After-Dinner Drinks

---

sherry, *n.* A fortified wine varying in color from light yellow to dark brown, made in the Jerez region of southwestern Spain. Sherries can be dry or sweet, light and ethereal, or robust, heavy, and rich. There are two general types of sherries, fino (lightest) and olorosso (heavier, higher in alcohol content).

*Roberto preferred a dry **sherry** after dinner.*

---

port, *n.* A sweet, usually dark-red, fortified, rich, alcoholic, and full-bodied wine, shipped from the Oporto region in the north of Portugal. Port wines are classic examples of fortified dessert wines that seem to age forever. There are several distinctive types of port, including ruby port, tawny port, vintage port, and crusted port.

*Edward chose a ruby **port** for its sweetness.*

brandy, *n.* An alcoholic liquor distilled from wine; a similar liquor distilled from the fermented juice of a specified fruit, such as cherry brandy.

*Lloyd and Melinda shared a **brandy**.*

cognac, *n.* (kahn-yak) from the French. A French brandy distilled from wine in the classic brandy region of France, located along the Atlantic coast north of Bordeaux; loosely, any French brandy.

*Gina celebrated by ordering an expensive **cognac**.*

cordial, *n.* An aromatic, syrupy alcoholic drink; liqueur.

*The entire group retired to the study for **cordials**.*

Also Explore: *aqua vitae, espresso, liqueur,* snifter.

Required

obligatory, *adj.* Legally or morally binding. An obligation implies a binding contract, promise, or moral responsibility or a duty imposed legally or socially.

As required by his employment contract, Richard spent the ***obligatory*** *two weeks at the management training program.*

prerequisite, *adj.* Something required beforehand, especially as a necessary condition for something following.

Working in the warehouse was a ***prerequisite*** *for joining the manufacturing department.*

dictate, *n.* An authoritative command.

Without consulting the board, Mr. Big issued a ***dictate*** *that forbade wearing shorts on casual Fridays.*

mandate, *n.* An authoritative order or command, especially a written one. A dictate can be verbal or written; a mandate must be written.

Dawn received a copy of the no-smoking ***mandate*** *in her inbox.*

request, *n.* The act of asking, or expressing a desire, for something.

It was a simple ***request:*** *Come into work this Saturday to help finish the project on time.*

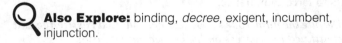 **Also Explore:** binding, *decree,* exigent, incumbent, injunction.

Permanent

entrench, *vt.* To establish securely. Entrench implies a permanence, something firmly fixed and not likely to be uprooted. Entrench is often used pejoratively to refer to a practice or belief that is undesirable and next to impossible to eliminate.

> *The inward focus was an **entrenched** part of the company culture in spite of its potentially disastrous effect on marketplace performance.*

constancy, *n.* The state or quality of being unchanging; a firmness of mind or purpose, a steadiness of affections or loyalties, or a freedom from variation or change.

> *The numbers showed a **constancy** from month to month.*

resolute, *adj.* Having or showing a fixed, firm purpose; determined; resolved; unwavering. Resolute implies having a goal and sticking to it.

> *Ann was **resolute** that she would purchase a new house by the end of the year.*

steadfast, *adj.* Not changing, fickle, or wavering; constant. Steadfast implies stable and unmoving.

> *The candidate's **steadfast** support of the antiabortion plank cost him the nomination.*

resilient, *adj.* Recovering strength, spirits, good humor, and so on quickly. Resilient implies the ability to withstand repeated efforts to force compliance.

> *Despite the numerous setbacks, Roger showed **resilience** and continued to progress on his chosen career path.*

 Also Explore: abiding, interminable, *perennial*, *tenacious*.

Temporary

---

ephemeral, *adj.* Short-lived. Ephemeral literally means existing only one day and, by extension, applies to that which is markedly short-lived.

> *Donald knew his glory was **ephemeral** because new results were being announced the next day.*

---

transitory, *adj.* Of a passing nature; not enduring or permanent. Transitory refers to that which by its very nature must sooner or later pass or end.

> *As he gazed down into his father's casket, Richard realized that life was **transitory**.*

fleeting, *adj.* Passing swiftly; not lasting. Fleeting implies of a thing that it passes swiftly and cannot be held.

> *Alas, it was only a **fleeting** thought, lost forever to the recesses of her mind.*

evanescent, *adj.* Tending to fade from sight; vanishing. Evanescent applies to that which appears momentarily and fades quickly away.

> *For however briefly, Sherry cherished the **evanescent** image of his face.*

vicissitude, *n.* A condition of constant change or alternation, such as a natural process. Vicissitude implies a regular succession or alternation, such as of night and day.

> *After many **vicissitudes** of fortune, Don conquered his demons and rose to a higher level.*

 Also Explore: ad hoc, diversity, meteoric, *mutable*, transient.

Original

progenitor, *n.* A forefather; ancestor in direct line. Also used to refer to a source from which something develops, such as an originator or precursor.

> *The government's ARPANET was the **progenitor** of today's Internet.*

prototype, *n.* The first thing or being of its kind; original. Prototype implies that others will ensue from the original—that is, that the prototype is not the only one made.

> *VisiCalc was the **prototype** for all spreadsheet software that followed.*

archetype, *n.* The original pattern, or model, from which all other things of the same kind are made. An archetype infers something that serves as a symbol. Archetype and prototype are often used interchangeably.

> *The **archetype** for all representative bodies was the House of Commons.*

exemplar, *n.* A person or thing regarded as worthy of imitation. Exemplar doesn't necessarily imply that a thing will be imitated, only that it is worthy of being imitated.

> *Michael Jordan was an **exemplar** of success for all would-be basketball stars.*

icon, *n.* An image; figure; representation. An icon is not the original but is often held as an ideal.

> *The bald eagle stood as an **icon** of America's fighting spirit.*

 Also Explore: *aboriginal,* innovative, *model, primordial.*

Football

---

kickoff, *n.* A place kick that puts the ball into play at the beginning of each half or after a touchdown or field goal.

*After the **kickoff,** the Colts had possession at their 20-yard line.*

---

down, *n.* One of four consecutive plays in which a team, in order to keep possession of the ball, must either score or advance the ball at least ten yards. Down also describes the state of a player who has just been tackled and a ball that a player touches to the ground in the end zone to get a touchback.

*After the 30-yard gain, it was first **down** at the 50-yard marker.*

audible, *n.* A play decided upon and called by the quarterback at the line of scrimmage.

*The quarterback decided that the planned play wouldn't work, so he called an **audible.***

fumble, *n.* When a ball carrier loses possession by dropping the ball or having it knocked away before a play ends; the first player to regain possession of the loose ball is said to make the recovery, and his team becomes the offense.

*The Chiefs' possession ended with a **fumble** when the quarterback lost the ball during a pass rush.*

line of scrimmage, *n.* An imaginary line, parallel to the goal lines, on which the ball rests at the start of each play and on either side of which the teams line up.

*The ball was returned to the **line of scrimmage.***

Also Explore: possession, quarterback, snap, tackle, touchback.

Fired Up

incite, *vt.* To urge to action; stir up. Incite implies an urging or stimulating to action, either in an favorable or an unfavorable sense.

*Leaping to the platform, Marvin tried to **incite** the crowd to rush the gates.*

embroil, *vt.* To draw into a conflict or fight; involve in trouble.

*Against his will, Jack became **embroiled** in the controversy.*

perpetrate, *vt.* To do or perform; be guilty of. Perpetrate implies something evil, criminal, or offensive.

*Glynneth was charged with **perpetrating** the foul deed.*

engender, *vt.* To bring into being; bring about; cause; produce. One can engender anything, conflicts included.

*Winona **engendered** a show of support for her downsized colleagues.*

exhort, *vt.* To urge earnestly by advice, warning. Exhort implies urging others to do what is proper or required.

*Juliet **exhorted** her group to get back to work so they could meet the assigned deadline.*

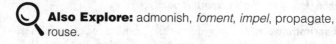 **Also Explore:** admonish, *foment*, *impel*, propagate, rouse.

Courage

---

intrepid, *adj.* Not afraid; bold; fearless; very brave. Intrepid implies absolute fearlessness, especially in facing the new or unknown.

> *Sir William's **intrepid** journey to the wilds of Africa captivated the reading audience.*

---

valiant, *adj.* Full of or characterized by courage or bravery; resolute or determined. Valiant emphasizes a heroic quality in the courage or fortitude shown.

> *Johnson made a **valiant** effort to save his employees from the downsizing, knowing full well it could cost him the support of the senior management team.*

audacious, *adj.* Bold or daring; fearless. Audacious suggests an imprudent or reckless boldness.

> *Joan's **audacious** accusations proved unfounded.*

bravado, *n.* Pretended courage or defiant confidence where there is really little or none.

> *Brad put on a show of **bravado** even though he was trembling in his boots.*

machismo, *n.* Overly assertive or exaggerated masculinity, especially as characterized by a show of virility, domination of women, and so on. In many cultures, the exaggerated posturings of machismo behavior are not well received.

> *Josef's **machismo** alienated him with his female superior.*

 Also Explore: dauntless, élan, mettle, plucky.

Winning and Losing

Rubicon, *n.* A point beyond which engagement is unavoidable. The Rubicon is a small river in northern Italy that formed a boundary between Cisalpine Gaul and the Roman Republic; when Caesar crossed the Rubicon in 49 B.C., it led irrevocably to war with Pompey. Meeting one's Rubicon refers to reaching a turning point.

> *Oliver had met his **Rubicon;** from this point on, there was no turning back.*

---

massacre, *n.* The indiscriminate, merciless killing of a number of human beings. Can also refer to an overwhelming defeat in business or sports.

> *The launch of the new product was so successful it resulted in a marketplace **massacre** of the other competitors.*

blood bath, *n.* A killing of many people. A blood bath does not have to be indiscriminate (as does massacre); it can also be a ruthlessly planned mass killing. Blood bath can also refer to a huge money-losing endeavor.

> *ReallyBig Co. took a **blood bath** on the failed launch of the new product.*

pillage, *vt.* To deprive of money or property by violence; loot. Pillage implies an assault for gain of some kind.

> *InterGlobal Corp. **pillaged** the units of the new acquisition, leaving only the top performers intact.*

stalemate, *n.* Any unresolved situation in which further action is impossible or useless; draw.

> *It was a **stalemate** between the company and the union; neither side would budge on its demands.*

 Also Explore: booty, checkmate, plunder, *theft.*

Financial Statements

---

balance sheet, *n.* A financial statement summarizing the assets, liabilities, and net worth of an individual or a business at a given date. The balance sheet is so called because the assets equal the sum of the liabilities and the net worth; that is, the two parts of the sheet must be in balance.

> *The **balance sheet** showed that the firm was in a cash positive situation.*

P & L, *n.* Profit and loss statement, also called an income statement; a financial statement that summarizes the various transactions of a business during a specified period, showing the net profit or loss. Note that the balance sheet shows net worth, whereas the P & L shows net profits.

> *The **P & L** showed a net loss for the period.*

asset, *n.* All the entries on a balance sheet showing the entire resources of a person or business, tangible and intangible, including accounts, cash, inventory, equipment, etc.

> *The company needed to sell some long-term **assets** to improve its liquidity.*

liability, *n.* The debts of a person or business, such as notes payable or long-term debentures. For a corporation, current liabilities are debts payable within 12 months; long-term liabilities are debts payable over a period of more than 12 months.

> *The current **liabilities** exceeded the estimated cash flow, putting the firm in a precarious position.*

net worth, *n.* The difference between the value of assets that are owned and the debts that are owed; total assets minus total liabilities.

> *Because of his huge debts, Richard had a negative **net worth**.*

 Also Explore: arrears, *encumbrance*, insolvency, receivable, reimbursement.

Openness

---

candid, *adj.* Very honest or frank in what one says or writes. Candid implies a basic honesty that makes deceit or evasion impossible, sometimes to the embarrassment of the listener.

> *Dana **candidly** addressed the company's performance, warts and all.*

---

frank, *adj.* Open and honest in expressing what one thinks or feels; straightforward. Frank applies to a person, remark, and so on that is free or blunt in expressing the truth or an opinion, unhampered by conventional reticence.

> *Moira was **frank** with her boss about her reasons for leaving.*

outspoken, *adj.* Unrestrained in speech. Outspoken suggests a lack of restraint or reserve in speech, especially when such might be preferable.

> *Beverly remained **outspoken** on the issue, despite warnings from her superiors.*

uninhibited, *adj.* Free from the usual social or psychological restraints, such as in behavior.

> *Ava's **uninhibited** behavior at the party was shocking to her co-workers' spouses.*

glasnost, *n.* (glas-nost) from the Russian (opportunity to be heard). The official internal policy of candor in publicizing the problems and weaknesses of Soviet or Russian society.

> *In the spirit of **glasnost,** the ex-party official admitted that the funds had been mismanaged.*

 Also Explore: explicit, reticence, sincere, unrestrained.

Sex (Same)

---

bisexual, *n.* A sexual orientation in which one feels attracted to both males and females. A bisexual is sometimes referred to as AC/DC or "going both ways."

*Woody Allen once joked that being **bisexual** doubles one's chances of getting a date on Saturday night.*

---

gay, *n.* Homosexual. Gay typically refers to a male homosexual.

*John came out of the closet and told his parents that he was **gay**.*

lesbian, *n.* A female homosexual.

*The bar was a gathering place for gays and **lesbians**.*

transsexual, *n.* A person who is predisposed to identify with the opposite sex, sometimes so strongly as to undergo surgery and hormone injections to effect a change of sex. A transsexual in the process of undergoing a sex change is referred to as pre-op; one who has completed the process is referred to as post-op.

*Roberta was a post-op **transsexual** who used to be known as Robert.*

transvestite, *n.* A person who derives sexual pleasure from dressing in the clothes of the opposite sex. Transvestites are not necessarily homosexual or transsexual; they just like wearing the other gender's clothing.

*Edward was a closet **transvestite**, dressing in his wife's clothing when she wasn't at home.*

Also Explore: androgynous, gender, hermaphrodite, orientation, Sapphic.

Duplicate

---

replica, *n.* A reproduction or copy of a work of art, especially a copy by the maker of the original. Loosely, replica can refer to any very close reproduction or copy.

*He couldn't afford the real thing, but Daniel did own a **replica** of the original Shelby Cobra.*

---

facsimile, *n.* An exact reproduction or copy.

*The dip was a reasonable **facsimile** of that served at the prestigious restaurant.*

imitation, *n.* Artificial likeness; copy. Imitation implies a counterfeit.

*The figure was a clever **imitation** that only experts could tell from the original.*

clone, *n.* A person or thing very much like another. In scientific terms, a clone is a genetically identical duplicate of an organism produced by replacing the nucleus of an unfertilized ovum with the nucleus of a body cell from the organism.

*The Southpark office was a **clone** of the Richfield branch.*

surrogate, *n.* A deputy or substitute. A surrogate mother is a woman who substitutes for another unable to become pregnant, such as by undergoing artificial insemination.

*Higgins acted as Mr. Big's **surrogate** for the out-of-town meeting.*

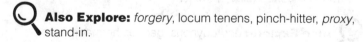 **Also Explore:** *forgery*, locum tenens, pinch-hitter, *proxy*, stand-in.

258

Rejuvenate

renaissance, *n.* (ren-eh-zans) from the French (to be born anew). A new birth; rebirth. From the Renaissance, the great revival of art, literature, and learning in Europe in the 14th, 15th, and 16th centuries. A Renaissance man is a highly cultivated individual who is skilled and well-versed in many or, ideally, all the arts and sciences.

> *The art of flag making was enjoying a* **renaissance** *in the world of crafts.*

revitalize, *vt.* To bring vitality, vigor, and so on back to after a decline.

> *The mayor announced a program to* **revitalize** *the downtown area.*

revivify, *vt.* To put new life or vigor into; cause to revive. Revivify implies a living thing, where any type of thing, living or otherwise, can be revitalized.

> *A shot of whiskey was all that was needed to* **revivify** *Uncle Bob after the long walk in the cold.*

reclaim, *vt.* To recover useful materials from waste products; to make wasteland, desert, etc. capable of being cultivated or lived on.

> *The neighbors vowed to* **reclaim** *their streets from the drug dealers.*

transfigure, *vt.* To change the figure, form, or outward appearance of; transform. Transfigure sometimes implies a deeper spiritual improvement.

> *The city was completely* **transfigured** *by the renovation of the downtown area.*

 Also Explore: metamorphose, regenerate, resuscitate, transmogrify, transubstantiate.

Golf (Part 2)

---

drive, *n.* A shot from the tee, usually with a driver. A drive is the initial shot on a given hole.

*Doug's initial **drive** was close to 200 yards.*

---

chip, *n.* A short, lofted shot, made especially from just off the putting green.

*He faced a short **chip** shot to the green.*

putt, *n.* A shot made on the putting green in an attempt to roll the ball into the hole.

*Unfortunately, he blew par with a two-**putt** on the eighth hole.*

rough, *n.* Any part of the course where grass, weeds, and so on are allowed to grow, uncut, forming a hazard or obstacle.

*The ball was in the **rough;** it was going to be a difficult shot.*

sand trap, *n.* A pit or trench filled with sand, serving as a hazard on a golf course.

*He blasted out of the **sand trap** to within inches of the hole.*

 Also Explore: driver, green, hazard, loft.

Doctors (Part 2)

psychiatrist, *n.* A doctor of medicine who specializes in the study, treatment, and prevention of disorders of the mind, including psychoses and neuroses, emotional maladjustments, etc.

*The **psychiatrist** prescribed Prozac to control Buck's mood swings.*

psychologist, *n.* A specialist in the science dealing with the mind and with mental and emotional processes. A psychologist is a person trained in methods of psychological analysis and counseling.

*Renee's **psychologist** suggested additional counseling sessions to address her fear of flying.*

pediatrician, *n.* A doctor of medicine who specializes in the study of the development and care of infants and children and with the treatment of their diseases, illnesses, and so on.

*The twins got booster shots at the **pediatrician's** office.*

gynecologist, *n.* A doctor of medicine who specializes in the study and treatment of the diseases of the female reproductive system, including the breasts.

*Margot made an appointment with her **gynecologist** for her annual pelvic exam.*

obstetrician, *n.* A medical doctor who specializes in the care and treatment of women during pregnancy, childbirth, and the ensuing period. An ob-gyn is a doctor that is both obstetrician and gynecologist.

*When Linda's **obstetrician** performed an ultrasound, she found out she was carrying a baby boy.*

 Also Explore: dermatologist, endocrinologist, *homeopathy*, neurologist, psychoanalyst.

False

---

mock, *adj.* Sham; false; imitation; pretended. Can also designate a food that imitates another. A mock-up is a scale model, usually a full-sized replica, of a structure or apparatus used for instructional or experimental purposes.

> *The attorneys put Orville through **mock** questioning before the trial; they needed to be sure he could keep his cool under pressure.*

---

faux, *adj.* (foh) from the French (false). False or artificial. A faux pas is a social blunder or error in etiquette that causes embarrassment.

> *Marsha wore **faux** diamonds to the charity event, preferring to leave the real gems in their safe deposit box.*

fraudulent, *adj.* Acting with intentional deception; deceitful.

> *The used car salesman engaged in **fraudulent** activity when he rolled back the car's odometer.*

erroneous, *adj.* Containing or based on error; mistaken; wrong.

> *I was **erroneous** in my assumption that Carol wanted me to ask her out; she laughed in my face!*

apocryphal, *adj.* Of doubtful authorship or authenticity; not genuine; counterfeit. Apocryphal suggests in particular that which is of doubtful authenticity or authorship.

> *Professor Ryan began to think that Joseph's dissertation was largely **apocryphal**. He'd never known the young man to possess such writing skill; it had to be someone else's work.*

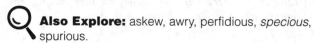

Also Explore: askew, awry, perfidious, *specious,* spurious.

Imitations

parody, *n.* A literary or musical work imitating the characteristic style of some other work or of a writer or composer in a satirical or humorous way, usually by applying it to an inappropriate subject.

> Airplane! *was a* **parody** *of the whole genre of airport disaster movies.*

satire, *n.* A literary work in which vices, follies, stupidities, abuses, and so on are held up to ridicule and contempt. Satire can also refer generally to any use of ridicule, sarcasm, or irony to expose, attack, or deride vices, follies, etc.

> Dr. Strangelove *was a broad* **satire** *about the follies of nuclear proliferation.*

burlesque, *n.* Any broadly comic or satirical imitation, such as of a writing, play, and so on. Burlesque implies the handling of a serious subject lightly or flippantly or of a trifling subject with mock seriousness.

> *The comedy troupe presented a* **burlesque** *that made light of a recent airplane disaster.*

lampoon, *n.* Lampoon refers to a piece of strongly satirical writing that uses broad humor in attacking and ridiculing the faults and weaknesses of an individual.

> *The college paper printed a* **lampoon** *of the university president.*

caricature, *n.* A picture or imitation of a person, literary style, etc. in which certain features or mannerisms are exaggerated for satirical effect.

> *He was dismayed to see his* **caricature** *hanging on the wall of the restaurant.*

 Also Explore: *affectation, deride,* incongruous, spoof.

263

Market Presence

brand, *n.* The kind or make of a commodity. Marketers strive to create a brand identity for products or lines of products, that describes (in psychographic terms) how people feel about a particular brand and how they incorporate it into their lifestyles.

*The marketing department discovered that only consumers from the lower income bracket were asking for their product by the **brand** name.*

label, *n.* An identifying brand of a company producing recorded music. For example, the Atlantic music label is part of the Time-Warner company.

*The artist formerly known as Bob decided to jump **labels** when his last CD didn't receive adequate promotion.*

logo, *n.* A distinctive company signature, trademark, colophon, motto, newspaper nameplate, and so on. For example, the Simon & Schuster logo is a distinctive drawing of a sower "sowing the seeds of knowledge."

*The brand group needed a dynamic **logo** for the new product's package.*

slogan, *n.* A catch phrase used to advertise a product. For example, Nike's original slogan was "Just do it."

*Now that they had the logo and the package, they needed a catchy **slogan** for the new product line.*

market share, *n.* The percent of sales in a given market for a specific product or company. One point of market share equates to one percent of total sales in the category; market share can be measured in either units sold or revenues generated.

*The new product attained five points of **market share** in its first six months on the market.*

 Also Explore: colophon, emblem, insignia, *psychographic*, trademark.

Selling

e-commerce, *n.* E-commerce (also known as electronic commerce) refers to online sales transacted over the Internet. Commerce in general refers to the buying and selling of goods, especially when done on a large scale between cities, states, or countries; trade.

> *As a result of its new website, the consulting firm expected* ***e-commerce*** *to grow to $2 billion by the year 2000.*

commodity, *n.* Anything bought and sold; any article of commerce. Commodity implies an interchangeability between two or more virtually indistinguishable products.

> *Toilet paper has become a* ***commodity;*** *the different brands are hard to tell apart.*

transaction, *n.* A business deal or agreement. A transaction is an individual sale to a person or entity.

> *Each online* ***transaction*** *was verified by a third-party security firm.*

trade *n.* The buying and selling of commodities or the bartering of goods; commerce. Dealings or the market involving specified commodities, customers, seasons, etc. In a comprehensive sense it refers to all the persons or companies in a particular line of business or work.

> *In the soft drink* ***trade,*** *ReallyBig Co. was known to be practically unassailable due to its market clout.*

traffic, *vt.* To buy and sell; barter. Somewhat historically, traffic means to trade over great distances; commerce. Specifically, it refers to commerce of a wrong or illegal kind.

> *The veterinarian was* ***trafficking*** *in a potent drug designed for cats every Friday and Saturday night along the disco strip.*

 Also Explore: barter, conferring, liquidate, *procure,* *solicit.*

Persuasion

---

proselytize, *vt.* To try to convert a person to one's religion. To proselytize is to persuade another to follow a new faith; preach to others the superiority of a new religion, idea, philosophy, and so on.

*Kurt insisted on **proselytizing** the values of Buddhism to his disinterested co-workers.*

---

propaganda, *n.* Any systematic, widespread dissemination or promotion of particular ideas, doctrines, or parties to further one's own cause or to damage an opposing one.

*The anti-union **propaganda** was surreptitiously sponsored by the company.*

tract, *n.* A propagandizing pamphlet, especially one on a religious or political subject.

*June read the libertarian **tract** with open skepticism.*

treatise, *n.* A formal, systematic article or book on some subject; a discussion of facts, evidence, or principles and the conclusions based on these.

*The professor's **treatise** on nuclear power was well received by the academic community.*

jingoistic, *adj.* Boasting of patriotism and favoring an aggressive, threatening, warlike foreign policy. Someone who is jingoistic is blindly and aggressively nationalistic.

*The Senator's **jingoistic** exhortations were a prelude to recommending military action against the terrorist state.*

 Also Explore: colporteur, *entice, inveigle,* missionary, revivalist.

Pretty Darned Good

Utopian, *adj.* Founded upon ideas envisioning perfection in social and political organization. Utopian implies idealism; someone who is Utopian is a visionary.

*Dan's dreams of a **Utopian** society were dashed by the reality of the American workplace.*

---

idyllic, *adj.* Pleasing and simple; having to do with the country life.

*Uncle Ben looked forward to an **idyllic** retirement in the country.*

impeccable, *adj.* Not liable to sin, incapable of wrongdoing; without defect or error; faultless; flawless.

*The new process was **impeccable;** the team had considered every contingency.*

optimal, *adj.* Most favorable or desirable; best. Optimal implies the most efficient or effective choice.

*The **optimal** solution didn't maximize revenues but did maximize profits.*

superb, *adj.* Rich or splendid; extremely fine; excellent. Superb is pretty good but not impeccable or optimal.

*Madeline found the meal **superb,** a dining experience par excellence.*

Also Explore: exquisite, irreproachable, pastoral, picturesque, visionary.

Center of Attention

---

protagonist, *n.* The main character in a drama, novel, or story around whom the action centers. A person who plays a leading or active part in any action is also referred to as a protagonist.

*Winnie was a chief **protagonist** in the upcoming sexual harassment lawsuit.*

---

authority, *n.* A person with much knowledge or experience in some field, whose information or opinion is hence reliable; expert. Also refers to the self-assurance and expertness that come with experience.

*Dr. Benjamin was the leading **authority** on skin disease among the geriatric homeless.*

pundit, *n.* A person who has or professes to have great learning; actual or self-professed authority.

*The **pundits** predicted that ReallyBig Co. would fail with their new line of products.*

braggart, *n.* An offensively boastful person.

*Yes, Jim was a **braggart,** but he also had much to boast about.*

antihero, *n.* The protagonist of a novel or play who lacks the virtues and estimable traits of a traditional hero.

*The character of Remington Wolcott was a classic **antihero,** a detective with questionable values and unclear motivation.*

Also Explore: artiste, braggadocio, maven, vaunter, virtuoso.

Spectators

box, *n.* A small, enclosed group of seats, such as in a theater, stadium, and so on. Seats in a box are, naturally, called box seats—and typically command a premium price.

*The company leased a luxury **box** for all home hockey games.*

balcony, *n.* An upper floor of rows of seats in a theater or auditorium, often jutting out over the main floor; gallery.

*Jim and Mary liked to sit in the **balcony,** where they could get a birds-eye view of the action.*

mezzanine, *n.* In some theaters, the first few rows of the balcony, separated from the others by an aisle.

*Winnie paid extra for the **mezzanine** seats.*

floor, *n.* The bottom part of a hall, theater, auditorium, or stadium. Floor-level seats refer to seats on the playing level at an indoor sporting event, such as a basketball game; for outdoor events, the same seats would be called field-level.

*As a special treat, John got four tickets on the **floor** to the next basketball game.*

bleachers, *n.* A section of cheaper seats, usually bare benches in tiers without a roof, for spectators at outdoor sporting events.

*The ambience more than made up for the view when sitting in the **bleachers** for a Cubs game.*

 Also Explore: arcade, balustrade, gallery, loggia, tier.

Indirect

oblique, *adj.* Not straight to the point; not straightforward; indirect. Oblique implies a brief and largely irrelevant or inaccurate response, kind of a glancing blow.

*At first the witness' answers were rather **oblique**; however, when prompted, she gave a more straightforward response.*

meandering, *adj.* Wandering or rambling aimlessly. To meander is to move from one place to the next without purpose; an uneventful, unfocused, unproductive effort. Meandering suggests completely irrelevant movement or discourse.

*Mrs. Ricketts responded to the question with a **meandering** response that never really addressed the central issue.*

skew, *vt.* To bias, distort, or pervert. To skew is to distort by causing to emphasize one response over another.

*The questions on the survey were worded in such a way as to **skew** the responses in a favorable direction.*

circuitous, *adj.* Roundabout; indirect; devious.

*James gave a long, **circuitous** explanation for why the orders had not arrived as expected.*

tangential, *adj.* Merely touching a subject, not dealing with it at length. Tangential implies emphasizing only one small part of a larger issue—and not necessarily the most important part.

*The rookie stockbroker collected a voluminous amount of information, most of it only related to the new offering in a **tangential** way.*

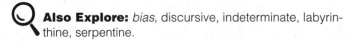 **Also Explore:** *bias*, discursive, indeterminate, labyrinthine, serpentine.

Getting Help

confidant, *n.* A close, trusted friend, to whom one confides intimate matters or secrets, especially those relating to affairs of love. Confidant implies a closer and more intimate relationship than does advisor or consultant.

> *Steve was honored to be one of Mr. Big's **confidants;** he knew what was going to happen days before the rest of his peers.*

advisor, *n.* One who gives advice, opinions, or counsel. An advisor can be retained in an official or an unofficial capacity.

> *The president consulted his **advisors** to determine how to respond to the latest union demands.*

consultant, *n.* An expert who is called on for professional or technical advice or opinions. A consultant is an expert advisor.

> *Annabelle hired a **consultant** who was experienced in direct mail.*

aide-de-camp, *n.* An officer in the army, navy, and so on serving as assistant to a superior. Now used generically for an assistant to an official person such as a Mayor or Senator. Usually just shortened to aide.

> *As **aide-de-camp,** Max did everything: getting her cups of coffee, and reviewing drafts of legislation for spelling and grammar.*

counsel, *n.* A mutual exchange of ideas, opinions, etc. Advice resulting from such an exchange or any advice, for that matter. More specifically, counsel refers to a lawyer giving advice about legal matters. Do not confuse with council, which simply refers to a meeting—advice exchanged or not.

> *Blaine served as Mr. Big's legal **counsel,** which put him in the public eye more than he personally cared for.*

 Also Explore: cabinet, confabulate, intimate, *mentor,* preceptor.

Moderating

buffer, *n.* Any person or thing that serves to lessen shock or prevent sharp impact, such as between antagonistic forces. Employing too much of a buffer in-between layers of an organization will tend to leave upper levels out of touch with what is really happening at the ground level.

> *The marketing department served as a **buffer** between the engineers and the sales force; the engineers couldn't understand sales-speak, and the sales reps didn't care about the technical details spouted by the engineers.*

countervail, *vt.* To make up for; compensate; to counteract; avail against.

> *Management **countervailed** the unexpected loss by closing down two unprofitable branch offices.*

stabilize, *vt.* To make steady or firm; to keep from changing or fluctuating, such as in price.

> *Closing the offices **stabilized** the firm's profit level.*

balance, *n.* A weight, force, effect, or piece of information that counteracts another or causes equilibrium.

> *Herman's conservative position served as a crucial **balance** to Suzanne's more liberal leanings.*

equilibrium, *n.* A state of balance or adjustment of conflicting desires, interests, and so on.

> *After a time, the marketplace reached a state of **equilibrium,** with no one player making gains at another's expense.*

Also Explore: counteract, counterpoise, DMZ, mitigation, negate.

Just Say No

DAY
273

---

deny; *vt.* To declare a statement untrue; to refuse to accept as true or right. Deny implies a refusal to accept as true, real, valid, existent, or tenable.

> *Mr. Big emphatically **denied** having any prior relationship with Andi.*

---

contradict, *vt.* To assert the opposite of what someone else has said. Contradict not only implies emphatic denial, but, in addition, often suggests belief or evidence that the opposite or contrary is true.

> *Andi **contradicted** Mr. Big's account of the story, outlining a totally different series of events.*

impugn, *vt.* (im-pyoon) To attack by argument or criticism; oppose or challenge as false or questionable. Impugn implies a direct, forceful attack against that which one calls into question.

> *Mr. Big **impugned** Andi by attacking her character and motivation.*

refute, *vt.* To prove a person to be wrong. Refute not only denies something, but also it goes the extra step of trying to prove it wrong.

> *Andi **refuted** Mr. Big's personal attacks by showing how honest she had been in the past.*

repudiate, *vt.* To refuse to have anything to do with; disown or cast off publicly.

> *In the end, Mr. Big **repudiated** the charges and refused to acknowledge Andi when he saw her in the halls.*

 Also Explore: balk, confute, demur, disown, *untenable.*

Cults

zealot, *n.* A person who is ardently devoted to a purpose to an extreme or excessive degree. Zealot implies vehement activity in support of a cause. Zealous behavior is often seen by those not closely involved as irrational and baseless.

*Because of her extreme anti-abortion views, Max thought Maddie was a right-wing **zealot**.*

indoctrinate, *vt.* To instruct in, or imbue with, doctrines, theories, or beliefs, such as of a sect.

*The cult tried to **indoctrinate** Paula in its history and methods.*

deprogram, *vt.* To cause to abandon a rigid commitment to certain beliefs or values, such as those of a religious cult, by undoing the effects of indoctrination.

*Paula needed to be **deprogrammed** before she could fully leave the cult behind.*

intervention, *n.* The act of coming between as an influence to modify, settle, or hinder some action. More formally, when one or a group of people confront a person who is an addict or member of a cult and intervene in a way to modify that person's behavior.

*Don's friends participated in an **intervention** to keep him from joining the cult.*

martyr, *n.* Any person tortured or killed because of his or her beliefs; any person who assumes an attitude of self-sacrifice or suffering to arouse feelings of pity, guilt, etc. in others.

*The cult leader dreamed of becoming a **martyr** to the cause by sacrificing himself in a terrorist act.*

 Also Explore: *denomination*, intercession, *propaganda*, *proselytize*.

Obsess

---

preoccupy, *vt.* To occupy the thoughts of to the virtual exclusion of other matters. Preoccupy implies that vital matters are ignored or left undone while one is occupied elsewhere.

*Joan was **preoccupied** with the details of her upcoming nuptials, and her work suffered for it.*

---

engross, *vt.* To take the entire attention of; occupy wholly. One can be engrossed with something yet not entirely preoccupied—meaning other matters will still be taken care of.

*David was **engrossed** in the latest Stephen King novel; he found it difficult to put down the book.*

immerse, *vt.* To absorb deeply. Immerse implies a rapid and intense learning process.

*Greg **immersed** himself in preparing for his new assignment, poring over reams of research reports and industry analysis.*

enthrall, *vt.* Literally means to make a slave of; enslave. Now of course, this is used figuratively to describe someone who is completely at something or someone's command. Not entirely a bad thing, enthrall can also mean to hold as if in a spell; fascinate.

*Paul was **enthralled** by the possibilities of the new product. He worked day and night to ensure its success.*

consume, *vt.* To destroy, to use up. It can mean to spend wastefully; squander (time, energy, money). Also, to eat or drink up; devour. Finally, it can mean to absorb completely; engross or obsess. In this latter sense, consume means all of these things; a person who is consumed by something often feels used up and even destroyed.

*The project **consumed** Dwight for six months. When it was finished he felt like a mere shadow of his former self.*

 Also Explore: bewitch, captivate, engage, *fanatic,* monopolize.

275

Internet Programming

HTML, Hypertext Markup Language, the language behind documents on the World Wide Web. A subset of Standard Generalized Markup Language (SGML), HTML includes capabilities that enable authors to insert hyperlinks.

*Marcus learned to code in **HTML** so he could fine-tune the appearance of his personal Web pages.*

Java, *n.* A high-level programming language, similar to C/C++, widely used for programming on Web sites and pages.

*After he mastered **Java**, Marcus could add some snazzy applets to his Web pages.*

Perl, Practical Extraction and Report Language, a UNIX-based interpreted scripting language that is specifically designed for scanning text files, extracting information from these files, and preparing reports summarizing the information. Perl is widely used to create CGI scripts that handle the output of HTML forms.

*To better interface his Web site to the UNIX server, Marcus needed to learn **Perl**.*

CGI, Common Gateway Interface, a standard that describes how World Wide Web servers should access external programs so that the data is returned to the user in the form of an automatically generated Web page. CGI programs, called scripts, often come into play when a Web user fills out an on-screen form.

*By incorporating **CGI** scripts, Marcus could add forms to his Web pages.*

script, *n.* A series of instructions that tells a program how to perform a specific procedure; a very simple type of programming language. Perl, CGI, and HTML are all scripting languages.

*Marcus wrote a **script** that let users automatically send him e-mail direct from his home page.*

 Also Explore: applet, interpret.

Hypothetical

---

theoretical, *adj.* Limited to or based on theory; hypothetical. Theoretical implies something proceeding as according to theory, even though actual practice might not prove this out.

> *The application of the vaccine was only **theoretical;** it had yet to undergo laboratory testing.*

---

academic, *adj.* Having no direct practical application.

> *The argument was **academic** because no one had actually applied for the post.*

speculative, *adj.* Of, characterized by, or having the nature of thought or conjecture.

> *All comments were **speculative;** no one really knew what was going to happen.*

conceptual, *adj.* Of a generalized idea of a thing or class of things; abstract notion.

> *Lyle favored a **conceptual** approach that embodied the Apostolic ideals.*

reputed, *adj.* Generally accounted or supposed to be such.

> *Ralph was the **reputed** owner of the unwashed coffee cup sitting on the lunchroom counter.*

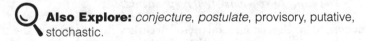

Also Explore: *conjecture, postulate,* provisory, putative, stochastic.

Research

margin of error, *n.* The difference between a computed or estimated result and the actual value, such as in mathematics. The statistical margin of error is the percentage difference between reported results from the sample group and estimated results in the population at large.

*There was a **margin of error** of ± 2 percent, meaning the actual results in the general population could range from 18 to 22 percent.*

focus group, *n.* A panel interview of a small group of people led by a moderator. Focus groups—typically with 10 to 15 participants—provide a forum for discussion, ideas, and feedback and can generate valuable qualitative market research information

*The **focus group** was convened to determine consumer attitudes towards the company's core brand.*

questionnaire, *n.* A written or printed form used in gathering information on some subject or subjects, consisting of a set of questions to be submitted to one or more persons.

*There were 2000 **questionnaires** returned.*

sample, *n.* A sample is a subset of a population from which data are collected and then used to estimate parameters of the total population.

*The **sample** size was 1000 respondents.*

accuracy, *n.* Precision; exactness. Accuracy in research is the degree to which a sample statistic would correspond to the population parameter it is meant to estimate if there were no random errors. Accuracy is high when bias is low.

*Due to the careful screening process, there was a high degree of **accuracy** in the results.*

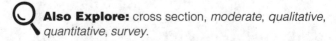 **Also Explore:** cross section, *moderate, qualitative, quantitative, survey.*

Leaning Toward

bias, *n.* A mental leaning or inclination; partiality. In statistical research, bias is a non-random error that causes survey estimates to differ from population values. Biases often associated with survey procedures include those caused by questionnaire wording, interviewing techniques, coding, incomplete coverage, and so on.

The survey was suspect because the questions reflected the ***bias*** *of the testing firm.*

inclination, *n.* A particular disposition or bent of mind; a liking or preference. Inclination refers to a more or less vague mental disposition toward some action, practice, or thing.

Bob had an ***inclination*** *toward the blue package.*

propensity, *n.* A natural inclination or tendency. Propensity implies an inherent inclination, as well as an almost uncontrollable attraction.

Sue's ***propensity*** *to say what was on her mind got her into hot water with her boss.*

predilection, *n.* A preconceived liking; partiality or preference. Predilection implies a preconceived liking formed as a result of one's background or temperament that inclines one to a particular preference.

When it came to buying books, Ralph had a ***predilection*** *for murder mysteries.*

penchant, *n.* A strong liking or fondness; taste.

Ned's ***penchant*** *for tall blondes didn't sit well with his wife, a short brunette.*

 Also Explore: *affinity,* appetite, preconceived, *prejudice,* proclivity.

Government

PAC, Political action committee, an organization created and managed by a private group to provide financial support to candidates seeking public office. They solicit campaign contributions from private individuals and distribute these funds to political candidates who share their political, economic, or social agendas.

*The **PAC** contributed to the Senator's campaign and tried to influence his vote on the upcoming legislation.*

lobbyist, *n.* A person, acting for a special interest group, who tries to influence the introduction of or voting on legislation or the decision of government administrators.

*The **lobbyist** took the representative out to dinner in an attempt to woo his vote for the bill.*

Congress, *n.* The legislature of the U.S., consisting of the Senate and the House of Representatives. Even though members of both the House and the Senate are members of Congress, only members of the House are called Congressmen.

***Congress** is one of the three branches of government in the U.S.*

House, *n.* Short for House of Representatives, the lower house of the legislature of the U.S. A member is referred to as either a Congressman or a Representative. Members of the House are elected to two-year terms.

*All members of the **House** were up for reelection in the fall.*

Senate, *n.* The upper house of the legislature of the U.S. A member is called a Senator. Senators are elected to six-year terms.

*The **Senate** would be back in session in January.*

 Also Explore: bicameral, *bureaucracy, executive,* judicial, legislative.

Groups (Part 2)

cabal, *n.* A small group of persons joined in a secret, often political intrigue. A cabal is a group whose members craftily formulate a plan for deceiving others. More generally, it can refer to any group whose objectives are self-serving and whose methods are deceptive and suspect.

> The **cabal** secretly plotted to overthrow the government in a surprise coup.

cadre, *n.* An operational unit, such as of staff officers or other key personnel, around which an expanded organization can be built. A cadre is a small, unified group organized to instruct or lead a larger group and becomes the nucleus for the larger group.

> A small **cadre** of managers was sent to build the company's European operations.

cartel, *n.* An association of industrialists, business firms, etc. for establishing a national or international monopoly by price fixing, ownership of controlling stock, and so on. Cartel is the European term for a trust and usually implies an international trust.

> The oil barons formed a **cartel** for the expressed purpose of inflating gasoline prices.

coalition, *n.* A temporary alliance of factions or nations, for some specific purpose, such as a group of political parties in times of national emergency.

> The **coalition** of manufacturers lobbied the government for tax breaks that would be specific to their industry.

consortium, *n.* A partnership or association. A consortium can be, but not always, a temporary alliance of two or more business firms in a common venture.

> The three firms formed a **consortium** to set standards for e-commerce transactions.

 Also Explore: *alliance*, cooperative, junta, *syndicate*.

On Your Own

---

ostracize, *vt.* To banish, bar, or exclude by common consent, such as from a group or from acceptance by society. To ostracize someone is to deliberately exclude him or her from a social circle.

*After his embarrassing behavior at the picnic, Ray was **ostracized** by the entire neighborhood.*

---

outcast, *n.* A person or thing cast out or rejected, such as by society.

*Nick's liberal views made him an **outcast** in the traditionally Republican household.*

pariah, *n.* Any person despised or rejected by others.

*After alienating the entire staff, Jeff was a **pariah** in the company.*

hermit, *n.* A person who lives alone in a lonely or secluded spot, often from religious motives.

*Dharma decided to leave the materialistic world behind and become a **hermit.***

iconoclast, *n.* One who attacks and seeks to destroy widely accepted ideas, beliefs, and so on.

*Bernie was labeled an **iconoclast** by attacking the ideals originally set forth by the company's founder.*

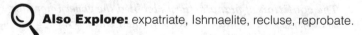

Also Explore: expatriate, Ishmaelite, recluse, reprobate.

---

investment, *n.* The amount of money put into a business, real estate, stocks, or bonds for the purpose of obtaining an income or profit. All of your investments collectively are called your portfolio.

> *Jack's upfront* **investment** *in the business gave him a 25 percent equity.*

---

equity, *n.* The value of property beyond the total amount owed on it in mortgages or liens. Can also refer to the funds contributed by the owners of a business.

> *Monica's total* **equity** *was over $100,000.*

ownership, *n.* Legal right of possession; lawful title to something. The word ownership is sometimes used to imply accountability, such as an individual taking ownership of a project.

> *Elroy took* **ownership** *of the project, rather than abandon it to the black hole of bureaucracy.*

accountability, *n.* Obliged to account for one's acts. Accountability implies liability for which one may be called to account.

> **Accountability** *for the performance of the new product line rested squarely on Shawnia's shoulders.*

responsible, *adj.* Expected or obliged to account for something or to someone; answerable. Responsible applies to one who has been delegated some duty or responsibility by one in authority and who is subject to penalty in case of default.

> *The board held Gordon* **responsible** *for the acquisition.*

 Also Explore: *appropriate, hostile takeover,* lien, title.

Obtaining Things

procure, *vt.* To get or bring about by some effort; obtain. Suggests active effort or contrivance in getting or bringing to pass.

> *It took some effort, but Joel was able to* ***procure*** *the documents from senator Randolph's safe deposit box.*

secure, *vt.* To make sure or certain; guarantee; ensure, as with a pledge. To get hold or possession of; obtain. To bring about; cause. Implies difficulty in obtaining something and perhaps in retaining it.

> *Karen talked to each board member individually to further* ***secure*** *in writing the acceptance of her radical proposal.*

acquire, *vt.* To get or gain by one's own efforts or action. To come to have as one's own; get possession of (to acquire certain traits). Implies a lengthy process in the getting and connotes collection or accretion (he acquired a fine education).

> *Carmen* ***acquired*** *her black belt only after seven years of arduous training and competition.*

buydown, *n.* A financing technique used to reduce the monthly payments for the first few years of a loan. Funds in the form of discount points are given to the lender to buy down or lower the effective interest rate paid by the buyer, thus reducing the monthly payments for a set time.

> ***Buydown*** *mortgages make a home more affordable in the early years; homeowners can refinance if rates drop.*

mortgage, *n.* The pledging of property to a creditor as security for the payment of a debt. A mortgage is typical type of loan used to buy a house.

> *Lane and Darlene calculated that they could afford a $200,000* ***mortgage*** *for their new home.*

 Also Explore: *collateral,* consideration, lease, *point.*

Real Estate (Part 2)

closing, *n.* The conclusion or consummation of a transaction. In real estate, closing includes the delivery of a deed, financial adjustments, the signing of notes, and the disbursement of funds necessary to the sale or loan transaction.

*The agent set the **closing** on the Hausers's house for Friday.*

commission, *n.* A fee or a percentage of the proceeds paid to a salesperson, broker, and so on, either in addition to, or in lieu of, wages or salary. In real estate, a commission is the payment to a broker for services rendered, such as in the sale or purchase of real property.

*The two agents split the **commission** on the sale because one represented the seller and the other represented the buyer.*

ARM, Adjustable rate mortgage, a loan characterized by a fluctuating interest rate, usually one tied to a bank or savings and loan association cost-of-funds index.

*Looking for ways to reduce their monthly payments, Bob and Karen investigated an **ARM**.*

balloon mortgage, *n.* The balance of the mortgage is due in a lump sum at the end of the term and is considerably larger than the required periodic payments because the loan amount was not fully amortized.

*Bob and Karen took a 5/25 **balloon mortgage;** their five years are fixed at a 7 percent interest rate, and the balloon payment comes due at the end of the fifth year.*

fixed-rate mortgage, *n.* A loan characterized by a single unchangeable interest rate. Fixed-rate mortgages are not adjustable and have no balloon payments.

*The 5/25 balloon was one point lower than a traditional **fixed-rate mortgage**.*

 Also Explore: *amortize,* disbursement, interest, *periodic, principal.*

Legalese

conditional, *adj.* Containing, implying, or dependent on a condition or conditions; qualified; not absolute. In legal terms, a condition is a clause in a contract, will, and so on that revokes, suspends, or modifies one or more of its stipulations upon the happening of an uncertain future event.

> *The closing was **conditional** on the seller making the listed repairs.*

clause, *n.* A particular article, stipulation, or provision in a formal or legal document.

> *His lawyer added a **clause** dealing with the future sale of the property.*

amendment, *n.* A revision or addition proposed or made in a bill, law, constitution, contract, etc.

> *The company's attorney wanted an **amendment** to the contract guaranteeing stay bonuses for the senior management staff.*

proxy, *n.* The authority to act for another; a document empowering a person to act for another, such as in voting at a shareholder's meeting.

> *Mr. Big assigned power of **proxy** to Jameson in the case of his absence.*

indemnify, *vt.* To repay for what has been lost or damaged; compensate for a loss; reimburse. Legally, the indemnified party is protected against liabilities or penalties from that party's actions; the indemnifying party provides the protection or reimbursement.

> *The company **indemnified** Hart from any liabilities resulting for his actions while he was acting for the company.*

 Also Explore: *abrogate, atone, countervail,* remunerate.

Verdicts

decree, *n.* An official order or decision; a decision or order of the court. A final decree is one that fully and finally disposes of the litigation. An interlocutory decree is a preliminary decree that is not final.

*The court issued a final **decree** in the Higgins case.*

writ, *n.* A formal legal document ordering or prohibiting some action. A writ is a court order requiring the performance of a specified act or giving authority to have the act done.

*The **writ** prohibited the firm from building on the disputed property.*

acquittal, *n.* A setting free or being set free by judgment of the court. In legal terms, an acquittal is the legal certification of the innocence of a person who has been charged with a crime, setting the person free from a charge of guilty by a finding of not guilty.

*The attorney argued for **acquittal** on all counts.*

appeal, *n.* The transference of a case to a higher court for rehearing or review. In legalese, a proceeding by which a party seeks an appellant court review of the action taken by a trial court; notice of appeal from the trial court must be filed within a specified period of time after the judgment is rendered.

*On **appeal,** the higher court reversed the previous decision.*

punitive damages, *n.* Damages awarded to the plaintiff beyond the actual loss, imposed as a punishment for the defendant's wrong. Also known as exemplary damages.

*RealluBig Co. was fined $2 million in **punitive damages.***

 Also Explore: edict, exonerate, *litigate*, *petition*, suit.

Exact

fastidious, *adj.* Not easy to please; very critical. A fastidious person is meticulous, exacting, and sensitive to procedure—sometimes to the point of obsession.

*Paul's office was **fastidiously** maintained with not a single detail out of place; he even alphabetized all the business cards in his Rolodex.*

punctilious, *adj.* Very careful about every detail of behavior, ceremony, and so on. As with fastidious, punctilious conveys an extreme behavior that may not be seen as normal in some quarters.

*Robinson was a **punctilious** host, attending to every detail of the affair.*

precise, *adj.* Strictly defined; accurately stated; definite. Precise implies something that strictly conforms to usage, rules, etc.

*The wording in the contract was **precise;** Jonathan could find no loophole.*

rigorous, *adj.* Rigidly precise; thoroughly accurate or exact.

*The new boxes were designed to meet **rigorous** standards for shipping damage.*

veracity, *n.* Habitual truthfulness; honesty; accuracy or precision, as of perception; that which is true.

*Nina confirmed the **veracity** of Darlene's story; all the facts were true.*

Also Explore: *accuracy,* definitive, discriminating, pedantic.

Mostly

effectively, *adv.* In effect; actually. Effectively implies something in actuality, not merely potential or theoretical, and is used to moderate what might otherwise be too extreme a statement for the actual circumstances.

> *As the group's de facto number two, John **effectively** ran the department while his boss was on vacation.*

essentially, *adv.* Basically. Essentially implies something fundamentally so. As with effectively, essentially tones down the nature of a statement, providing some "wiggle room" in case the statement is challenged.

> *The new product was **essentially** the old product in new packaging.*

primarily, *adv.* Mainly; principally. Primarily implies something mostly—but not completely—so.

> *Jim's feelings towards Jane were **primarily** platonic— except for when she wore that low-cut red dress!*

substantially, *adv.* Considerably; in a large part. Substantially implies something large enough to be considered so.

> *His work record **substantially** qualified him for the promotion.*

predominantly, *adv.* Having ascendancy, authority, or dominating influence over others; superior. Also, most frequent, noticeable, and so on.

> *Motosportif motorcycle company was **predominantly** represented at the trade show.*

 Also Explore: immeasurably, preponderant, prevailing, principally, prodigiously.

Air Travel

---

hub and spoke, *n.* The routing system employed by most major airlines that incorporates a main "hub" airport and multiple outlying "spoke" airports. The primary purpose of the hub and spoke system is to increase the airline's load factor by bringing passengers together (to the hub airport) from smaller markets (the spoke airports).

> The **hub and spoke** *system meant that there were few direct flights from the Midwest to the West coast that didn't stop at the Chicago hub first.*

---

direct flight, *n.* A flight that is routed directly from one city to another with no stops in-between. Contrast a direct flight with a connecting flight, which routes the traveler through an interim airport and includes a layover between flights.

> *Francis preferred to take a* **direct flight,** *thus avoiding time-wasting layovers.*

cabin, *n.* The enclosed section of an aircraft where the occupants sit. The cabin includes the passenger section and the cockpit, which is where the pilot, copilot, and flight crew operate.

> *The* **cabin** *was completely full.*

bulkhead, *n.* Any of the upright partitions separating parts of the airplane. Typically, there is a bulkhead separating the cockpit from the main passenger cabin and another bulkhead separating the first class section from the coach class section.

> *Patty hated* **bulkhead** *seats because she couldn't stretch her legs or store her bag under the seat in front of her.*

emergency exit row, *n.* The rows of seats adjacent to the emergency exit doors. Seats in this row typically have slightly more legroom than regular seats.

> *Patty requested a seat in the* **emergency exit row.**

 Also Explore: layover, load factor.

Stopping

paralysis, *n.* Any condition of helpless inactivity or of inability to act. Paralysis suggests not being able to act for some reason and implies a degree of helplessness. Paralysis is sometimes used figuratively to refer to the inability of a person or institution to take action in a given situation.

> *Hemmings suffered a **paralysis** of nerve after his three prior initiatives crashed and burned.*

cessation, *n.* A ceasing, or stopping, either forever or for some time. Cessation implies a temporary halt.

> *Immediately after Christmas the sales force noticed a **cessation** of new account orders.*

desist, *vi.* To cease; stop. Desist implies a permanent halt.

> *The court ordered the parties to **desist** from discussing the case with the media.*

discontinuance, *n.* The stopping of a legal action prior to trial, either voluntarily by the plaintiff or by order of the court.

> *Before the trial could begin, the court issued a **discontinuance**.*

belay, *vt.* To hold; stop; cancel.

> ***Belay** that order!*

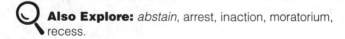 **Also Explore:** *abstain*, arrest, inaction, moratorium, recess.

Giving Up

---

capitulate, *vi.* To give up (to an enemy) on prearranged conditions; surrender conditionally. Capitulate comes from the practice of settling or drawing up the heads or chapters of an agreement. (The Latin word caput means "head.")

> *The company **capitulated,** conditional on the union agreeing to a new vote in 12 months.*

---

forfeit, *vt.* To lose, give up, or be deprived of as a penalty for some crime or fault. Forfeit implies a loss dictated by a third party or because of a breaking of a rule.

> *Agreeing that it had infringed on an existing trademark, ReallyBig Co. **forfeited** use of the slogan in the U.K.*

concede, *vt.* To admit as certain or proper.

> *After examining all his options, Smith **conceded** victory to Jones.*

conciliatory, *adj.* Tending to win over or reconcile. Conciliatory implies a degree of friendly behavior.

> *Trying a different tactic, the head of the union made **conciliatory** remarks to senior management.*

facilitate, *vt.* To make easy or easier.

> *The newfound communication **facilitated** an agreement between the two sides.*

Also Explore: *ameliorate, desist,* forgo, relinquish, succumb.

Still Going Strong

---

inertia, *n.* A tendency to remain in a fixed condition without change; disinclination to move or act. In physics, inertia is the tendency of matter to remain at rest if at rest, or, if moving, to keep moving in the same direction, unless affected by some outside force. Note that inertia does not imply a lack of movement, simply a lack of change.

> *Sheer **inertia** contributed to some degree of continuing sales, even after the promotion had ceased.*

---

momentum, *n.* Strength or force that keeps growing.

> *The campaign gathered **momentum** in its closing weeks.*

impetus, *n.* Anything that stimulates activity; driving force or motive; incentive; impulse. Impetus implies initiative, a pushing forward, or an energetic beginning.

> *The Senator gave **impetus** to the school standards movement when he proposed the abolition of social promotion.*

inexorable, *adj.* That which cannot be moved or influenced by persuasion or entreaty. Can also refer to that which cannot be altered, checked, and so on.

> *The unions made three **inexorable** demands that they refused to compromise on.*

unrelenting, *adj.* Refusing to yield or relent; inflexible. Can imply a lack of mercy or compassion.

> *The competition was **unrelenting,** pouring increasing amounts of funds into advertising and promotion.*

 Also Explore: *adamant*, dogged, dynamism, implacable, stamina.

Exit

---

egress, *n.* The act of going out or forth; a way out; exit. Egress can be a place or means to depart or the act of departing.

*The hall monitor barred the students from all **egress** without a hall pass.*

---

emerge, *vi.* To come forth into view; become visible; to become apparent or known.

*The new market leader **emerged** from the rest of the pack.*

hatch, *vt.* To bring (a plan or idea) into existence; especially to plan in a secret or underhanded way; plot.

*Lonnie and Veronica **hatched** a scheme to steal funds from the store's petty cash.*

decamp, *vi.* To go away suddenly and secretly; run away.

*The executives decided to **decamp** and close down the remote office.*

excise, *vt.* To remove by cutting out or away.

*Higgins **excised** all connection to the prior administration by reassigning the last of the former team.*

Also Explore: *abscond*, emanate, exodus, *extricate*, vacate.

Floor Plans

---

open floor plan, *n.* An office design incorporating large open spaces, few permanent walls, and individual offices comprised of short, portable walls. The individual offices in an open floor plan are called cubicles (or cubes). An open floor plan hopes to inspire a nonterritorial environment that is easily reconfigured when necessary.

> *Dennis liked everything about the new **open floor plan** except the fact that he would have to give up his private office for a cubicle in the center of the staff bullpen.*

---

compression, *n.* The act of squeezing the square footage of space allotted to each employee in an office. The current U.S. average square foot per employee is 100 square feet—and shrinking.

> *Dennis was a victim of **compression** as the facilities department downsized average cube size to fit more employees into the main building.*

pollution, *n.* The cacophony of audio and visual noise that infects open floor plans.

> *To shield himself from the **pollution,** Dennis wore a headset tuned to a white noise generator.*

recycling, *vt.* The act of reclaiming old factories, warehouses, and so on as offices.

> *ReallyBig Co. **recycled** its old warehouse to use as the office for the new telemarketing group.*

programming, *vt.* The collaboration between architect and client that uncovers the true corporate organization and culture.

> *In the **programming** process, the architect discovered that ReallyBig Co. only cared about profits, not about employee comfort.*

 Also Explore: cubicle, *environment, facility,* space.

---

justice, *n.* The use of authority and power to uphold what is right, just, or lawful. Justice is also the administration of law and the procedure of a law court. To many people, justice implies someone getting what one is due—either positively or negatively.

*Perry believed that **justice** would be served and the culprits appropriately punished.*

---

castigate, *vt.* To punish or rebuke severely, especially by harsh public criticism.

*Warren was **castigated** at the company meeting by Mr. Big.*

incarcerate, *vt.* To imprison; jail. Using legal terminology, incarceration is described as imprisonment or confinement in a jail or penitentiary.

*The prosecutor asked the judge to **incarcerate** the defendant.*

penal, *adj.* Specifying or prescribing punishment, especially legal punishment. The penal code is a body of law dealing with various crimes or offenses and their legal penalties; penal servitude is imprisonment, usually at hard labor.

*The **penal** code provided for harsh penalties for crimes of violence.*

rehabilitate, *vt.* To put back in good condition; to bring or restore to a normal or optimal state.

*After years in prison, Morgan had lost faith in the system's ability to **rehabilitate** prisoners.*

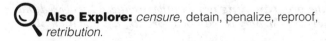 **Also Explore:** *censure*, detain, penalize, reproof, *retribution*.

Characters

---

curmudgeon, *n.* A surly, ill-mannered, bad-tempered person; cantankerous fellow. To be curmudgeonly is to be ill-tempered and difficult. For some reasons, most curmudgeons are males, and most are older.

*Uncle Walter was a **curmudgeon,** complaining all the time and ordering the other family members about.*

---

raconteur, *n.* A person skilled at telling stories or anecdotes. Raconteurs are welcomed at most social gatherings, made popular by the stories they tell—and the way they tell them.

*Uncle Ted was a true **raconteur,** entrancing all who would listen with his marvelous stories.*

Cassandra, *n.* A person whose warnings of misfortune are disregarded. A Cassandra is a person who prophesies or warns of approaching evil and is usually disregarded. Derived from classical mythology, where Cassandra was a prophet cursed by Apollo so her prophecies, although true, were fated never to be believed.

*Aunt Louise was a **Cassandra,** constantly warning of the ills that might befall others—who, most of the time, didn't bother to listen to her.*

sycophant, *n.* A person who seeks favor by flattering people of wealth or influence.

*Cousin Brett was a **sycophant,** always buttering up rich Uncle Ralph.*

misogynist, *n.* One who has a hatred of women. Misogynists are almost exclusively male.

*Uncle Jim was a lifelong bachelor, a **misogynist** who preferred to avoid what he called "the evil sex."*

 Also Explore: churl, clairvoyant, fabulist, parasite, toady.

Lodging

accommodations, *n.* In the plural, accommodations refers to lodgings or room and board. It can also generally refer to traveling space, such as on a train or airplane; seat, berth, etc.

> *The **accommodations** aboard PanWorld airlines made the more expensive ticket worthwhile for a transatlantic flight.*

amenities, *n.* Pleasant quality; attractiveness. An attractive or desirable feature, as in a place or climate. Anything that adds to a person's comfort; convenience. In the plural it refers to the courteous acts and pleasant manners of polite social behavior.

> ***Amenities** such as the salad bar and the ATM machine made the Tumbleweed Inn a real find.*

resort, *n.* A place to which people go often or generally for rest or recreation, such as on a vacation. A resort typically is a hotel with expanded amenities, such as tennis courts, a spa, and so on.

> *Two miles away was an upscale ski **resort,** complete with spa and conference facilities.*

spa *n.* Any place, especially a health resort, having a mineral spring. However, "spa" can be used generally to describe any fashionable resort or any business with exercise rooms, sauna baths, etc. As a single entity a "spa" refers to a large whirlpool bath, with ledges for seating several people.

> *Sulfer Springs was everything a **spa** should be: a resort hotel replete with mineral springs, a gymnasium and private whirlpool baths.*

bed-and-breakfast, *adj.* Accommodations, in a hotel or private home, in which breakfast is provided as part of the price. B&Bs are known for their quaint, non-commercial atmosphere.

> *Mike and Sandy decided to convert the old house into a **bed-and-breakfast.***

 Also Explore: chalet, *concierge*, hostel, sanctuary, *valet*.

Other Offices

---

headquarters, *n.* The main office, or center of operations and control, in any organization. Headquarters often dictates policy to other offices and in many cases contains a centralized backoffice operation.

> *The orders came down from* **headquarters** *to close early on Christmas Eve.*

---

branch, *n.* A division or a separately located unit of an organization.

> *The bank opened a* **branch** *in the suburban shopping center.*

satellite, *n.* Something subordinate or dependent; specifically, a small office that is organizationally and financially dependent on, and hence adjusts its policies to, a larger, more central office.

> *The* **satellite** *office was located inside the large grocery store, sharing resources with the main office.*

remote, *adj.* Far off and hidden away. A remote office is one physically or geographically far removed from central headquarters.

> *The* **remote** *office did its own hiring locally.*

centralize, *vt.* To organize under one control; concentrate the power or authority in a central organization.

> *ReallyBig Co. decided to* **centralize** *all purchasing and hiring at corporate headquarters.*

 Also Explore: division, general office, *unit*, secluded.

In Order

adjacent, *adj.* Near or close (to something). Adjacent things may or may not be in actual contact with each other, but they are not separated by things of the same kind. Two buildings side-by-side are adjacent; if a new building is built in-between them, the two older buildings are no longer adjacent.

*The new office was **adjacent** to the fast food restaurant.*

contiguous, *adj.* In physical contact; touching along all or most of one side.

*The four stores were **contiguous** with the main highway.*

consecutive, *adj.* Following in order, without interruption; successive. For example, the series "A A A" contains three consecutive letter A's; the series "A A B A" only contains two consecutive letter A's.

*The promotion ran for four **consecutive** months.*

abutting, *vi.* Ending on or leaning upon at one end; bordering on.

*The shopping center's parking lot **abutted** the farmer's field.*

annex, *vt.* To add on or attach, such as a smaller thing to a larger; append. An annex is typically a wing added to a building or a nearby building used as an addition to the main building.

*The owner decided to **annex** the field to his existing property in order to enlarge the parking lot.*

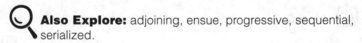

Also Explore: adjoining, ensue, progressive, sequential, serialized.

Move Beyond

excel, *vt.* To be better or greater than or superior to (another or others). Excel implies superiority in some quality, skill, or achievement over all or over the one (or ones) specified.

> *Robert **excelled** in physics, getting straight A's in all his college courses.*

exceed, *vt.* To go or be beyond. Exceed implies going beyond a stated limit, limiting regulation, measure, and so on.

> *The output of the new plant **exceeded** the original goals.*

surpass, *vt.* To excel or be superior to. Surpass implies a going beyond (someone or something specified) in degree, amount, or quality.

> *Kimberly's work **surpassed** her manager's expectations.*

transcend, *vt.* To go beyond the limits of; exceed. Transcend suggests a surpassing to an extreme degree.

> *The art exhibit **transcended** all boundaries of good taste.*

overstate, *vt.* To give an extravagant or magnified account of the facts or truth.

> *The prior year's P & L **overstated** the actual net income by $100,000.*

 Also Explore: eclipse, exaggerate, outpace, overstep, surmount.

On the Edge

---

marginal, *adj.* Close to a margin or limit, especially a lower limit; limited; minimal. Marginal implies something of trifling significance, not important enough to bother with.

*The gains on the stock were **marginal** and did not inspire him to maintain it in his portfolio.*

---

borderline, *adj.* On the boundary of what is acceptable, valid, or normal. Borderline implies having a questionable or indefinite status.

*Randy's caustic remark was **borderline** insubordination.*

collateral, *adj.* Accompanying or existing in a subordinate, corroborative, or indirect relationship.

*The salesperson left a catalog and **collateral** materials.*

peripheral, *adj.* Only slightly connected with what is essential or important; merely incidental.

*The incident was only **peripheral** to the discussion at hand.*

nominal, *adj.* In name only, not in fact.

*Frederick was the **nominal** leader; William was really in control.*

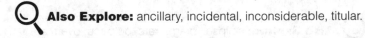

Also Explore: ancillary, incidental, inconsiderable, titular.

Leading Edge

---

bellwether, *n.* Anything suggesting the general tendency or direction of events, style, etc. Bellwether can also refer to a person who assumes leadership of a movement or activity.

> *New Hampshire was always a **bellwether** for the November presidential election.*

---

vanguard, *n.* The leading position or persons in a movement, field of endeavor, and so on.

> *Dr. Benjamin was in the **vanguard** of research into acne therapy.*

breakthrough, *n.* A strikingly important advance or discovery.

> *The new product was a **breakthrough** in high performance laser printing.*

revolutionary, *adj.* Bringing about or constituting a great or radical change.

> *The new PC included a **revolutionary** new storage medium.*

scout, *n.* A person sent out to observe the tactics of an opponent, to search out new talent, etc.

> *The **scouts** in the field reported that Biggie Mart was testing a new store concept in the Midwest.*

 Also Explore: a priori, *harbinger, progenitor,* presage, *prognosticate.*

Record

archive, *vt., vi.* To place or keep records or papers. An archive is a place where public records, documents, and so on are kept. Archive can also refer to old computer files stored on backup disks or tapes.

> *Randy decided it was time to **archive** all the old cash flow records, so he told his assistant to take the boxes out to the warehouse.*

transcribe, *vt.* To write out or type out in full (shorthand notes, a speech, etc.). Transcribe can also refer to the process of arranging or adapting a piece of music for an instrument, voice, or ensemble other than that for which it was originally written.

> *Marty **transcribed** the notes from the meeting into electronic format.*

chronicle, *vt.* To tell or write the history of; put into a historical record or register of facts or events.

> *Donna set out to **chronicle** the events of the past decade.*

catalog, *vt.* To make a complete or comprehensive list, usually with descriptive comments.

> *Sean **cataloged** all the forms available from the HR department.*

enumerate, *vt.* To name one-by-one; specify, as in a list.

> *Betsy **enumerated** the various benefits offered by ReallyBig Co.*

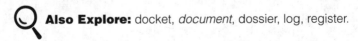 **Also Explore:** docket, *document*, dossier, log, register.

Expenses

---

variable costs, *n.* Those expenses of a business that increase directly in proportion to the level of sales in dollars or units sold. Variable costs can include cost of goods sold, sales commissions, shipping charges, delivery charges, costs of direct materials or supplies, wages of part-time or temporary employees, and sales or production bonuses.

> *The **variable costs** made up 20 percent of the product's total cost.*

---

fixed costs, *n.* Those expenses of a business that remain the same regardless of the level of sales. Fixed costs can include rent, interest on debt, insurance, plant and equipment expenses, business licenses, and salary of permanent full-time workers.

> *The plant's **fixed costs** were so high that the break-even level was unrealistic.*

overhead, *n.* The general, continuing costs involved in running a business, such as rent, maintenance, utilities, and so on. Overhead is a fixed cost.

> *The company decided to reduce **overhead** as a means of cutting fixed costs.*

break-even, *adj.* Designating that point, as in a commercial venture, at which income and expenses are equal. Any profitable sales once break-even has been reached put a business firmly in the black.

> *The **break-even** level on the new product was 20,000 units.*

black ink, *n.* A profit shown in the accounts of a bank, company, etc. (Contrast with red ink, which refers to a deficit or loss.) A profitable business is sometimes said to be "in the black."

> *If fixed costs could be brought in line, the new product line could be generating **black ink** within 12 months.*

 Also Explore: *deficit, income,* outlay, per diem, *profit.*

Jobs

vocation, *n.* A call, summons, or impulsion to perform a certain function or enter a certain career, especially a religious one. Generally, vocation can simply refer to any trade, profession, or occupation.

*Selling real estate was a **vocation** for Marvin. He felt impelled to find each of his clients their dream home.*

appointment, *n.* A naming or selecting for an office or position. Usually used to designate a promotion to a prestigous position by virtue of past accomplishments or particular skills.

*Melissa received the news of her **appointment** to the president's cabinet with a feeling of self satisfaction.*

work ethic, *n.* A system of values in which central importance is ascribed to work, or purposeful activity, and to qualities of character believed to be promoted by work.

*The **work ethic** of the Gen X employees paled to that of their baby boomer predecessors.*

white-collar, *adj.* Designating of clerical or professional workers or others employed in work not essentially manual. Contrast with blue-collar, referring to industrial workers, especially the semi-skilled and unskilled.

*The **white-collar** workers would be unaffected by a strike.*

workers' compensation, *n.* The compensation to an employee for injury or occupational disease suffered in connection with employment, paid under a government-supervised insurance system contributed to by employers.

*After developing carpal tunnel syndrome, Christine filed for **workers' compensation.***

 Also Explore: *executive, mission,* occupation, Protestant ethic, *retainer.*

Without a Home

destitute, *adj.* Lacking the necessities of life; living in complete poverty. Destitute implies being poor enough to need help from others.

> *After six months without a job, Allen was* **destitute;** *he was forced to ask his brother for cash to buy groceries for his family.*

homeless, *n.* Those typically poor or sometimes mentally ill people who are unable to maintain a place to live and therefore often may sleep in the streets or parks.

> *Higgins contributed to a shelter for the* **homeless.**

itinerant, *n.* A person who travels from place to place. Itinerant applies to persons whose work or profession requires them to travel from place to place.

> *ReallyBig Co. was criticized for hiring* **itinerant** *workers to harvest its seasonal crops.*

peripatetic, *adj.* Moving from place to place; walking about. Peripatetic implies a walking or moving about in carrying on some activity and is applied humorously to persons who are always on the go.

> *Ronnie's husband lived the* **peripatetic** *lifestyle of a traveling salesman.*

downtrodden, *adj.* Oppressed; tyrannized over. Downtrodden does not necessarily imply an economic condition, but rather a social one.

> *The workers in the border town were* **downtrodden,** *their rights nonexistent.*

 Also Explore: *displaced,* impoverished, mendicant, prodigal.

Ask for It

---

supplicant, *n.* A person who makes a humble request or supplication. A supplicant can be either someone who asks humbly or someone who prays. A supplication is a prayer or a request.

*The minister greeted the **supplicants** in his sanctuary for the weekly prayer session.*

---

prayer, *n.* A humble and sincere request, such as to God. A prayer is sincere; a plea is urgent; a petition is formal.

*He said a **prayer,** asking for the safety of the ones he loved.*

plea, *n.* An earnest and urgent request.

*He made a **plea** to the two parties to put aside their differences and help the community in its time of need.*

petition, *vt.* To ask formally or earnestly.

*She **petitioned** the city-county council to waive the zoning ordinance for her home business.*

solicit, *vt.* To ask or seek earnestly or pleadingly; appeal to or for.

*He **solicited** her advice on the new project.*

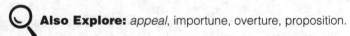

Also Explore: *appeal,* importune, overture, proposition.

Approval and Control

approbation, *n.* Approval or commendation. Approbation implies declaring or recognizing something or someone as good.

> *The crowd nodded their* **approbation** *during the Senator's speech.*

ratify, *vt.* To approve or confirm, especially to give official sanction to. Ratify implies a formal or official approval.

> *The board* **ratified** *the new contract.*

endorse, *vt.* To give approval to; support. Ratify is formal; endorse is not necessarily so.

> *Mr. Big* **endorsed** *Joe Pike in the mayoral campaign.*

command, *vt.* To have authority or jurisdiction over; control.

> *Stephenson took* **command** *of the group when Higgins left.*

entrust, *vt.* To assign the care of; turn over for safekeeping.

> *Williams* **entrusted** *the group to Gwen in his absence.*

Also Explore: acquiesce, *benediction*, carte blanche, countenance, *sanctioned*.

Protect

---

harbor, *vt.* To serve as, or provide, a place of protection to; shelter or house; conceal or hide. Harbor implies a place of security and comfort.

> *Deana **harbored** her sister-in-law after she ran away from her abusive husband.*

---

insulate, *vt.* To set apart; detach from the rest.

> *Mr. Big was **insulated** from the concerns of the workers.*

precaution, *n.* A measure taken beforehand against possible danger, failure, and so on.

> *Roy took certain **precautions** in case he was stranded in his car during a snow storm.*

guardian, *n.* A person who guards, protects, or takes care of another person or property. In legal terms, a guardian is a person legally placed in charge of the affairs of a minor or of a person of unsound mind.

> *Harry acted as Sally's **guardian** when they walked through a rough section of town.*

ward, *n.* Any person under another's protection or care. In legal terms, a child or legally incompetent person placed under the care of a guardian or court.

> *After her parents were killed in a car crash, Betty was made a **ward** of the court.*

Also Explore: asylum, custodian, garrison, haven, refuge.

Punishment (Part 3)

---

reparation, *n.* A making of amends; making up for a wrong or injury. Anything paid or done to make up for something else; compensation. Compensation by a nation defeated in a war for economic losses suffered by the victor or for crimes committed against individuals, payable in money, labor, goods, etc.

> The **reparations** segment of the victim's rights bill proved to be a stumbling block.

---

atone, *vi.* To make amends or reparation (for a wrongdoing, a wrongdoer, and so on).

> While in prison, Jordan promised to **atone** for his sins.

recompense, *vt.* To repay (a person, etc.). Recompense means to compensate for a loss.

> Mary realized that there was no way to be **recompensed** for the loss of her son.

reimburse, *vt.* To compensate for expenses, damages, losses, and so on.

> The insurance company **reimbursed** Johnson for his stolen property.

reconstitute, *vt.* To reconstruct, reorganize; to restore. Reconstitute implies to make whole.

> The court ordered ReallyBig Co. to **reconstitute** Mrs. Shields for the losses she suffered after her unjustified dismissal.

 **Also Explore:** compensate, propitiate, recompose, *reparation.*

Taking Action

---

alacrity, *n.* Eager willingness or readiness, often manifested by quick, lively action. Alacrity implies mental alertness and clarity of perception. Someone who is willing to extend herself politely and quickly for another is said to show alacrity.

> *Williams' usual **alacrity** diminished; he felt he needed a nap to restore his energy.*

---

incur, *vt.* To become subject to through one's own action; bring upon oneself.

> *By complaining to his supervisor about the late payment of his expenses, Geoff **incurred** the wrath of the accounting department.*

unilateral, *adj.* Done or undertaken by one side only; not reciprocal.

> *Jones decided to take **unilateral** action to break the stalemate.*

bilateral, *adj.* Participated in by both sides equally; reciprocal.

> *Both sides agreed to the **bilateral** action.*

multilateral, *adj.* Participated in by more than two parties, nations, etc.

> *The three companies issued a **multilateral** statement.*

 Also Explore: exploit, *incite*, *manifest*, promote.

Orderly

linear, *adj.* Made of or using lines. Two or more things arranged in a straight line are linear, as is a straight line of thought. In addition, linear can be used to a type of thinking that is logical and not complex.

*Frank's **linear** thinking kept him from recognizing a more creative alternative.*

random, *adj.* Not uniform; especially of different sizes. Random can also refer to a type of thinking that lacks aim or method and appears purposeless or haphazard.

*Tina's **random** thoughts only touched on the problem at hand.*

parallel, *adj.* Extending in the same direction and at the same distance apart at every point, so as never to meet, such as lines, planes, and so on. Two lines running side-by-side (and never meeting) are parallel.

*The two projects were running on **parallel** tracks.*

perpendicular, *adj.* At right angles to a given plane or line. A line that intersects another line at a right angle is perpendicular to the second line.

*Miles arranged his desk **perpendicular** to the wall.*

concentric, *adj.* Having a center in common. For example, circles inside of other circles are concentric.

*The bullseye was nothing more than a series of **concentric** circles.*

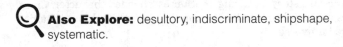

Also Explore: desultory, indiscriminate, shipshape, systematic.

Changing the Past

retcon, *n.* Retroactive continuity, a situation in continuity fiction where a new story "reveals" heretofore unknown details about events in previous stories. The most common retconning occurs in pulp fiction, especially comic books or soap operas, where the events revealed leave the "facts" the same (thus preserving continuity) while completely changing their interpretation. Prequels often retcon events presented in the original stories.

*The **retcon** changed the character's origin.*

prequel, *n.* A film, novel, etc. about events that preceded and often led up to those of another novel, film, or whatever that was produced or published earlier. Don't confuse with sequel, which is a continuation of an existing story.

*In the **prequel**, we learned just why the antagonist turned bad.*

revamp, *vt.* To renovate or revise; make over. In literature or media, a revamp takes an existing character or situation and changes it in a way that makes it fresher or more appealing.

*The writer decided to **revamp** the character for the millenium.*

revisionist, *adj.* Changed or revised, especially some accepted theory, or doctrine. Revisionist history refers to changing the documentation of historical characters or events to reflect the attitude of the current power structure or culture.

*The **revisionist** explanation was simpler, if not historically accurate.*

crossover, *n.* A fictional story in which one established character appears in a story featuring another established character. Crossovers are rare because two fictional characters seldom inhabit a shared universe.

*When Spider-Man met Superman, it was the first **crossover** between Marvel and DC Comics.*

 Also Explore: amend, rectify, renovate, sequel.

Beforehand

harbinger, *n.* A person or thing that comes before to announce or give an indication of what follows. A harbinger (person) is a forerunner; a harbinger (thing) is an omen. A harbinger foreshadows a future event or trend.

> *The slow Labor Day weekend was a **harbinger** of a disappointing holiday sales season.*

predecessor, *n.* A person who comes before another, such as in office.

> *Janet's **predecessor** left her department in disarray.*

predestined, *vt.* Decreed beforehand.

> *Hamilton was **predestined** for success; his family was wealthy and influential.*

foreshadow, *vt.* To be a sign of something to come; indicate or suggest before hand.

> *The high turnover rate **foreshadowed** the labor problems the company would encounter in the coming months.*

foreboding, *n.* A prediction, portent, or presentiment, especially of something bad or harmful.

> *Neil had a sense of **foreboding** that something bad was about to happen.*

Also Explore: foregone, herald, preordained, prefigure.

New Staff

newbie, *n.* Any person new in a position or with an organization. Newbie is specifically used online to refer to an Internet neophyte.

> *As a **newbie** to USENET newsgroups, Donna got flamed whenever she committed a breach of etiquette.*

rookie, *n.* Any novice in an activity or in an organization or business.

> *Florence was a **rookie** in the accounting department, having started two weeks ago.*

apprentice, *n.* A person who is acquiring a trade, craft, or skill under specified conditions, usually as a member of a labor union. Apprentice can be used in broader terms to refer to any learner or beginner.

> *Josef signed on as an **apprentice** fork-lift operator in the warehouse.*

intern, *n.* An intern is an employee, usually recruited from a school or university (and in most cases still a student), who is working in an organization for a limited time (normally a semester) in exchange for on-the-job training and, in most cases, school credit.

> *Melinda worked as an **intern** at ReallyBig Co. during her senior year, receiving class credit and getting real-world experience for her resumé.*

probation, *n.* A period of testing or trial. New employees often have to serve through a probationary period before they attain full employment status.

> *All new employees were put on **probation** for their first 90 days, after which they started to receive full benefits.*

 Also Explore: amateur, inductee, neophyte, novitiate, postulant.

Headhunting

recruiter, *n.* An agent or agency specializing in the recruitment of executive or highly skilled personnel. Recruiters are also known as headhunters, management consultants, executive search consultants, etc.

> *After the human relations department drew a blank, ReallyBig Co. hired an executive recruiter to help fill the vacant vice president position.*

contingency, *n.* Payment made only when certain stated conditions are met. A contingency recruiter is paid by an employer only if and when a job seeker submitted by the recruiter is actually hired.

> *Normally, ReallyBig Co. engaged recruiters on a contingency basis, paying a percentage of the new hire's first-year salary when the position was filled.*

retainer, *n.* A fee paid in advance to make services available when needed. A retainer recruiter is paid by the employer regardless of whether anyone they submit is actually hired.

> *Knowing that the VP search could take quite some time, the company decided to pay the recruiter a retainer for his ongoing search activities.*

negotiate, *vi.* To confer, bargain, or discuss with a view to reaching agreement.

> *After the lead candidate was identified, ReallyBig Co. had the recruiter negotiate a compensation package with the prospective hire.*

offer, *n.* Terms of employment proposed by an employer to a prospective employee. A job offer typically includes base salary, bonus, benefits, and any relocation expenses.

> *The offer included a $200,000 base, 40 percent performance bonus, and full relocation package.*

 Also Explore: agent, proffer, tender.

Pieces and Parts

---

comprise, *vt.* To include; contain; consist of. In careful usage, the whole comprises the parts; the whole is not comprised of the parts.

*The solution **comprised** elements from several working theories.*

---

compose, *vt.* To form in combination; make up. In careful usage, the whole is composed of all the parts.

*The team was **composed** of five talented staff members.*

component, *n.* Any of the main constituent parts of a system or thing. Component refers to any of the simple or compound parts of some complex thing or concept.

*There were three **components** to the agreement.*

element, *n.* A component part or quality, often one that is basic or essential. Element is a broad term for any of the basic, irreducible parts or principles of anything, concrete or abstract.

*The **elements** of success were carefully delineated.*

ingredient, *n.* Any of the things that a mixture is made of. Ingredient refers to any of the substances (sometimes nonessential) that are mixed together in preparing a food, medicine, and so on.

*Hard work was just one **ingredient** in the project's success.*

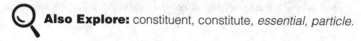

Also Explore: constituent, constitute, *essential, particle.*

Computer Parts

microprocessor, *n.* A chip used as the central processing unit (CPU) of a computer. The microprocessor provides the speed and capabilities of a computer; it is the main internal component where instructions are executed and calculations are performed.

*Jim's new computer was a real screamer with a 300MHz Pentium II **microprocessor.***

memory, *n.* A device or medium that provides temporary storage of programs and data during program execution. Memory is a computer's temporary storage capacity, measured in megabytes (Mb) of RAM (random-access memory).

*Windows needed at least 16Mb of **memory,** although it ran better with 32Mb.*

disk, *n.* A small, flat, magnetic disk for storing data permanently. There are two types of computer disks: floppy diskettes (typically with 1.4Mb of storage capacity) and hard disks (with capacity ranging from 100Mb to over 4Gb).

*Drew needed to defragment his hard **disk** to improve its performance.*

modem, *n.* A device that converts data to a form that can be transmitted by telephone. Modem is short for modulation/demodulation, modulates a digital signal into analog form (for transmittal), and then demodulates it back into digital format.

*Rhoda installed a faster **modem** to improve her connection to the Internet.*

mouse, *n.* A small, hand-held device that is moved about on a flat surface in such a way as to move or position the cursor or part of the computer's display screen. A mouse has one or more buttons on top and a cable connected to the computer.

*Sean clicked the right **mouse** button to display a pop-up menu.*

 Also Explore: CPU, cursor, defragment, DSL, ISDN.

Slow . . .

torpid, *adj.* Sluggish in functioning; slow and dull. Torpid implies slowness because of lethargy and stupidity or something or someone not capable of necessary and meaningful change.

*Nate's **torpid** performance was negatively impacting the group's workload.*

stunt, *vt.* To check the growth or development of; to hinder (growth or development).

*The lack of proper equipment **stunted** the group's progress.*

debilitate, *vt.* To make weak or feeble.

*The loss of two key players **debilitated** the group.*

placid, *adj.* Undisturbed; tranquil; calm; quiet. Placid implies peaceful, not making waves.

*Kay longed for a **placid** weekend with no interruptions from beepers or voice mail.*

latent, *adj.* Present but invisible or inactive; lying hidden and undeveloped within a person or thing, such as a quality or power.

*Tom's **latent** leadership abilities emerged during the crisis.*

Also Explore: *apathetic, dormant, enervate,* lethargic, unexcitable.

And Slower

---

dilatory, *adj.* Inclined to delay; slow or late in doing things. Dilatory implies irresponsibility in not attending thoroughly or quickly enough to what might be an important matter.

*Wally's **dilatory** work record was grounds for dismissal; he had yet to complete a project on time.*

---

deliberate, *adj.* Unhurried and methodical. Deliberate implies purposeful, measured, unhurried behavior or decision-making or a thoroughly considered action.

*Everyone thought Raymond was slow, but he was actually **deliberate;** he made sure everything was right before proceeding.*

lackadaisical, *adj.* Showing lack of interest or spirit. Lackadaisical implies a casual, disinterested attitude, attributed to mental outlook.

*A **lackadaisical** attitude toward deadlines cemented Richard's fate at the bottom of the secretarial pool.*

somnolent, *adj.* Drowsy, sleepy. Somnolent implies inattentiveness.

*The audience grew **somnolent** towards the end of Mr. Big's annual speech.*

dormant, *adj.* As if asleep; inoperative; inactive.

*The brand was **dormant,** present in the market but showing few signs of life.*

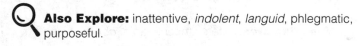 **Also Explore:** inattentive, *indolent*, *languid*, phlegmatic, purposeful.

Solid

stolid, *adj.* Having or showing little or no emotion or sensitivity; unexcitable. Stolid implies mental lethargy and a lack of appropriate empathy and suggests dullness, obtuseness, or stupidity in one who is not easily moved or excited. One who is stolid is typically indifferent to and unconcerned about interesting or compelling events.

*The mayor was **stolidly** indifferent to the pleas from the minority community, knowing that his fat cat friends in the business community could buy him the next election.*

stoic, *adj.* Showing austere indifference to joy, grief, pleasure or pain; calm and unflinching under suffering, bad fortune, and so on. Stoic specifically suggests the ability to endure suffering without flinching.

*He received the bad news with **stoic** calm.*

expressionless, *adj.* Lacking expression; blank and impassive. An expressionless face is a poker face.

*Gwendolyne sat **expressionless** during her job review, afraid to show concern over how her boss viewed her performance.*

immovable, *adj.* That cannot be changed; unyielding.

*Geoff's faith in the product was **immovable**.*

monolithic, *adj.* Something like a single large block or piece of stone in size; unity of structure or purpose; unyielding quality.

*The **monolithic** bureaucracy proved an insurmountable barrier for all but the most resolute.*

 Also Explore: austere, impenetrable, *obtuse*, *steadfast.*

Furniture (Part 2)

DAY 323

---

etagère, _n._ (ay-ta-zher) from the French. A free-standing set of open shelves that can be utilized as a room divider behind a sofa or as a modular wall unit. An etagère can also be used for displaying small art objects, ornaments, mementos, etc.

> _Bruce placed the **etagère** between the living room and the dining area._

---

inlay, _n._ Pieces of wood, metal, and so on set into a surface to make a design that is usually level with the surface. Inlays are typically decorative patterns created with pieces of different colored woods or ivory, bone, shell, or brass that have been set into cut-out sections of the base, solid wood.

> _The dining room table had an ornate **inlay** that formed a diamond pattern._

ottoman, _n._ A low, cushioned footstool. An ottoman can be either an upholstered footstool or a low seat without arms or back.

> _At the end of the day, nothing is better than stretching back and putting your feet up on the **ottoman**._

sectional, _n._ A sofa made up of sections or parts that may be used as separate units; a sofa in several segments. The sections may be used in combination or separately, as the shape of the room dictates.

> _The **sectional** was arranged in an L shape in the corner of the living room._

veneer, _n._ A thin surface layer of fine wood or costly material laid over a base of common material. A veneer can also be made of wood sheets applied to a furniture surface to create decorative inlay patterns of wood grain.

> _The etagère had an oak **veneer**._

 Also Explore: bevel, grain, modular.

Replace

cannibalize, vt. To take any or all personnel or components from (one organization) for use in building up another. Often used to refer to a new thing that may detract from the existence of a previous, similar thing.

> *The new sports coupe **cannibalized** sales from the older four-door sedan.*

supersede, vt. To cause to be set aside or dropped from use as inferior or obsolete and replaced by something else. Supersede implies a substitution with more modern and effective policies or devices.

> *The personal computer **superseded** the typewriter for word processing chores.*

supplant, vt. To remove or uproot in order to replace with something else. Supplant does not necessarily imply replacement with something better, only something different.

> *When the lease is up, the current office will be **supplanted** by a new building across town.*

rebuild, vt. To repair or remodel extensively, as by taking apart and reconstructing, often with new parts.

> *To restore the department to its former luster, Jones needed to **rebuild** it with entirely new staff.*

replenish, vt. To make full or complete again, as by furnishing a new supply. Rebuilding is a tearing down and building back up; replenishment is just a filling up.

> *The retailer needed to **replenish** his supply of the company's product.*

 Also Explore: glean, reconstruct, remodel, substitution, usurp.

Basketball

---

fast break, *n.* A play in which a team quickly moves down the floor in an attempt to score before an adequate defense can be set up. Also called the run-and-shoot offense, the fast break is in contrast to the half-court game, where a team slows down the play and takes the time to develop a play in its front court.

> *The team scored a quick two points on a **fast break** fed by a defensive rebound.*

---

in the paint, *adj.* Being in the foul lane area, which is typically painted a different color than the rest of the floor.

> *The team's center was dominant **in the paint**.*

back court, *n.* The half of the court that contains the basket a team is defending. (Back court can also refer to the two guards of one team in the game as a unit.) Compare with front court, the half of the court that contains the team's offensive basket.

> *The team was slow setting up its defense in the **back court**.*

high post, *n.* An imaginary area outside either side of the foul lane at the free-throw line. Compare to low post, an imaginary area outside either side of the foul lane close to the basket.

> *The forward took the **high post** and fed the ball inside to the center.*

triple double, *n.* When a player scores double-digits in three categories during one game, such as points, assists, and rebounds.

> *The star forward had a **triple double,** scoring 14 points with 10 assists and 12 rebounds.*

 Also Explore: defense, foul lane, free-throw, offense, rebound.

Clever

---

sagacious, *adj.* Having or showing keen perception or discernment and sound judgment or foresight. Sagacious implies showing insight and wisdom in one's understanding and judgment of things. Sagacious can also refer to someone skillful in statecraft or management.

*Polly respected Uncle Ed's **sagacious** advice; his years of experience lent his opinions special credence in this particular matter.*

---

shrewd, *adj.* Keen-witted, clever, or sharp in practical affairs. Shrewd implies keenness of mind, sharp insight, and a cleverness in practical matters.

*Veronica's **shrewd** perceptions proved accurate.*

resourceful, *adj.* Able to deal promptly and effectively with problems, difficulties, etc.

*Arnold was **resourceful** in finding resources for the upcoming project.*

ingenuity, *n.* Cleverness, originality, skill, and so on.

*Danny showed great **ingenuity** in figuring out a solution to the problem that had been plaguing the group.*

artifice, *n.* Trickery or craft; a sly or artful trick. Artifice implies trickery or an unusually clever tactic.

*Sandy's gift for **artifice** was better used against the competition than internally.*

 Also Explore: apt, astute, *discern*, glib, keen.

Words

---

intellectual property, *n.* Something produced by the mind, of which the ownership or right to use may be legally protected by a copyright, patent, trademark, and so on. Books, articles, songs, and artwork are all different types of intellectual property.

> *George granted his publisher perpetual rights to all of his* **intellectual property,** *including both magazine articles and books.*

---

content, *n.* All that is contained in something; everything inside. In any media, content is the substance; the way content is presented is the style. Content is sometimes thought of as media-independent so that content can be ported from one medium to another.

> *Sadly, Lindsay's presentation was* **content**-*free; it looked nice but didn't really say anything.*

context, *n.* The whole situation, background, or environment relevant to a particular event, personality, creation, etc.

> *Taken out of* **context,** *it looked as though Higgins was unsupportive of the new product.*

diction, *n.* A manner of expression in words; choice of words; wording. A manner of speaking or singing.

> *The professor gave Maria two A's for* **diction** *on her presentation: one for her style of writing and the other for her style of delivery.*

lingua franca, *n.* Any hybrid language used for communication between different peoples; a common language.

> *C is the* **lingua franca** *for software programmers.*

 Also Explore: enunciation, gist, locution, *style*, substance.

Rights and Royalties

---

copyright, *n.* The exclusive right to the publication, product, or sales of the rights to a literary, dramatic, musical, or artistic work or to the use of a commercial print or label, granted by law for a specified period of time to an author, composer, artist, distributor, etc.

>*The author retained the **copyright** to his story, so it couldn't be reprinted or reused without his permission.*

---

right, *n.* An interest in property, real or intangible. One can license rights to intellectual property. A copyright is a specific type of right.

>*The publishing house sold the foreign **rights** to a series of local translators.*

license, *n.* Formal permission to use something. Typical licenses are for use of copyrighted items, such as logos, brand names, and so on.

>*The sporting apparel manufacturer produced a line of shirts and jerseys under **license** from the NBA.*

syndicate, *vt.* To sell content (an article, feature, etc.) through an agency or syndicate for publication in many newspapers, periodicals, Web sites, etc.

>*The writer tried to **syndicate** his column to a chain of newspapers.*

royalty, *n.* A share of the proceeds or product paid to the owner of a right, such as a patent or copyright, for permission to use it or operate under it.

>*He received a 15 percent **royalty** on each copy sold.*

Also Explore: *grant, honorarium,* permission, prerogative, share.

Coming Soon

---

forthcoming, *adj.* About to appear; approaching. Forth-coming implies something about to happen or something available when required or as promised.

> *If my **forthcoming** book sells as well as my last book, I'll be able to buy a new home theater system with the proceeds.*

---

imminent, *n.* Likely to happen without delay. Imminent implies the anticipation of something threatening.

> *From the tense atmosphere at the White House, it was clear that the invasion was **imminent**.*

eventual, *adj.* Happening at the end of, or as a result of, a series of events; ultimate; final. Eventual implies a sense of inevitability.

> *Samantha anticipated the **eventual** outcome of the case.*

looming, *adj.* Appearing, taking shape, or coming in sight indistinctly as through a mist, especially in a large, portentous, or threatening form.

> *The grim specter of bankruptcy was **looming** on the horizon for the beleaguered merchant.*

portentous, *adj.* That is an omen or warning of evil.

> *The skies were of **portentous** darkness and fury.*

 Also Explore: *anticipated*, emerged, ineluctable, offing.

Weather

El Niño, *n.* A major warming of the equatorial waters in the Pacific Ocean, occurring every three to seven years and characterized by shifts in normal weather patterns. El Niño can seriously alter weather patterns over a widespread area.

> *The weathercasters blamed **El Niño** for the wet winter in southern California.*

front, *n.* The boundary between two air masses of different density and temperature. A front preceding a cold air mass is called a cold front; a front preceding a warm air mass is called a warm front.

> *The cold **front** brought with it cooler, dryer air.*

humidity, *n.* The amount or degree of moisture in the air. The relative humidity is the amount of moisture in the air as compared with the maximum amount that the air could contain at the same temperature, expressed as a percentage.

> *The relative **humidity** in New Orleans was 95 percent; you couldn't walk a block without breaking out in a sweat.*

barometric pressure, *n.* The pressure due to the weight of the earth's atmosphere; one standard atmosphere measures 29.92 inches of mercury. (Also called atmospheric pressure.)

> ***Barometric pressure** typically falls preceding a storm.*

Doppler radar, *n.* A type of weather radar that determines whether atmospheric motion is toward or away from the radar. Doppler radar uses the Doppler effect to measure the velocity of particles suspended in the atmosphere.

> *The **Doppler radar** indicated a line of showers moving to the east at ten miles per hour.*

 Also Explore: *atmosphere*, density, elements, inclement, isobar.

Guessing Game

prognosticate, *vt.* To foretell or predict, especially from signs or indications. To prognosticate is to prophesize based on some current symptoms or indications.

> *James refused to **prognosticate** the outcome of the Super Bowl.*

forecast, *vt.* To estimate or calculate in advance; predict or seek to predict. A forecast can also refer to a prediction of future weather conditions.

> *The sales force **forecast** an increase in orders for the second quarter.*

estimate, *vt.* To judge or determine generally but carefully (size, value, cost, requirements, and so on); calculate approximately.

> *Johnson **estimated** that repairs could run into the four figures.*

budget, *vt.* To plan expenditures or activities according to a schedule. An estimate is a guess; a budget is a plan.

> *Nadine's **budget** didn't allow any frivolous expenses.*

scenario, *n.* An outline for any proposed or planned series of events, real or imagined.

> *The events played out according to Mitchell's **scenario**.*

 Also Explore: *conjecture*, predict, presume, prophesize.

In the Middle

---

average, *n.* The numerical result obtained by dividing the sum of two or more quantities by the number of quantities.

*The **average** of 5, 6, and 10 is 7.*

---

mean, *n.* A number intermediate between the smallest and largest values of a set of quantities. The arithmetic mean is the average.

*The **mean** of 5, 6, and 10 is 7.5.*

median, *n.* The middle number or point in a series containing an odd number of items or the number midway between the two middle numbers in a series containing an even number of items.

*The **median** of 5, 6, and 10 is 6.*

mode, *n.* The value, number, and so on that occurs most frequently in a given series.

*The **mode** of 5, 6, 6, and 10 is 6.*

typical, *adj.* Having or showing the characteristics, qualities, etc. of a kind, class, or group so fully as to be a representative example.

*Holly grew up in a **typical** middle-class neighborhood.*

 Also Explore: criterion, gauge, norm, standard.

Short

terse, *adj.* Free of superfluous words; concise in a polished, smooth, way. Terse language is elegantly concise and cleanly written or spoken.

> *Joe Friday's **terse** style set the tone for dozens of fictional detectives to follow.*

pithy, *adj.* Terse and full of substance or meaning. Terse is concise; pithy is concise yet full of content.

> *Sarah's **pithy** comments said volumes.*

succinct, *adj.* Clearly and briefly stated. Succinct is characterized by brevity and conciseness of speech.

> *Oliver's **succinct** summarization of the facts brought everyone up to speed quickly.*

trenchant, *adj.* Keen; penetrating; distinct. Trenchant is not necessarily short, just effective and clear-cut.

> *Dinah's **trenchant** analysis helped Larry understand what was really going on.*

brief, *n.* A summary or abstract; a concise statement of the main points. Brief emphasizes compactness.

> *Pete prepared a **brief** of the situation for Mr. Big.*

 Also Explore: *abstract*, brevity, *concise*, incisive.

Quickly

---

expedient, *adj.* Useful for effecting a desired result; suited to the circumstances or the occasion; advantageous; convenient. Expedient is sometimes used derogatorily in reference to precipitous action meeting pragmatic needs but not in concert with overarching principles.

*Carter took the **expedient** route to complete his project, even though it ultimately made the results less effective.*

---

impetuous, *adj.* Acting or done suddenly or without little thought. Impetuous is an obviously hasty and usually problematic decision or action and implies an action having negative or unflattering consequences.

*Madeline was an **impetuous** young girl, always running off on her own and getting into trouble.*

capricious, *adj.* Tending to change abruptly and without apparent reason; changing on a whim. Capricious implies not having a good reason for change, an unfair or groundless behavior or action.

*The H.R. department warned that by changing the structure frequently and **capriciously,** the company could lose some of its most important workers.*

impulsive, *adj.* Acting or likely to act suddenly, usually without premeditation. Capricious is sudden change; impulsive is sudden action.

*Johnson's **impulsive** reaction to his boss's request cost him his job.*

hasten, *vt.* To cause to be or come faster; speed up; accelerate.

*The poor fourth quarter sales **hastened** the closing of the remote office.*

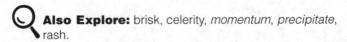 **Also Explore:** brisk, celerity, *momentum*, *precipitate*, rash.

334

Start-ups and Shutdowns

venture capital, *n.* Funds invested or available for investment at considerable risk of loss in potentially highly profitable enterprises. Venture firms seek new companies—often in high-tech or emerging industries—to invest in, with the hopes of the company ultimately hitting it big and going public through an IPO.

The small start-up sought **venture capital** *to finance its expansion plans.*

IPO, *n.* Initial public offering; the first sale of stock by a company to the public. IPOs are often smaller, newer companies seeking equity capital to expand their businesses.

The start-up's investors urged the owner to float an **IPO.**

capsize, *vt.* To cease business operations, especially as a result of sustained losses or negative cash flow.

The small company **capsized** *under the weight of its losses.*

bankruptcy, *n.* The state of being legally declared unable to pay one's debts. The property involved in a bankruptcy is administered for the benefit of any and all creditors and divided among them appropriately.

With mounting debt and no job prospects, Ken and Karen declared **bankruptcy.**

chapter 11, *n.* A proceeding under the Federal Bankruptcy Act whereby a company or corporation may, through a court order, remain in business for a time as long as it pays current debts but must eventually reorganize and pay its creditors or cease operations.

The company kept its doors open under **chapter 11** *while it worked out a plan to repay its creditors.*

 Also Explore: *cash flow,* creditor, *equity, investment, stock.*

Making Your Presence Known

---

advocate, *vt.* To speak or write in support of; be in favor of. Advocacy refers to the action of supporting, vindicating, or recommending publicly, usually through use of an argument of some sort. An advocate is one who pleads or argues another's cause, such as a lawyer.

> *Ellen was Warren's biggest **advocate,** arguing to her boss that he should be assigned the lucrative new account.*

---

conduct, *n.* The process or way of managing or direction; management; handling. Conduct implies a supervising by using one's executive skill, knowledge, and wisdom.

> *Henri's **conduct** of the situation was effective.*

control, *vt.* To exercise authority over; direct; command. Control implies firm direction by regulation or restraint and often connotes complete domination.

> *ReallyBig Co. sought to **control** the distribution channel for its core products.*

impact, *n.* The power of an event or idea to produce changes, move the feelings, and so on.

> *The new product launch made a major market **impact.***

clout, *n.* Power or influence; especially political power.

> *The Senator had considerable **clout** in the subcommittee.*

Also Explore: connections, leverage, prominence, puissance, sway.

How to Do It

---

opportunistic, *adj.* Adapting one's actions, judgments, and so on to circumstances to further one's immediate interests without regard for basic principles or eventual consequences.

*Scott prided himself on being an **opportunistic** reactor, always ready to exploit any new opportunities.*

---

reactive, *adj.* Tending to respond to a stimulus; be affected by some influence or event. Contrast with proactive, which means to take the initiative.

*The company's **reactive** behavior put it one step behind its more proactive competitors.*

efficacious, *adj.* Producing or capable of producing the desired effect; having the intended result.

*Robert believed that the new software problem would be an **efficacious** remedy to their accounting problems.*

efficient, *adj.* Producing a desired effect or product with a minimum of effort, expense, or waste; working well. Efficient implies skill and economy of energy in producing the desired result.

*Pam's team was the most **efficient,** finishing the project two weeks ahead of the other groups.*

effective, *adj.* Having an effect; producing a result. Efficient means getting it done with a minimum of effort; effective means getting it done, period.

*Russell's team was the most **effective,** producing the strongest results—even though Pam's team finished sooner.*

 Also Explore: adept, effectuate, execute, reciprocate.

Overused

cliché, *n.* An expression or idea that has become trite. A cliché is an expression or idea that, although once fresh and forceful, has become hackneyed and weak through much repetition.

*Nike's "Just Do It" slogan had become a **cliché**.*

platitude, *n.* A commonplace or trite remark or idea, especially one uttered as if it were fresh, original, novel, or momentous.

*Nora took Dick's speech and weakened it by adding numerous **platitudes**.*

trite, *adj.* Worn out by constant use; no longer having freshness, originality, or novelty; stale. Trite is applied to something, especially an expression or idea, that through repeated use or application has lost its original freshness and impressive force.

*Hank grimaced when Judy used the **trite** metaphor "quick as a whip."*

hackneyed, *adj.* Made trite or commonplace by overuse. Hackneyed refers to such expressions that through constant use have become virtually meaningless.

*The reporter's use of **hackneyed** expressions raised the ire of his editor.*

truism, *n.* A statement the truth of which is obvious or well known. A truism is a statement whose truth is widely known and whose utterance, therefore, seems superfluous.

*"A penny saved is a penny earned," although trite, is a **truism**.*

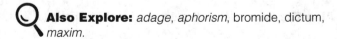
Also Explore: *adage, aphorism,* bromide, dictum, *maxim.*

Vows and Acknowledgments

kudos, *n.* Credit or praise for an achievement; glory or fame. Note that kudos is both singular and plural; there is no such word as kudo.

*Marlon received **kudos** from the board for his outstanding presentation at the annual shareholder's meeting.*

recognition, *n.* Recognizing or being recognized. Acknowledgment and approval, gratitude, and so on. Recognition by a group is high praise for achievements or actions and is usually done in some official capacity.

*The Mayor gave Cal the key to the city in **recognition** of his diligent work in revitalizing the downtown.*

acknowledgment, *n.* Something done or given in acknowledgment as an expression of thanks. Usually an acknowledgment in less formal, and perhaps less public, than recognition.

*Dawn received a thank-you card from her boss in **acknowledgment** of her hard work on the year-end reports.*

commendation, *n.* Mention of someone or something as worthy of attention; recommend. An expression of approval of; praise. A commendation is usually relatively private; sometimes it is just a letter of praise in a personnel file.

*June called Tom into her office to show him the **commendation** she was about to place into his file.*

accolades, *n.* Anything done or given as a sign of great respect, approval, appreciation, and so on; words of praise. Interestingly, an accolade was also an embrace (a touch on the shoulder with the flat side of a sword) formerly used in conferring knighthood.

*George's performance received **accolades** from most of the critics. He became a star overnight.*

Also Explore: credit, *distinguished,* esteem, renown, tribute.

Related To

---

codependent, *adj.* Mutually dependent. In psychological terms, codependent defines someone who is influenced or controlled by, reliant on, or needing another person who is addicted to alcohol, drugs, etc.

*Julie was **codependent** on her abusive, alcoholic husband; she refused to leave him, even when he beat her.*

---

symbiosis, *n.* The intimate living together of two things, especially if such association is of mutual advantage. A codependent relationship is a negative and needy relationship; a symbiotic relationship is a positive and synergistic relationship.

*There exists a **symbiosis** between plant life and animal life.*

correlation, *n.* A mutual relationship or connection.

*There was a **correlation** between the amount of advertising and the sell-through rate.*

causal, *adj.* Of anything producing an effect or result. Causal implies a direct effect as a result of an act.

*In spite of the correlation, Marge couldn't establish a **causal** relationship between the two items.*

affinity, *n.* Close relationship; connection.

*George felt an **affinity** to his retailers.*

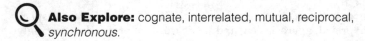 **Also Explore:** cognate, interrelated, mutual, reciprocal, *synchronous.*

Part Of

intrinsic, *adj.* Belonging to the real nature of a thing; not dependent on external circumstances. Intrinsic implies fundamental in character.

*The international monetary system is based on the **intrinsic** value of gold.*

integral, *adj.* Necessary for completeness; essential. Integral implies acting as a constituent and essential member of the whole.

*The shape of the carton was **integral** to the product's package.*

inherent, *adj.* Existing in someone or something as a natural and inseparable quality, characteristic, or right. Inherent implies an important part of something.

*Sherry had an **inherent** goodness that shone through no matter what the circumstances.*

innate, *adj.* Existing naturally rather than acquired; that seems to have been in one from birth. Innate describes that which belongs to something as part of its nature or constitution; inborn.

*Beth could always rely on her **innate** sense of right and wrong.*

congenital, *adj.* Existing as such at birth. Congenital implies existence at or from one's birth, specifically as a result of prenatal environment.

*The Stevens child suffered from a **congenital** heart defect.*

 Also Explore: aggregate, *component*, *core*, *essential*.

Same As

---

tantamount, *adj.* Having equal force, value, effect; equal to. Derives from a phrase that means "to amount to as much."

*The President's speech was **tantamount** to a declaration of war.*

---

commensurate, *adj.* Equal in measure or size. Commensurate implies corresponding in extent or degree or proportionate.

*His compensation was **commensurate** with his experience.*

equidistant, *adj.* Equally distant. Equidistant refers to things that are the same length away from each other.

*The two remote offices were **equidistant** from the main headquarters.*

equitable, *adj.* Characterized by impartiality; fair; just.

*The settlement was **equitable** for both parties.*

invariable, *adj.* Not changing; constant; uniform.

Invariably, *sales picked up over the Christmas season.*

Also Explore: coextensive, consubstantial, impartial, indistinguishable.

Vary

---

vacillate, *vi.* To waver in mind; show indecision. Vacillate implies someone who wavers between options or cannot decide which course of action to settle on.

*The two health plans were so similar that Kent **vacillated** on which one he would choose.*

---

fluctuate, *vt.* To be continually changing or varying in an irregular way.

*Speculation over quarterly earnings caused the stock price to **fluctuate** wildly.*

oscillate, *vi.* To swing or move regularly back and forth.

*The high winds caused the bridge to **oscillate** dangerously.*

undulate, *vt.* To move in or as in waves.

*The belly dancer's hips began to **undulate**.*

flux, *n.* A continuous movement or continual change.

*The high turnover rate kept the org chart in a state of **flux**.*

 Also Explore: *dither*, irresolute, variable, *mutable*.

Doing and Undoing

---

consolidate, *vt.* To combine into a single whole; merge; unite. Consolidate implies a strengthening or stabilization by the combination of many parts.

The board voted to **consolidate** *the two offices into one central location.*

---

catenate, *vt.* To form into a chain or linked series.

The retailer decided to **catenate** *his stores under a single name.*

diversify, *vt.* To divide up (investments, liabilities) among different companies, securities, and so on; to expand (a business, line of products) by increasing the variety of things produced or of operations undertaken.

Robert instructed his broker to **diversify** *his portfolio.*

divest, *vt.* To disencumber or rid (of something unwanted). Diversify means to expand or dilute; divest means to get rid of.

ReallyBig Co. decided to **divest** *its smaller, less synergistic operating units.*

rescind, *vt.* To repeal or cancel (a law, order, and so on). Rescind implies to abolish.

The company **rescinded** *its formal dress code.*

Also Explore: deprive, dilute, disencumber, *merger*, revoke.

---

transpire, *vi.* To come to pass; happen. Transpire means for some event to take place but can also refer to an escape from secrecy or becoming public.

> *As events **transpired,** it became clear that the acquisition was a bad business decision.*

---

eventuate, *vi.* To happen in the end; result.

> *The new tax laws will **eventuate** a lower tax rate for most Americans.*

occur, *vi.* To present itself; come to mind.

> *It **occurred** to Lyn that she could make more money if she added a few extra services to the menu.*

commence, *vi.* To begin; start; originate.

> *It was time for the proceedings to **commence.***

chance, *vi.* To have the fortune, good or bad.

> *Peter **chanced** upon his old performance review while browsing through his desk drawer.*

 Also Explore: befall, broach, embark, ensue, inaugurate.

Forever

perennial, *adj.* Lasting or continuing for a long time; returning or becoming active again and again. Perennial implies reliability. Sometimes the word evergreen is also used in this fashion.

> How the Grinch Stole Christmas *is a **perennial** favorite with children; it gets high ratings every holiday season.*

perpetual, *adj.* Continuing indefinitely without interruption; constant. Perpetual differs from perennial or periodic in that it never goes away, and it never ends.

> *The world's population was **perpetually** increasing.*

periodic, *adj.* Occurring, appearing, or recurring at regular intervals. Periodic differs from perpetual in that it is not constant but rather comes and goes at fixed intervals.

> *The **periodic** appearance of El Niño played havoc with long-range weather forecasts.*

annuity, *n.* A payment of a fixed sum of money at regular intervals of time, especially yearly. An annuity can also be an investment yielding periodic payments during the annuitant's lifetime, for a stated number of years, or in perpetuity.

> *As he grew older, John looked for investments that would provide an **annuity** in his old age.*

immemorial, *adj.* Extending back beyond memory or record; ancient.

> *The act of lighting a candle or fire to facilitate prayer or meditation extends back to time **immemorial**.*

 Also Explore: evergreen, imperishable, interminable, sempiternal, unceasing.

Complete

extensive, *adj.* Having a wide scope, effect, influence, etc.; far-reaching. Extensive refers to the effect something has; expansive refers to the size of the thing itself.

> *The fallout from the product failure was **extensive;** the project team was reassigned, the team leader was banished to a remote office, and the entire second shift in the factory had to be let go.*

expansive, *adj.* Having great size, bulk, scope, and so on. Can also refer to someone of a free and generous nature.

> *The company's **expansive** campus contained more than five miles of walkways.*

exhaustive, *adj.* Leaving nothing out; covering every possible detail; thorough.

> *His research was **exhaustive,** leaving no stone unturned.*

encyclopedic, *adj.* Of or like an encyclopedia; giving or knowing information about many subjects; comprehensive in scope.

> *His **encyclopedic** knowledge of the subject was impressive.*

encompassing, *adj.* Shutting in all around; surrounding; encircling.

> *Microsoft's domination of the software industry was all-**encompassing.***

Also Explore: comprehensive, demonstrative, encircling, scope.

Global Finances

neomercantilism, *n.* A revival of the mercantilist doctrine that proposes that the economic interests of the nation could be strengthened by the government by protection of home industries, as through tariffs, by increased foreign trade, as through monopolies, and by a balance of exports over imports. Neomercantilism today refers not only to the compulsion of the state to use the economy to generate wealth but also the tendency to adopt a variety of protectionist trade, investment, and other policies.

> *Neomercantilism suggests a country cannot be strong without the state helping business and industry along.*

prosperity, *n.* Good fortune; wealth and success. In global terms, prosperity refers to an economic state of growth with rising profits and full employment

> *The Western economies enjoyed an unprecedented period of **prosperity.***

austerity, *n.* Tightened economy, such as because of shortages of consumer goods.

> *As the wartime economy took hold, the region entered a period of forced **austerity.***

deficit, *n.* The amount by which a sum of money is less than the required amount; specifically, an excess of liabilities over assets, of losses over profits, or of expenditure over income.

> *The country ran a foreign-trade **deficit.***

dump, *vt.* To sell (a commodity) in a large quantity at a low price, especially in a foreign market at a price below that of the domestic market.

> *The Asian countries were accused of **dumping** products in the U.S. in order to dominate the market.*

 Also Explore: *commodity,* protectionist, tariff, *trade.*

To Rule

usurp, *vt.* To take or assume (power, a position, property, rights, and so on) and hold in possession by force or without right. To usurp is to take over, such as by a coup.

*ReallyBig Co. **usurped** control of the distribution channel from its wholesalers, leaving them with no new product to distribute.*

conquer, *vt.* To get possession or control of by or such as by winning a war. Conquer implies gaining mastery over someone or something by physical, mental, or moral force.

*The new product **conquered** the marketplace through sheer force of sales.*

vanquish, *vt.* To defeat in any conflict, such as in an argument. Vanquish implies a thorough overpowering or frustrating, often in a single conflict or battle.

*The competitor was **vanquished** to a subsidiary market position.*

subdue, *vt.* To bring into subjection or control. Subdue is to defeat so as to break the spirit of resistance.

*When the union battle was lost, the workers became **subdued**.*

master, *vt.* To gain control over; to become an expert in; to gain a thorough understanding of.

*Rodney sought to **master** the programs on his personal computer.*

Also Explore: ascendancy, coup, dominate, regime, subjection.

Improve

ameliorate, *vt.* To make or become better; to improve. Ameliorate implies reducing the intensity of a harmful or painful influence. When an unacceptable situation has been made better, it is said to have been ameliorated.

> *Dr. Benson prescribed an analgesic to help **ameliorate** Henrietta's pain.*

ambition, *n.* A strong desire to gain a particular objective; the drive to succeed or to gain fame, power, wealth, and so on.

> *Nicki's **ambition** was to be a college professor.*

enhance, *vt.* To make greater, as in cost, value, attractiveness, etc.; heighten. To improve the quality or condition of something or someone. To improve electronically the quality or clarity of (a photograph or other image) by means of a computer.

> *The new painkiller **enhanced** Margaret's daily life so much that her doctor began a study on the drug to find out if it should be a controlled substance.*

upgrade, *vt.* To enhance or improve. In the software industry, upgrade refers to the movement from an older version to a newer version.

> *ReallyBig Co. was in the processing of **upgrading** all its desktops from Windows 95 to Windows 98.*

evolve, *vt.* To develop by gradual changes; unfold.

> *The plan **evolved** over time.*

 Also Explore: *augment*, cultivate, gentrify, mature.

Lessen

mitigate, _vt._ To make or become milder, less severe, less rigorous, or less painful. In legal terms, a mitigating circumstance is a circumstance that may be considered to reduce the degree of moral culpability, although it does not entirely justify or excuse an offense.

> _The severity of his offense was **mitigated** by the fact that he thought he was protecting his family._

temper, _vt._ To make suitable, desirable, or free from excess by mingling with something else; reduce in intensity, especially by the admixture of some other quality. Temper suggests deliberate self-restraint.

> _Randy **tempered** his criticism of the company's performance by pointing out the many good things that had happened in the past year._

decrease, _vt._ To become or cause to become less, smaller; diminish. Decrease suggests a growing gradually smaller in bulk, size, volume, or number.

> _The bonus levels **decreased** year after year._

attenuate, _vt._ To lessen in severity, value, amount, intensity, etc.; weaken.

> _Raising the walls of the cubicles served to **attenuate** the noise level._

eliminate, _vt._ To take out; remove; get rid of.

> _Mr. Big wanted to totally **eliminate** his chief competitor._

Also Explore: admixture, assuage, _moderate_, mollify.

Avoid

eschew, *vt.* To keep away from (something harmful or disliked). Eschew implies deliberately avoiding and staying away from something or someone.

> *Deliberately playing to his frugal image, the chairman* ***eschewed*** *the use of a private limo and took a taxi instead.*

evade, *vt.* To avoid or escape from by deceit or cleverness; elude. Evade also refers to avoiding doing or answering directly; getting around (something or some point).

> *Mr. Big* ***evaded*** *the question by talking about the new puppy his wife had given him for Christmas.*

circumlocution, *n.* A roundabout, indirect, or lengthy way of expressing something. Circumlocution helps one avoid saying something directly.

> *Jeremy's* ***circumlocution*** *helped him sidestep the tough question.*

forswear, *vt.* To renounce on oath; promise earnestly to give up.

> *I* ***forswear*** *fatty foods for the good of my health.*

abstain, *vi.* To hold oneself back; voluntarily do without; refrain (from).

> *Ronald* ***abstained*** *from smoking while his wife was pregnant.*

 Also Explore: malinger, periphrasis, renounce, shirk, shun.

Looking Forward To

---

expectant, *adj.* Looking for as likely to occur or appear. Expectant implies a considerable degree of confidence that a particular event will happen.

*Ralph was **expectant** that his bonus check would be in this week's pay envelope.*

---

anticipate, *vt.* To look forward to; expect. Anticipate implies a looking forward to something with a foretaste of the pleasure or distress it promises or a realizing of something in advance and a taking of steps to meet it.

*Lori eagerly **anticipated** her summer vacation.*

eager, *adj.* Feeling or showing keen desire; impatient to do or get.

*Mark was **eager** to start his new job.*

anxious, *adj.* Uneasy in mind; worried. Don't confuse eager with anxious; eager implies impatience, whereas anxious implies dread.

*Phyllis was **anxious** about her upcoming performance review; she didn't think her boss appreciated the work she'd done.*

concerned, *adj.* Involved or interested. Can also mean being uneasy or anxious.

*Shelly was **concerned** about the increasing turnover in the marketing department.*

Also Explore: apprehensive, ardent, foretaste, tenterhooks, vigilant.

Sayings

---

aphorism, *n.* A short, pointed sentence expressing a wise or clever observation or a general truth. An aphorism employs cleverness or wit to make an observation.

"The early bird catches the worm" is a classic **aphorism.**

---

maxim, *n.* A concisely expressed principle or rule of conduct or a statement of a general truth. A maxim employs conciseness to state a principle or truth.

Nicole adhered to the **maxim** *"Love is love's reward."*

proverb, *n.* A short, traditional saying that expresses some obvious truth or familiar experience. An adage may or may not be true but is accepted as such; a proverb is a story or saying that illustrates an actual truth.

Uncle Mike told his nephews a **proverb** *that illustrated why it pays to be kind to your fellow man.*

adage, *n.* An old saying that has been popularly accepted as a truth.

As the **adage** *says, "A stitch in time saves nine."*

axiom, *n.* An established principle or law of a science, art, and so on.

The axiom of choice is one of the most discussed **axioms** *of mathematics, perhaps second only to Euclid's parallel postulate.*

 Also Explore: bromide, saying, *platitude*, truth, *cliché.*

Figures of Speech

DAY 355

---

irony, *n.* A combination of circumstance or a result that is the opposite of what is or might be expected or considered appropriate. In speech or writing, a method of humorous or subtly sarcastic expression in which the intended meaning of the words is the direct opposite of their usual sense.

> *The **irony** of the situation is that the one person who didn't care about the size of his office was assigned the largest office in the building.*

---

metaphor, *n.* A figure of speech containing an implied comparison, in which a word or phrase ordinarily and primarily used of one thing is applied to another.

> *Shakespeare's famous line "All the world's a stage" is actually a **metaphor.***

simile, *n.* A figure of speech in which one thing is likened to another dissimilar thing typically by the use of like or as.

> *Even ad slogans employ **similes;** a case in point is "A day without orange juice is like a day without sunshine."*

allegory, *n.* A story in which people, things, and happenings have a hidden or symbolic meaning. Allegories are used for teaching or explaining ideas, morals, principles, etc.

> *The teacher found that she could teach moral lessons to her class through the use of **allegory.***

sarcasm, *n.* A taunting, sneering, cutting, or caustic remark; gibe or jeer, generally ironic. Sarcasm implies an intent to hurt by taunting with mocking ridicule, veiled sneers, and so on.

> *With **sarcasm** dripping from her voice, Ronnie assured Jim that of course she'd wait up for him when he went out drinking with his friends.*

 Also Explore: *burlesque*, gibe, parable, paradox, *truism.*

Malicious Intent

---

calumny, *n.* A false and malicious statement meant to hurt someone's reputation. Calumny is not a formal or legal term as is libel, having a more general connotation.

*Sophie tried to ignore the hateful **calumnies** shouted at her by the crowd.*

---

libel, *n.* Any false and malicious written or printed statement, or any sign, picture, or effigy, tending to expose a person to public ridicule, hatred, or contempt or to injure a person's reputation in any way. In a general sense, libel is any publication that is injurious to the reputation of another.

*Johnson was accused of **libel** for the story he wrote about Mr. Richmond.*

slander, *n.* The utterance in the presence of another person of a false statement or statements, damaging to a third person's character or reputation. Libel and slander both are methods of defamation—the former being expressed by print, writings, pictures or signs, the latter orally.

*Johnson filed a suit for **slander** when Mr. Richmond cast aspersions on Johnson's integrity in a television interview.*

defame, *vt.* To attack or injure the reputation or honor of someone or something by false and malicious statements.

*Gloria claimed she was **defamed** by the rumors spread at school.*

malign, *vt.* To speak evil of; to defame or slander. Malign does not necessarily involve a lie but does imply a deliberate showing of ill will.

*Buffy was **maligned** by Cher's cutting comments about her clothing sense.*

 Also Explore: *censure*, opprobrious, ridicule, scandalize, traduce.

Clothing

---

business casual, *adj.* Casual clothing accepted as proper dress in a business environment. Business casual is typified by khakis, corduroys, denim shirts, polo shirts, sweaters, and loafers—not suits, ties, and wingtips. This move away from traditional business attire reflects a general blurring of the line between work and home; as of 1997, 9 out of 10 U.S. companies had some sort of casual dress policy, usually including some form of "dress-down Fridays," and 40 percent of all companies allowed casual clothing every day.

Levon had to buy a whole new wardrobe when his company switched to **business casual** *five days a week.*

---

black tie, *adj.* A tuxedo and the proper accessories. Black tie implies a formal affair where tuxedo and appropriate evening wear, such as a formal, is required.

The invitation stipulated **black tie,** *so Calvin dug his tuxedo out of the closet.*

décolletage, *n.* A low-cut neck of a dress, exposing the neck and shoulders of the wearer. Associated with women's formals.

Kristi's parents thought her **décolletage** *plunged too low for a girl her age.*

braces, *n.* Suspenders. Suspenders worn with business clothing (suit, tie, etc.) are typically called braces; suspenders worn with casual clothing (or suspenders that clasp rather than button in place) are still called suspenders.

Miles liked wearing **braces** *with his bow tie.*

dart, *n.* A short, stitched fold that tapers to a point, used to shape a garment. Similar to pleat, except that a dart tapers to a point, where a pleat is of uniform width and pressed or stitched in place.

Jenny sewed the **darts** *into her new skirt.*

 Also Explore: formal, khaki, pleat, tuxedo, wingtip.

Managing Staff

---

headcount, *n.* The total number of employees in an organization or department. Open headcount refers to those positions planned in the budget but currently unfilled.

*Senior management decided to increase **headcount** in the new unit by 10 percent in the second half.*

---

head, *n.* One position within an organization. A head can be either filled (with a current employee) or open (waiting for an employee to be hired).

*Marcie had three open **heads** to fill within the next 30 days.*

freeze, *vt.* To fix employment, hiring, spending, and so on at a given level or place by authoritative regulation. Under a headcount freeze, new employees can be hired as long as they replace someone who has left the company; under a hiring freeze, no new employees can be hired, period.

*To keep expenses in check, Mr. Little ordered a headcount **freeze** for the balance of the fiscal year.*

human resources, *n.* A department in a company or institution that looks after personnel records, company benefits, hiring and training of employees, and so on; personnel department. Ironically, many HR departments are so consumed with bureaucracy that they have little time to deal with the human needs of a company's employees.

***Human resources** distributed the benefits forms for all employees to complete.*

severance, *n.* Extra pay given to employees who are dismissed through no fault of their own, such as during a downsizing.

*All downsized employees will receive one week's **severance** for each year they were employed.*

 Also Explore: *benefits, bonus,* downsize, *outplacement, rightsize.*

Exercise

---

aerobic, *adj.* Exercise, such as running or swimming, that conditions the heart and lungs by increasing the efficiency of oxygen intake by the body. Aerobic exercise is designed to strengthen the cardiopulmonary system.

*Forty-five minutes on the exercise bike is an excellent **aerobic** workout.*

---

anaerobic, *adj.* Anaerobic exercise focuses on short burst, intense training. The object is to continue exercise after the oxygen in the muscles has been utilized thus increasing endurance.

*Brad sprinted one full lap around the indoor track to push his training into the **anaerobic** envelope.*

calisthenics, *n.* Exercises, such as push-ups and sit-ups. Calisthenics is resistence training without weights. It is primarily concerned with improving muscular strength and tone.

*Jane signed up for the **calisthenics** program instead of aerobics; she wanted to focus on increasing her muscle strength.*

isometrics, *n.* A method of physical exercise in which one set of muscles is tensed, for a period of seconds, in opposition to another set of muscles or to an immovable object. Isometrics is another form of resistance training without weights.

*Kyle did daily **isometric** exercises with the physical therapist while he was confined to bed.*

anabolic steroid, *n.* Any of a group of synthetic steroid hormones that promote the growth of tissue, especially muscle tissue.

*The coach warned his wrestlers about the dangers of beefing up with **anabolic steroids.***

 Also Explore: drill, *healthful*, healthy, vigorous, *wellness.*

Getting Smaller

---

minimax, *adj.* Of or having to do with a strategy for minimizing the maximum error or loss. Often used in gaming, where a player moves to maximize the minimum value of his opponent's possible following moves.

*Jason employed a **minimax** strategy against his opponent.*

---

minimize, *vt.* To reduce to a minimum; decrease to the least possible amount, degree, etc.

*The public relations flack worked to **minimize** the damage from the lawsuit.*

diminish, *vt.* To make, or make see, smaller; reduce in size, degree, importance, and so on; lessen.

*Steve saw his role on the team **diminish** over time.*

disparage, *vt.* To discredit; speak slightly of; show disrespect for; belittle. To disparage is to lower in esteem, such as by insinuation, invidious comparison, faint praise, etc.

*Arnold **disparaged** Steve's efforts on the project.*

minimalism, *n.* Action of a minimal or conservative kind. More formally, minimalism is a movement in art, dance, or music, beginning in the 1960s, in which only the simplest design, structure, forms, and so on are used, often repetitiously, and the artist's individuality is minimized. Minimalist can also refer to anything that employs a stripped-down approach.

*By eschewing Java applets and fancy graphics, Kayla applied a **minimalist** approach to her Web page.*

 Also Explore: *essential*, *abridge*, wane, abate, curtail.

Aging

---

planned obsolescence, *n.* The practice of making something obsolete or out of fashion before it actually wears out. Consumer goods manufacturers are sometimes accused of practicing planned obsolescence by adding new (but not necessarily needed) features on a yearly basis; the new models then obsolete the old ones, even though the old ones still work perfectly fine.

> *BigCar Co. practiced* **planned obsolescence** *by subtly changing the bumper style on the new models, as well as adding a second button on the keyless entry system.*

---

deteriorate, *vt.* To make or become worse; lower in quality or value. Many things deteriorate with age; other things deteriorate because of poor construction.

> *Conditions at the old plant continued to* **deteriorate.** *One week, the toilets refused to flush; the next week, the HVAC system broke down.*

decrepit, *adj.* Broken down or worn out by old age, illness, or long use. Decrepit implies enfeebled.

> *The aging facilities were* **decrepit;** *the elevators didn't work half the time, and the phone system was continually breaking down.*

disintegrate, *vt.* To separate into parts or fragments; break up; disunite.

> *The old chair practically* **disintegrated** *when he sat down on it.*

decompose, *vt.* To break up or separate into basic components or parts; to rot.

> *Michael carefully picked up the* **decomposing** *paper, taking care not to further its deterioration.*

 Also Explore: *depreciation*, enfeebled, *erode,* rot, wane.

Weaken

---

enervate, *vt.* To deprive of strength, force, vigor, and so on; weaken physically, mentally, or morally. Do not confuse enervate (to weaken) with the similar-sounding energize, which has the opposite meaning (to invigorate).

*Thomas found that growing old was **enervating;** by the end of the day, he had barely enough strength to drag himself to bed.*

---

devitalize, *vt.* To make listless or ineffective; lower the vitality of; weaken.

*As he grew older, he became more and more **devitalized.***

demoralize, *vt.* To lower the morale of; weaken the spirit, courage, discipline, or staying power of.

*Losing that last account **demoralized** him; he wasn't sure he had the discipline to go on.*

demotivate, *vt.* To stifle some drive, impulse, intention, etc..

*Carolyn was **demotivated** by the cut in her commission rates.*

diffuse, *vt.* To pour, spread out, or disperse in every direction; spread or scatter widely.

*As the company grew, the management team became more **diffuse.***

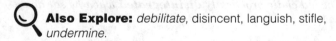 **Also Explore:** *debilitate,* disincent, languish, stifle, undermine.

Injuries

triage, *n.* A system of assigning priorities of medical treatment based on urgency and chance for survival and used on battlefields and in hospital emergency wards. Triage can also refer to any system of establishing the order in which acts of assistance are to be carried out in any emergency or any plan for an organization to divest itself of units, properties, or products during a downturn.

> *The board ordered the COO to perform **triage** on the organization, dispassionately cutting those units that were not worth saving.*

sprain, *n.* A wrench or twist of a ligament or muscle of a joint without dislocating the bones, characterized by swelling, pain, and disablement of the joint.

> *Martha thought she **sprained** her wrist playing tennis.*

dislocate, *vt.* To displace a bone from its proper position at a joint.

> *It turns out it wasn't a sprain; her wrist was **dislocated.***

fracture, *n.* A break in a body part, especially in a bone, or a tear in a cartilage. A compound fracture is a bone fracture in which broken ends of bone have pierced the skin.

> *Mark had a compound **fracture** of his left arm due to the auto accident.*

contusion, *n.* A bruise or injury in which the skin is not broken.

> *Despite the hard fall, Marty only suffered a **contusion.***

Also Explore: abrasion, impairment, laceration, rupture, splint.

Death

epitaph, *n.* An inscription on a tomb or gravestone in memory of the person buried there; a short composition in prose or verse, written as a tribute to a dead person. Do not confuse with epithet, which is a disparaging word or phrase. Few people would want an epithet engraved on their tombstone.

*Ned wanted a simple **epitaph** on his tombstone: "He lived, he worked, he died."*

corpse, *n.* A dead body, especially of a person. Also refers to something once vigorous but now lifeless and of no use. Similar to cadaver, which is a corpse used for dissection.

*The **corpse** needed to be prepared for burial.*

cremate, *vt.* To burn up, to burn a dead body to ashes. Cremation is a space-saving alternative to burial.

*Edward wanted to be **cremated** when he died and his ashes strewn over the ocean.*

euthanasia, *n.* Act or practice of causing death painlessly to end suffering; advocated by some as a way to deal with persons dying of incurable, painful diseases.

*Dr. Benjamin was a proponent of **euthanasia;** he had watched his grandmother suffer from the pain of a debilitating illness and wanted to ease the suffering for others in her position.*

Grim Reaper, *n.* Death, often personified as a shrouded skeleton bearing a scythe.

*When your time comes, the **Grim Reaper** will be knocking at your door.*

 **Also Explore:** annihilation, cadaver, demise, necrosis, Pale Horse.

The End

denouement, *n.* The outcome, solution, unraveling, or clarification of a plot in a drama or story; any final revelation or outcome. Denouement implies the clearing up at the end of a play or story of the complications of a plot or the outcome of a tangled sequence of events.

> *In the **denouement,** we discover who killed Mrs. Jones and what happened to the missing million dollars.*

climax, *n.* The final, culminating element or event in a series; highest point, as of interest or excitement.

> *Being named employee of the year was the **climax** to Ferguson's long career at the company.*

zenith, *n.* The highest point; peak.

> *His career was at its **zenith;** he had two books on the bestseller list, and his agent was negotiating a six-figure advance for his next work.*

apocalypse, *n.* The ultimate destruction of evil and triumph of good. As written in the book of Revelation, a cosmic cataclysm in which God destroys the ruling powers of evil.

> *The parishioners began to prepare for what they believed would be the coming **apocalypse.***

finale, *n.* The conclusion or last part; end.

> *This is the **finale** to this book; thanks for reading!*

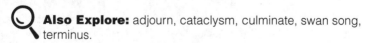 **Also Explore:** adjourn, cataclysm, culminate, swan song, terminus.

PART
2

Negotiate and Win!

TOP 20 WORDS TO...

Deal with a Lawyer—Without Ending Up in Jail!

TOP 20 WORDS TO...

Talk with an Accountant Without Your Eyes Glazing Over

TOP 20 WORDS TO...

Build or Destroy Professional Relationships

Survive a Boring Cocktail Party

TOP 20 WORDS TO...

Establish and Sustain Marketplace Success

Ensure Gainful (and Continuous) Employment

Generate Publicity
(Good or Bad)

Run a Successful Campaign

Look Good at Your Class Reunion

Build a Successful Team

Enjoy a Successful Vacation

TOP 20 WORDS TO...

Conduct a Successful Charity Drive

Buy and Sell Real Estate Without Losing Your Shirt

TOP 20 WORDS TO...

Successfully Buy and Sell Stocks

Live a Healthy Lifestyle

TOP 20 WORDS TO...

Sound Like You Have a Life

Critique the Fine Arts

TOP 20 WORDS TO...

Play with High-Tech Toys

TOP
20
WORDS TO...

Sound Like You're Computer Literate

TOP 20 WORDS TO...

Speak and Write ~~Good~~ Well

Index

393

Grant, 148
Graph, 187
Gratuity, 107
Grease, 241
Green, 207
Greenhouse effect, 129
Gregarious, 225
Grim Reaper, 364
Gross, 34
Guardian, 310
Guerilla, 141
GUI, 163
Guile, 137
Gynecologist, 261

H

Habitual, 205
Hackneyed, 338
Halcyon, 9
Hamstring, 39
Handheld, 143
Handoff, 113
Handout, 55
Happenstance, 228
Harassment, 97
Harbinger, 315
Harbor, 310
Hard news, 41
Harmony, 35
Hasten, 334
Hatch, 294
Haughty, 178
Havoc, 166
HDTV, 163
Head, 358
Headcount, 358
Headquarters, 299
Healthful, 206
Hearsay, 86
Heartland, 144
Hedonist, 3
Heinous, 175
Hermit, 282
High post, 325
Historical, 205
Histrionic, 157
Hoax, 100
Hobbyist, 64
Hoi polloi, 117
Holistic, 37
Homeless, 307
Home office, 102
Homeopathy, 37
Home theater, 50
Homicide, 110
Homogenous, 211
Honorarium, 148

Horsepower, 170
Hostile, 221
Hostile takeover, 127
House, 280
HTML, 276
Hub and spoke, 290
Human resources, 358
Humidity, 330
Hybrid, 140
Hype, 157
Hypertension, 95
Hypertext, 244
Hypothesis, 84

I

Iatrogenic, 231
Ibuprofen, 73
Icon, 250
Iconoclast, 282
Idle, 114
Idyllic, 267
Ignorant, 57
Illicit, 43
Illiterate, 57
Imbibe, 241
IMHO, 80
Imitation, 258
Immemorial, 346
Immerse, 275
Imminent, 329
Immovable, 322
Impact, 336
Impair, 39
Impasse, 23
Impassive, 124
Impeach, 177
Impeccable, 267
Impedimenta, 194
Impel, 119
Imperious, 178
Impertinent, 135
Impetuous, 334
Impetus, 293
Imply, 45
Import, 242
Imposing, 118
Impressive, 118
Impromptu, 82
Impropriety, 61
Improvise, 82
Impudent, 135
Impugn, 273
Impulsive, 334
Inactive, 114
Inadmissible, 86
Inane, 192
Inappropriate, 105

Incarcerate, 296
Incentive, 30
Incite, 252
Inclination, 279
Incognito, 174
Income, 34
Incorrigible, 191
Incremental, 151
Incriminate, 45
Incur, 312
Indecorous, 160
Indemnify, 286
Indict, 177
Indifferent, 124
Indiscretion, 61
Indispensable, 104
Indisposed, 231
Indoctrinate, 274
Indolent, 114
Induce, 14
Ineffectual, 93, 121
Inertia, 293
Inevitable, 184
Inexorable, 293
Inexplicable, 74
Infirmity, 231
Inflation, 229
Infrangible, 205
Infrastructure, 2
Ingenuity, 326
Ingratiate, 153
Ingredient, 318
Inherent, 341
Initialize, 131
Initiate, 46
Inlay, 323
Innate, 341
Innocuous, 121
Insinuate, 88
Insipid, 72
Insolent, 176
Inspire, 14
Insulate, 310
Integral, 341
Integrity, 182
Intellectual property, 327
Intelligence, 174
Intelligentsia, 60
Interactive, 244
Interchangeable, 211
Interject, 88
Intern, 316
Internationalism, 242
Internet, 218
Interpolate, 88
Interrupt, 88
Intersperse, 88

400